Explorations *in the* Theology *of*
BENEDICT XVI

Explorations *in the* Theology *of*
BENEDICT XVI

Edited by
JOHN C. CAVADINI

University of Notre Dame Press
Notre Dame, Indiana

Library of Congress Cataloging-in-Publication Data
Explorations in the theology of Benedict XVI / edited by John C. Cavadini.
    p.   cm.
Festschrift delivered in 2012 at a conference at the University of Notre Dame.
    Includes index.
    ISBN 978-0-268-02309-6 (cloth : alk. paper)
    ISBN 0-268-02309-3 (cloth : alk. paper)—E-ISBN 978-0-268-07698-6
    1. Benedict XVI, Pope, 1927– —Congresses. 2. Catholic Church—
Doctrines—History—20th century—Congresses. 3. Catholic Church—
Doctrines—History—21st century—Congresses. 4. Catholic Church—
History—20th century—Congresses. 5. Catholic Church—History—21st
century—Congresses. I. Cavadini, John C.
  BX1378.6.E97   2012
  230'.2092—dc23
                                2012034402

CONTENTS

ACKNOWLEDGMENTS

I express my deep gratitude to those without whose assistance this volume could not have come to completion. This includes professors Lawrence S. Cunningham and Cyril J. O'Regan at the University of Notre Dame, who helped plan the original conference that this volume represents, and staff at the Institute for Church Life at Notre Dame who were instrumental in its success: Jennifer A. Monahan, assistant director; Brian R. Shappell, business manager; Virginia M. Nawrocki, office coordinator; and James H. Lee, research assistant; as well as Harriet E. Baldwin of the Institute for Scholarship in the Liberal Arts at Notre Dame. Funding for the conference came from the McGrath-Cavadini Director's Fund at the Institute for Church Life, and thus thanks are due to Robert and Joan McGrath for their enduring generosity.

I owe an enormous debt of gratitude to the staff at the University of Notre Dame Press, for their professionalism, plentiful supply of patience, wonderful enthusiasm, and just plain kindness in working on a significantly expedited schedule. This includes Harvey J. Humphrey, Jr., interim director; Rebecca R. DeBoer, managing editor; Sheila Berg, copyeditor; and many others who have worked on the manuscript already or will have guided it to final publication in the weeks to come, long after the writing of these acknowledgments.

The authors of the individual essays were all admirably, even zealously, cooperative in meeting deadlines to ensure timely publication, and I thank them. The Reverend John I. Jenkins, C.S.C., president of the University of Notre Dame, embraced this project from the outset and has enthusiastically supported it to its completion. Finally, I owe a special debt of gratitude to Nancy R. Cavadini, whose prodigious labor in the initial and final editing of the papers made it possible to have a volume ready for the press in the first place. Of course, in acknowledging these debts of gratitude, I reserve any errors that may remain to myself alone.

INTRODUCTION

JOHN C. CAVADINI

"God Is Love." Such is our faith, the faith of the Church. As theologians and colleagues from other disciplines, we seek to understand this profound truth ever more clearly, to discover it ever anew, and to be able to communicate what we have discovered ever more persuasively. In doing so, we acknowledge ourselves to be following the footsteps, most proximately, of Pope Benedict XVI, whose first encyclical was named after this passage from Scripture. For such is the task of the theologian according to Saint Augustine that there is the first phase, that of discovery, *modus inveniendi*, and then the second phase, that of communication, *modus proferendi*. The conviction of Saint Augustine is that God has himself spoken so precise, so persuasive, and so moving a Word of Love in the Incarnation that to "discover" it adequately and anew must mean to allow oneself to be informed, persuaded, and moved in one's own heart ever anew and ever more profoundly, and so to want to impart an understanding of that Word that can pierce through the hardness of our age—hard as the pavement on the streets that the indigent poor must walk every day, as

1

Dorothy Day put it—to allow God's Word of Love to be spoken in someone else's heart.

The two phases of theology are therefore mutually implicated; they are not really separable, because to want to discover God's Word of Love anew, to want to understand it better, means at the very same time to want to discover how to say it better, how to articulate it in a way that it can be heard in one's own time and that is true to the original Truth, the original Logos or Meaning, the original Light. "Love is the light—and in the end, the only light—that can always illuminate a world grown dim and give us the courage to keep living and working. . . . To experience love and in this way to cause the light of God to enter the world—this is the invitation I would like to extend with the present Encyclical," writes Pope Benedict just before the conclusion of the encyclical letter *God Is Love*. Is this the *modus inveniendi* or the *modus proferendi*? It is really the description of the union of both. Benedict's encyclical seeks understanding ("to experience love") in order to engender understanding ("to cause the light of God to enter the world"). It performs the union between the desire to understand and the desire to engender understanding and invites everyone in his or her own way, including theologians, to do the same. How else can a work of theology issue an "invitation" to "experience love and in this way to cause the light of God to enter into the world"? One seeks an "understanding" that can be the occasion for the original Understanding, the original Light, to find a place in someone's heart, to move someone deeply in the experience of being loved and cherished and so nourished by God, and thus to cause the light of God to enter, ever ancient and ever new, into the world.

We have chosen to study the theology of Benedict XVI not only out of what is called or sometimes passes for "academic" interest, by which is sometimes meant a neutral, objectifying (if not objective!) interest, but also in order to take up his invitation, and so to honor him, as theologians. We study his theology throughout his career, for its intrinsic interest but also so that we can understand how it surfaces and comes to a fruition in his letters and statements as Supreme Pastor. We hope thereby to hear the invitation he has issued as Benedict

XVI more precisely and more clearly, so that we can receive most fully the invitation "to experience love and in this way to cause the light of God to enter into the world more faithfully and fruitfully." We are convinced that one of Benedict's major achievements is the demonstration of Augustine's original insight into the unity of the theological tasks of understanding and of engendering understanding. We propose that, among other things, this is the "invention," in the sense of "discovery," of a new apologetics founded not so much on the desire to outdo one's opponent in dialectical victory but to allow the Love in which the original Word was spoken to be heard anew and to make its own case, its own "apologia," in the hearts of those who hear. If "love alone is credible," to borrow from Balthasar, love alone needs no apology, or, better, provides its own. "Let love speak," could perhaps be the motto of the encyclical letter *Deus Caritas Est* and, as such, the motto for Joseph Ratzinger/Benedict XVI's theology over his life's work as a theologian, and we take it as our own. Ultimately we will see that even this is actually not the discovery of a new apologetics so much as the recovery and reinterpretation of something ancient.

Cyril O'Regan's essay, first in this collection, offers an overview of Benedict's theology by analyzing it, as a whole, and so it stands by itself here. In characterizing Joseph Ratzinger/Pope Benedict XVI's theology as a "constitutively Augustinian" enterprise, a "figuring" of Augustinian theology for the contemporary period, O'Regan's essay opens up what we might call the interior life of this theology as a way of giving an account of its power and its depth. To denominate it as "constitutively" Augustinian means simultaneously displacing clichés about Benedict and, even more, about Augustine. "Ruled out from the beginning is deploying 'Augustinian' as a trope for a dialectical or negative view with regard to the saeculum," for such a view "fails to capture either Augustine's or Benedict's complex and highly nuanced negotiation with culture," as O'Regan puts it. Instead of dialectically opposed pairs, this means a series of thematic and structural integrations, beginning first and foremost with theology as "faith seeking understanding" which integrates faith and reason and results in a theology that is integrated with the pastoral. "Theology is irreducibly

pastoral," for both Augustine and Benedict. I take this to be a rede-
scription of the intrinsic connection between the *modus inveniendi*
and the *modus proferendi* I have already noted.

The "irreducibly pastoral" character of Benedict's theology signifies also the integration of the "faith of the theologian and simple
faith" as it exists in any member of the Church. These reflect and
enact the even more "constitutive" integration of faith and reason. For
Benedict, "faith and reason are made for each other," but "even more
than Augustine, Benedict is alive to the prospect that they will separate and become alien to each other and, as such, will be damaging to
the Church." In fact, for Benedict, "separate from each other, faith and
reason become pathologies." Other Augustinian-style integrations:
the balance between a critically informed approach to the Bible and
an overall hermeneutic of Scripture as the Word of God; the integration of Christianity as a cultural reality and at the same time the
bearer of a unique and unsurpassable revelation; the integration of
theology and prayer, each mutually implicating and recommending
and even enacting the other; and an apocalyptic sensibility that views
the consummation of history as still to arrive and yet as mysteriously
present in the sacramental life of the Church in the midst of the
"drama" of its journeying, pilgrimwise, through the ambiguities of history as we know them now.

If there is a critical edge to Benedict's theology, it is, like Augustine's, in defense of the integrations that his theology upholds as fundamental against the "pathologies" that would dis-integrate them. One
specific element of Augustinian theology, the relation between Christ
and culture as exposited in the *De Doctrina Christiana,* for example, is
brought forward in Benedict, and that is the uniqueness of the Christian claim that "Christ is the eschatological disclosure of God," and as
such offers an unsurpassable truth, even if elements of truth may be
found outside the sphere of Christian revelation and there is a valua-
tion of dialogue which is not one-sided and yet does not renounce
the claim to truth. Benedict, like Augustine, argues against the premature foreclosure of dialogue in the renunciation of the uniqueness
of the Christian claim, partly from failure to understand it and to respect the integrations that it entails. "That history," O'Regan points

out, "according to Benedict, will prove a battleground of claims does not provide sufficient reason to surrender them. In the meantime, other religions and cultures are to be treated with more than tolerance; they are to be treated with love."

Benedict's criticism of the contemporary tendency to accept no truth as universal, what he referred to as a "dictatorship of relativism," is addressed most specifically in the next group of essays in the volume, under the rubric "The Dynamic of Advent." Peter Casarella's essay on culture and conscience leads off here, reminding us that Benedict's opposition to the "dictatorship of relativism" is not to be taken "as if it were a blast from a bunker in the U.S. culture wars," or as if the dictatorship of relativism were ideally to be overturned only to be replaced by a new dictatorship, that of faith. The profoundly Augustinian character of Benedict's opposition to the dictatorship of relativism is reflected, as Casarella reminds us, in his invocation of an "advent dynamic" to describe the interaction of cultures and their progression "'toward the Logos of God, who became flesh in Jesus Christ.'" This is not a statement of triumphalism but an interpretation of the Augustinian drama of pilgrimage. It is based on the conviction of "the capacity of any culture—Christian or non-Christian—to remain open to an *encounter* with another culture without sacrificing *either* its religious foundation *or* the necessary stance of openness."

This is not to unsay a nonrelativistic conception of human nature. Instead, Casarella goes on to point out, "Ratzinger's resolute commitment to intercultural dialogue is nurtured by his confidence in the ability of our contemporaries to recover the lost language of human nature." Here is another integrative moment in the thought of Benedict XVI, in which intercultural dialogue is not set off against and opposed to the idea of a transcultural human nature but based on such an idea. The formation of conscience is seen not in a narrow, moralistic way but rather as a formation of the person in the freedom to bear witness to the truth of human nature and human dignity in such a way that it permits the renewal of the cultural imagination and preserves it from developing hardened complacencies about the relative nature of truth that in turn promote, rather than stem, violence and cultural decadence. Cannot one hear echoed the Augustinian claim, from *City of God,* book 5, that the witness of the martyrs demystifies the imperial chauvinism that marks the Roman quest for cultural prestige ("glory") as nothing other than the subjection of virtue to opinion rather than to truth? "Relativism," no matter how "liberal," is in its essence an imperial dynamic (and in that sense, a "dictatorship") that leads both for Augustine and for Benedict inevitably to cultural incoherence and social decline.

That relativism could become, paradoxically, a new dogmatism is the subject of the next essay by Fr. Edward T. Oakes. He begins with quotes from Allan Bloom that make it seem, contrary to Casarella's claim, that Benedict's opposition to the "dictatorship of relativism" does in fact come from a bunker in the U.S. culture wars after all. By the end of the essay, however, it is clear that the forceful evocation of these "paradoxes" of relativism serve only to emphasize the terms, and so to heighten the "resolution," of the "relativity paradox" of which the title speaks. The essay relates to the contemporary breakdown of the Augustinian balance between the uniqueness of Christ and the claims to (and presence of!) truth found in non-Christian cultural achievements.

Fundamentally the challenge, and therefore the resolution, is Christological. The "challenge of Christological relativism" is first posed in its modern form most acutely by Troeltsch's book *The Absoluteness of Christianity,* so, as Father Oakes demonstrates, the resolution of the paradoxes of relativism is itself Christological. Acceptance of the Incarnation in faith is acceptance of a "stumbling block" for reason. It "overturns" our "normal approach to reality," a "folly" that "requires the overthrow of worldly norms of rationality." This does not destroy reason but provides it with an ideal of love which amazes and informs reason, humanizes it and heals it as it plumbs the depths of a love it could not have imagined on its own. Reason is healed because on the one hand it accepts as the norm of truth something fixed and unsurpassable, rejecting the relativism that leads to the reduction of itself to the purely technical. Yet even as it does accept such absolute truth, because it is the truth of an absolute love, such acceptance opens reason to listening to the other instead of closing it off. Listening will be with an openness based on love, an openness hitherto unimaginable. It will not fail to discern as error anything which contradicts the truth that makes the listening possible, and yet it will be open to a depth of truth it may not have expected to hear. In any event it is precluded from "setting limits on God's behalf; the very heart of faith [and thus of reason] has been lost to anyone who supposes that it is only worthwhile, if it is, so to say, made worthwhile by the damnation of others," as Father Oakes quotes Benedict as saying.

The right kind of listening must in fact learn to appreciate a "depth" of otherness, if Robert M. Gimello is correct. He uses this idea in the main title for his essay, which is subtitled "Buddhism and Benedict's Theology of Religions." This essay comes from the depth of Gimello's lifelong scholarly acquaintance with Buddhism. Its erudition forestalls a superficial account of interreligious dialogue which requires each party, in effect, to "suspend, treat as merely provisional, and perhaps even relinquish one's own beliefs." This would mean, in the case of Christianity, that Christian doctrine could be understood as "'true' only in a 'relative' sense." For Benedict, as Gimello points out, such a dialogue is bound to be "superficial," and its listening to the other not very disciplined or deep. More than likely it will merely "conceal in the cloak of one's own desires the true, demanding otherness of the other."

The right kind of listening will be able truly to see in other religions, in this case Buddhism, "many things that are both true and holy," but it will also become aware of aspects "that are simply incompatible with Christian belief and the Christian life, or are deficient unto Christian ends, aspects overlooked in undisciplined haste to form liberating bonds with the other." Gimello lists eight examples of "sharp antinomies" that present themselves in the "depth of otherness" that Buddhism exhibits in relation to Christianity. These are fundamental differences, and unless one faces them, one does not really see the other, or oneself for that matter, very clearly. In fact, the other so construed can turn out to be an (imperial?) "misappropriation," an abuse of the other who is constructed—distorted—so as to serve as a critique of those aspects of one's own religious orthodoxy one does not like. In the process one loses a sense of what criteria one is using to judge what is true and what is not; what is revealed and what is not. How would one know that the Buddhist experience of emptiness, for instance, is the equivalent of the Christian experience of the grace of the Risen Lord, as some have claimed? In fact a sense of absolute truth is deployed in such claims to equivalency, only in a hidden way, masked by the assertion of relative truth itself in each concrete instance. Gimello offers an extended comparison of the Christian doctrine of love (charity) to Buddhist doctrines of compassion, opening our eyes to a vast landscape of beauty in either case, but also to an equally vast incommensurability between the two, if one resists the temptation to reduce both to a supposed position imperially hovering above either. For example, "the suffering beings who are the foci of the bodhisattva's compassion . . . have no independent, fixed identities, and, lacking such identities, they have neither intrinsic worth nor claim of their own on the bodhisattva's pity [and thus] are pitied, so to speak, not for their own sakes but as instantiations of the impersonal truth of pervasive suffering," but this is radically different from the Christian basis for love of the other.

Thus, also disclosed in a truly loving and disciplined "discriminate attention that other religions deserve" are "elements of the other religion that can . . . help Christianity more deeply to plumb its own depths." Gimello gives as an example of this the "epistemological sophistication" that discerns "the subtle and complex relations between desire and [ignorance,] the failure to know," the "inveteracy of cognitive concupiscence . . . to fabricate desired falsehood." Buddhism's "astute, fine-grained analysis of the psychology of error, the intricate ways in which the conscious and unconscious mind constructs falsehood," provides riches that can enhance Christianity's understanding of its faith rather than relativize its faith. A dialogue that arose out of a true sense of what is incommensurable *belief* and what arises from the kind of spermatic *reason* that Christians have held to have been available to non-Christians such as Socrates (as O'Regan pointed out for Benedict)—would not this dialogue be a participation in the "advent dynamic," the interaction of cultures and their progression "toward the Logos of God, who became flesh in Jesus Christ"? Would not such dialogue be an example of a loving encounter with the other, truly attempting to see the other instead of constructing him or her as merely an instrument to "think with" about one's own religious discomfitures? The work that it would then take to "understand" one's own faith in a way that can engender understanding of that faith in the concrete other before you would be a kind of self-giving, the giving of one's best self in love, a witness of the heart and thereby the creation of a kind of communion. Perhaps this would be the "apologetics of love" at its deepest level, the union of the *modus inveniendi* and the *modus proferendi* in the medium of frank, clear, and loving conversation. This is to recapture the balance advanced as an ideal in the *De Doctrina* of Saint Augustine in a wholly new context.

This mention of apologetics brings us to the concluding essay of this section of the book, "Reflections on *Introduction to Christianity*," by Lawrence S. Cunningham. Cunningham points to the consistency of Ratzinger's thought throughout his theological career that enables a return to the *Introduction* to serve in its turn as recapitulation. The *Introduction* originated in a series of lectures offered to an audience of both believers and nonbelievers. Therefore it has what Cunningham calls "the ring of both catechesis and apology." It is the attempt to engage in theology so that what one "discovers" in the *modus inveniendi* is discovered in the attempt to engender understanding of what Christians believe in a way that serves believers and nonbelievers at the same time. It is "both a proclamation of the faith and, however tacitly, an apologia for the faith."

Can the same exposition actually serve both purposes? If the very same exposition that can prompt conversion to Christianity can also provide "understanding" to what a Christian already believes, it implies that Christian conversion is never fully accomplished, is never a settled achievement that can be left behind once and for all with baptism, but is an ongoing reality. This balances the possession of the fullness of truth in Christianity with the humility required to possess the truth, larger than oneself and received as a gift, properly. One possesses it properly in an openness to others, in a way that the theological task of "faith seeking understanding" discovers the "understanding" that makes the faith "understandable" to others, not by giving up its uniqueness, but by interpreting it in terms that allow it to be heard as "reasonable" and so inviting at least to dialogue. If this seems like the opening of a dialogue that will be in medias res for a longer rather than a shorter time, that is probably a correct intuition of Ratzinger's sense of things. The overcoming of the dictatorship of relativism is not the replacement of it with another dicatatorship, this time of faith, but with an "understanding" that is at once an "invitation." The invitation is based not on a comfortable "imperial" sense of Truth as implying the equivalency of all "truths" but an uncomfortable bearing of witness in humility and generosity, "toward the Logos of God, who became flesh in Jesus Christ." Ratzinger speaks as "a pilgrim of faith inviting others to join that journey," as Cunningham puts it. Here we are, with the beginning as our end, in the advent dynamic mentioned by Casarella. And, as Cunningham points out, this integrating dynamic does arise from Ratzinger's lifelong dedication to holding together faith and reason in the fundamental belief that the Word, Reason itself, became flesh.

But how well does this theology translate into prescriptions for action in a world where not all are believers and yet all must learn to live together not in a distant future but now? If we really do believe that God is Love, then it must so translate. The next two essays, in the section "Caritas in Veritate," attempt to answer that question, by reviewing and by developing Benedict's theology. Daniel Philpott's essay, "God's Saving Justice: Faith, Reason, and Reconciliation in the Political Thought of Pope Benedict XVI," addresses the topic of the reconciliation of peoples after upheavals caused by aggression, war, persecution, and genocide. Philpott argues that at the heart of Benedict's perspective lies the synthesis, already insistently noted in the previous essays, of faith and reason. He explains that Benedict argues in the first instance for the purification of reason by faith. Justice is a concept accessible to reason alone, of course, but true justice presupposes something which reason cannot provide for itself or account for on its own, and that is love. The love in question is not just a subjective feeling but "the love of God in the Bible, revealed and shared through Jesus Christ." The justice enacted on our behalf by Jesus Christ discloses that "even justice itself depends on the love that exceeds justice." On the other hand, religion or faith alone—"religion decoupled from reason"—"is liable to collapse into sectarianism and violence." In terms of a logic of reconciliation, reason demands that justice be done in terms of the rights of all involved. But reconciliation, conceived in biblical terms received in faith, discloses a justice that goes beyond rights ("what is due to each") and thus beyond the limitation of the reconciling imagination simply to "what is due" based either on the pathology of reason alone, disconnected from faith, or of faith alone, disconnected from reason. "The justice of reconciliation . . . encompasses but exceeds rights," as Philpott summarizes, and it "takes on even more fullness through its connection with two other concepts derived from the Bible: peace and mercy."

Operating, then, on the principle, following Benedict, that the sustaining of justice, the justice of rights and due, "itself depends on love," Philpott enumerates six "wounds" and six corresponding "practices" that illustrate the need for a reconciliation that is effective because, while encompassing rights, it goes beyond rights. Perhaps in the context of this brief introduction, we can mention only one, the sixth practice, namely, forgiveness. "*Forgiveness* [is] the rarest of the six practices to take place in political orders but also the most distinctively Christian and," Philpott argues, "the most potentially transforming." It is of course not practiced in isolation from the other five practices, which include "punishment" and "apology," though it is not necessarily directly connected to these either. Philpott observes that "for societies recovering from past injustices, forgiveness helps to defeat the standing victory of injustice, contributes to the restoration of victims, and helps to work against cycles of revenge and counter-revenge." He concludes, "The balm of reconciliation redresses wounds that are wider than those that human rights can describe, involves measures wider than restoring human rights, and indeed effects the kinds of restoration that greatly strengthen a regime based on human rights." This reflects the justice that is rooted in reason, enhanced and given grounding in its dependence on the mercy, love, and grace found in faith, even as it also connects faith to the reasonableness that arises out of the sense of human nature and its concomitant sense of human rights.

The second essay in this section speaks directly out of the encyclical that has given the section its title. Simona Beretta's essay on Benedict's *Caritas in Veritate* is titled "Development Driven by Hope and Gratuitousness: The Innovative Economics of Benedict XVI." The question of Catholic social teaching arises here, with respect to the unique perspective it brings to the question of the economic and political development of peoples. One of Benedict's characteristic reminders is that Catholic social teaching loses what it uniquely has to offer if it cuts itself off from the rest of Catholic teaching, especially if it concentrates on "justice" apart from Catholic teaching on love, and on the faith and hope which provide the full dimensions of love. Economic development, if it is to be authentic human development and not simply technocratic solutions to technical problems, must be "driven" by values that are authentically human. Just social structures are necessary, but once established they do not function by themselves, and neither capitalism nor Marxism has been able to make good on the promise that just social structures, in themselves, can or have delivered a consistent justice. These structures are administered and supported by free agents and a free community who must be "animated" ever and anew "by convictions capable of motivating people to assent freely to the social order" and by a hope that is large enough to guarantee a place for the value of human freedom itself and for its proper exercise. In the economic sphere, "gratuitousness" plays a more important role than one might first imagine, even from the perspective of reason alone. There are many gifts given and received, gifts of trust, for instance, of initiative, of truth, of all kinds of "relational goods" that are more difficult to sustain than the material goods they help to create. Nor is the "gift" economy without its pathologies in a fallen world, for some of the worst corruption arises from bribes and other "gifts" and so-called gratuities that have taken on a life of their own. The economy of gifts cannot be noticed for what it is, assigned its true and fullest meaning, purified and supported apart from *caritas*. *Caritas* in turn has no objective dimensions apart from the faith that discloses the immensity and purity of God's love and the world as a place in which love is not a subjective illusion but is actually itself a gift. The idea of "gift" makes sense because it is engraved in the very nature of the cosmos as creation. Once again, we find that faith alone is not sufficient to create an economic or political solution but also that reason alone, unaided by faith, is not sufficient either because it can neither see nor support the person in his or her totality and full dignity *as* gift.

The final four essays constitute a study at the intersection of exegesis, sacrament, and Church. In one way or another, these are centered squarely on the love of which the Church is as a kind of sacrament, created and bound together by the outpouring of the love of Christ in the Eucharist, and so the section is titled "God Is Love." In this, the first of Benedict's encyclicals as pope, we can find the intersection of all these themes.

Francesca Aran Murphy's essay sets the tone with her remarkable synthesis, "Papal Ecclesiology." This title is a surprise because of the scope of her essay, which covers Benedict's entire theological career, not just his time as Peter's successor. It is also a surprise because this papal ecclesiology turns out to be just as ecumenical as it is papal. In fact, the eucharistic image of the Church at the origin of Benedict's "communio ecclesiology" was intended "to mediate between external conceptions of the Church, such as ultrapapalism, and internalist or charismatic ecclesiologies." And, while "Ratzinger is profoundly out of tune with what he sees as the absence of love in Luther's theology," this papal ecclesiology is also "an ecumenical ecclesiology," with conscious outreach and sympathy in other ways to, among others, Luther, Barth, and the Orthodox. Murphy locates the genius of Ratzinger's ecclesiology in its ability to articulate a Catholic ecclesiology which can, in turn, almost seem Lutheran, Barthian, even Orthodox, because of its attentiveness to all its Christian interlocutors. The interlocutors, however, go beyond the Christian audience, for he has also "within earshot" the secular culture to which the idea of the Church no longer seems to make any sense. The sensibilities of secular culture are formed by a relativism, arising from historical consciousness, that at once denies the uniqueness of the Church and with it of the Scriptures she has canonized and the sacraments she celebrates. Ratzinger's response, as Murphy sees it, is to direct his interlocutors' attention to faith in the Resurrection of the Lord. "The Resurrection reframes the past, refiguring all the historic biblical images around itself. Reading Scripture ecclesially means reading it in the resurrected body of Christ: this is the key to the problem of hermeneutics." The Church, as the creation of the Spirit, in the love of the Risen Lord, is the "subject" to whom God has spoken in revelation, and thus she can "see" the divine form of Christ, in Scripture, in the Eucharist, in the poor, since the love which forms the seeing is constitutive of her being. Citing Ratzinger himself, Murphy notes, "to 'say that the last supper is the origin of the Church ... means ... that the Eucharist links men and women ... with Christ and ... in this way ... turns people into the Church.' Hence the Church both as institution and as charismatic 'lives in Eucharistic communities.'" When the Church gives an account of her uniqueness, it is thus a "dispossessive" account, as "dispossessive" as the love which forms her, and so is the opposite of triumphalist even as such an account articulates uniqueness. It sees itself and the whole world from the perspective of the victory of the dispossessive love of Christ which is the Resurrection.

Gary A. Anderson's essay is an exposition, as it were, of the "seeing" of the Lord by the interpreter of Scripture in the exegesis of Scripture. Such a "seeing" does not require one to dissociate oneself from "history." After all, the Resurrection is a historical event. As a historical event, as well as an event that transcends history, it gathers and "reframes" all our seeing. We can "see" the mystery revealed in the history more clearly. Anderson offers an exegesis of the baptism of Jesus that takes its inspiration from Benedict's *Jesus of Nazareth,* without actually repeating it. Anderson builds on a clarifying distinction made by Msgr. John Meier which preserves the possibility, on historical-critical grounds, that Jesus accepted the baptism of John without assuming that Jesus, since he accepted John's baptism, thought he himself was a sinner. Meier warns against "'the psychologizing [tendencies] of the "liberal lives" [of Jesus]'" and points to the sense of "collective sin" in the Jewish tradition. This sense can be voiced by a righteous person who associates himself with the collectivity without necessarily implying personal sin of his own. Anderson amplifies these comments with a detailed analysis of the figures of Ezra and, even more, of Tobit. Tobit's sinless integrity is not an occasion to separate himself from his people but actually forms the basis of his solidarity with them to the point of accepting their sinfulness as his own. Thus, "Benedict's claim that Jesus' consent to baptism was intended to express 'solidarity with men who have incurred guilt but yearn for righteousness' is not some sort of apologetic veneer awkwardly posed over the more sober and searing historical judgment proposed by [others], but it is rather the likeliest historical reading of the event."

Can we "see" more? Anderson recommends we attend to an icon from the monastery of Saint Catherine on Mount Sinai. It has two registers. In the top register there is depicted the baptism of Jesus in the Jordan and, in the lower register, the descent of Jesus into Hades after his death. "Yet, strikingly, the movement is depicted along a single vertical axis; it is as though Jesus falls through the Jordan into Sheol," showing the influence of Romans 6 on the iconographer's imagination. In other words, here is a "reframing" of the image from the Gospels based on the Resurrection. Will "the historical-critical reader, however, have reason to worry? . . . Was Jesus conscious of the fact that his baptism was the first step in a journey that would lead to the cross?" But seeing the full truth of the meaning of the event from the perspective of the Resurrection does not mean we are required to "psychologize" Jesus' exact awareness as a human being. Jesus' complete and righteous trust in God is, from the perspective of the Resurrection, at least an implicit awareness of his future and identity. To think this way is in accord, Anderson would claim, with the Letter to the Hebrews which says Jesus was "made perfect" through his death and resurrection (Anderson cites from Tom Weinandy's opinion of the matter). Summarizing his treatment of the moment of the baptism of the Lord, Anderson says, "I have provided additional evidence as to why the Christian reader need not be embarrassed by the fact that Jesus submitted to John's baptism, and why a robust Christological account need not presuppose that Jesus knew precisely where that baptism would take him." The latter point, Anderson notes, is in disagreement with Benedict's exegesis in *Jesus of Nazareth*, though, he says, he hopes his alternative reading is seen as "congruent with the overall aim of [Benedict's] project, that is, a portrait of Jesus that strengthens faith even as it takes the questions of historical reconstruction with utmost seriousness." Here again, this time in the domain of biblical exegesis, as Anderson points out, "faith and reason are not at odds with one another, but each serves to enlarge the capacities of the other."

Kimberly Hope Belcher's wide-ranging essay, "The Feast of Peace: The Eucharist as a Sacrifice and a Meal in Benedict XVI's Theology," is an interpretation not only of Benedict's theology of the Eucharist, but really of his whole theology as it is almost sacramentally present and visible in his discussions of the Eucharist. The first thing we see, once again, is the integrative character of Benedict's theology, this time in a view "of the sacrifice of the Mass [that] . . . can overcome the dichotomy of meal and sacrifice as it has been portrayed all too often since the Reformation period." This is made possible by the recovery of the Augustinian doctrine that all worship is sacrifice, even the would-have-been worship of the unfallen: "sacrifice is a universal of human religion, according to Benedict, because human beings are transcendent and dependent." Benedict's view of sacrifice, as he himself writes, "has nothing to do with destruction or non-being: it is rather a way of being," a positive self-offering. Like the papal ecclesiology, the papal eucharistic theology is developed in conscious outreach to Protestant theology. Pope Benedict condemns as "mistaken ideas" the late medieval understandings of sacrifice that Luther protested, ideas that seemed to suggest that "the sacrifice of the Mass competed with or adds to the sacrifice of the cross." "Rather," Belcher notes, citing Benedict, "the eucharistic sacrifice is a witness to the fact that God does not save us without our participation but rather 'accepts us and takes us up, so that we ourselves become active with his support and alongside him, participating in the mystery ourselves.'" The Eucharist is the "transcultural" and therefore universal fulfillment of the "age-old problem of representative sacrifice." Representative sacrifice "is never sufficient, but it points us toward the possibility of our participating in the one sufficient sacrifice of Jesus on the cross."

The Eucharist fulfills this problem because "the sacrifice of the cross is made present and effective in the Eucharist. It is neither extrinsic to the structure of salvation history (not some 'other thing' that priests can offer an angry God to appease him) nor opposed to the Incarnation: rather, the sacrifice of the Eucharist is the presence of the unity of God and humanity which is definitively offered to humanity in the incarnation and consummated in the Pasch."

This view of the eucharistic sacrifice overcomes the dichotomy with the meal emphasis, and necessarily implicates it. Because the cross brings together human and divine self-offering, perhaps the ultimate integration of all, it also implies and forms the unity of those participating in a "feast of peace." In Benedict's encyclical *Deus Caritas Est* and his apostolic exhortation *Sacramentum Caritatis*, his culminating statements on the Eucharist thus far, Belcher summarizes, "the Eucharist has become the self-gift of the Trinity come to dwell at home with human beings," so that "in it, the sacrifice of Christ on the cross has given itself over and become complete in the community meal, and in it the eschatological call to community with God is recognized also as the moral call to be one in Spirit with my brothers and sisters." Thus, "the Eucharist is the fulfillment of human worship, 'Peace in the universe through peace with God, the union of above and below.'"

One could not do much better than that in summing up the significance of the theology of Pope Benedict XVI. Yet all his encyclical letters have ended, just as Blessed John Paul II's did, with an invocation of the Blessed Virgin Mary, and so we end there too, with Matthew Levering's essay, "Mary in the Theology of Joseph Ratzinger/Pope Benedict XVI."

Early in his career, Levering shows, Joseph Ratzinger argued that "Mariology be placed fully in the context of ecclesiology." His theology of Mary began, and remained, squarely there. The influence of Augustine is registered here. Even if some of the Marian doctrines defined later go beyond Augustine, Augustine provides the basal key in which to listen to and "understand" all of them. Levering quotes Joseph Ratzinger from an early speech, saying, "Mary 'is the living sign of the fact that Christian piety does not stand alone in isolation before God, . . . the sign that Christ does not intend to remain alone, but rather that redeemed, believing humankind has become one body with him, one single Christ, "the whole Christ, head and members," as Saint Augustine said with unsurpassable beauty."'

The doctrine of Mary is therefore intimately linked with the doctrine of the Church both now and in her eschatological state on behalf of all of us who will follow. The doctrines of the fullness of grace (Immaculate Conception) and the fullness of redemption (Assumption) are doctrines that help us understand the fullness of "Christ's presence to us" and "our presence to him" both now and in the future state of glory. Ephesians 2.6 proclaims that God has *raised us up with him [Christ] and made us sit with him in the heavenly places in Christ Jesus.*" Levering comments on Benedict's use of this passage in reference to Mary. The fullness of the baptismal gift as Paul sees it has in fact been given to Mary, such that in Mary we see the fullness of our own redemption even if that is for us a future state.

If our vision has been adequately reframed by the Passion and Resurrection of Christ, then seeing Christ, we also see his Spouse, the Bride of Christ. If our vision is reframed by the Resurrection, then we have learned the apocalyptic vision which irradiates the present even as it points off into the future. We see the Spouse, the Bride of Christ, in the hope provided by the Resurrection, since it is the victory of the Love of Christ from which the Spouse is created as Spouse. But we only see the Spouse in the full truth of her identity if we see Mary, not because she, as Jesus's Mother, *is* the Spouse, but rather because she is the exemplary type whose fullness of grace and fullness of redemption becomes the icon of the redemption of the Church. Seeing the Bride fully through seeing Mary means seeing the biblical images, from both Testaments, from the perspective of the Resurrection. Her virginal barrenness bears the bearer of life, and through him, all his sons and daughters. Mary fulfills the type of "daughter Zion" not by canceling out the Jewish people as the elect but vindicating it in the fulfillment. The types are not fully vindicated or fulfilled apart from Mary, and she in turn is not fully seen except typologically, the images being reframed from the "vision" afforded by the Resurrection. Levering reminds us, with Benedict, that typology is a manner of reading Scripture that is itself represented in inspired New Testament Scripture, and so endorsed as a valid "view." Even original sin is itself a doctrine based on typology (of the two Adams). "For Ratzinger, then, the Marian doctrines flow from the Church's typological exegesis and liturgical praise of Mary. These doctrines would fall to the ground without the acceptance of typology as a real way in which God communicates truth about the mysteries of salvation. That God has used typology in this way is shown to us by Scripture, and indeed by Jesus himself."

Our volume thus concludes on the note of the fullness of redemption in the Assumption of Mary. In this way we can see that "heavenly glory already includes the unity of man and woman, Christ and his Bride the Church. . . . [T]he first fruits of Christ's Resurrection have truly begun in the new family of God." Family and friends: these basic human joys, available and celebrated in all cultures, testimony to human nature in its solidarity, are elevated and struck into glory, accessible to but beyond the imagination afforded either by reason or by faith. And on that integrative vision, our volume ends.

We cannot but end on a suitably joyful note. The particular theological career celebrated in this volume ended (or rather continues!) with its protagonist having been elected pope and his theology surfacing and solidified, in high papal relief, in an encyclical of the sublimity of "God Is Love." How can we not also find ourselves, as we explore this theology, coming to appreciate more and more with gratitude, and with love, the gift of the life of the Church, whose authoritative proclamation that God is Love has been nourishing us with this faith for so many centuries, continuing today in the ministry of Pope Benedict XVI. We have been authoritatively admonished that love is as lively and compelling an option as ever, that indeed, "Love *is* possible, and we are able to practice it because we are created in the image of God!" It is a gift of the Church's authoritative proclamation, now amplified and enriched in Benedict's ministry, that "Love IS the Light," that has given us "the courage needed to keep living and working,"

and, we could add, hoping. On the occasion of the year of Pope Benedict's eighty-fifth birthday, we have the occasion to ponder with gratitude, in pondering his theology, the gifts of ecclesial life, the gift of
the ministry of Peter, the ecclesial vocation of the theologian, and the
privilege and responsibility we have to "build up the one Body" by
seeking understanding in a way that will engender understanding,
and so, in our own small ways, "to cause the light of God to enter into
the world."

Ad multos annos! With love and gratitude, the contributors, and all
who had a hand in the support and execution of this volume. The
Feast of Pentecost, 2012.

chapter one

BENEDICT THE AUGUSTINIAN

CYRIL O'REGAN

The title of this essay expresses the claim that the theology of Benedict XVI is constitutively Augustinian, that is, that "Augustinianism" is the proper description of Benedict's oeuvre in whole and in part. And although the point should be obvious, I will make it anyway: this is to deny that Benedict's theology is best described as Thomistic, transcendental, or political; even if should we look carefully we would find some measure of all three in the almost sixty-year writing career of the current pope. To avoid vacuity, criteria of ascription have to be adduced and satisfied. Ruled out from the beginning is deploying "Augustinian" as a trope for a dialectical or negative view with regard to the saeculum. This view not only suffers from an indeterminacy; it also dismally fails to capture either Augustine's or Benedict's complex and highly nuanced negotiation with culture. Criteria of ascription would minimally involve the following: (i) Benedict demonstrates real familiarity with and admiration of the classic texts of Augustine; (ii) correlatively, there is significant evidence in Benedict of the adoption of an Augustinian theological style; (iii) in his work Benedict illustrates significant overlap in terms of topic focus and self-consciously

21

articulates substantive theological positions which are Augustinian in kind; and (iv) the operation of the principle of historical analogy, that is, Benedict's sense that he is living in a time of crisis and senescence similar to that of Augustine, in which not only is there massive contestation of Christianity's truths, but Christianity is determined to be obsolete. I speak to all four of these elements here, even if a considerable portion of my efforts go into exploring the overlap in topic focus and Benedict's repetition of substantive Augustinian positions. This task is executed in the second and by far the longest section of the essay. I cover five theological topics that are important to both thinkers and indicate how, in each case, Benedict takes an Augustinian stance: (a) eschatology, (b) the relation of faith and reason and the dire consequences of separation, (c) biblical interpretation, (d) the relation of faith and culture, and (e) prayer and liturgy as indelible features of Christian faith. It is with the first two points that I begin. Evidence needs to be produced that throughout his career Benedict not only turns again and again to Augustine as his theological model, but also that in Benedict's self-understanding the basic figuration of his theology is Augustinian. The fourth and last of these elements, that is, Benedict's perception of the analogy between his situation and that of Augustine, functions as something of a free radical. Without giving it freestanding treatment, I recur to the point from time to time throughout the essay and conclude with a discussion of what I think is their shared apocalyptic sensibility, which both consider to be inscribed in the very nature of Christianity.

ADMIRING, FIGURING, AND REPEATING
A THEOLOGICAL STYLE

It is Heidegger who is fond of quoting the Hölderlinian line, "as you started so you will remain," with a view less to underscoring a thinker's integrity than pointing to the phenomenon of thought circling back to a beginning and deepening it.[1] This could well describe Benedict's engagement with Augustine over the years, from his dissertation on Augustine's *City of God* in the 1950s to his quite recent reflections on

Augustine given under the auspices of a kind of catechetical retrieval of the Church fathers in general.[2] These texts, one written as a theological tyro, the other as pope, offer, at once, Benedict's most express judgments on Augustine and provide boundaries that roughly mark beginnings and ends. "Roughly" needs to be underscored. Benedict's love of Augustine may well have preceded his dissertation. More important, it is obvious that the loyalty to the thought of Augustine is ongoing and expresses itself in Benedict's encyclicals, especially in *Deus Caritas Est* (2005) and *Spe Salvi* (2007), and also in his recent two-volume *Jesus of Nazareth* (2007, 2011).[3] I will make substantive comments on these texts in due course, but for the moment I wish to say a little more about what the two bookends tell us about Benedict's perception of what is enduringly valid in the thought of Saint Augustine. In his dissertation on the *City of God,* Benedict underscored and validated Augustine's judgment of the importance of history as the context in which the Church finds itself between a determinate past and an indefinite future, and as it is forced to deal with a complex and ambiguous world that proposes different goods and holds out different incentives for these goods. As such, the context cannot fail to be dramatic. Although it is less obvious, it is the case nevertheless that in validating Augustine's theology of history Benedict is also, to a considerable extent, validating theology in history; more specifically, he is validating theology as an intervention in disclosing the times, attending to the larger patterns of movement in history, and articulating the ways salvation relates negatively and positively to the rush of change as well as to imminent crisis and the prospect of chaos. It would be true, although a bit trivial, to say that here Benedict introduces the topic of eschatology, which will never leave him, which he critically addresses in his Habilitation on Bonaventure (1957), which finds classic expression in his enduring *Eschatology* (1971), and which gets powerfully expressed as recently as *Spe Salvi,* which he insists is "largely indebted to Augustine and his encounter with God."[4] It would probably be more accurate to say that Benedict discovers in Augustine, and thereafter never forgets, that theology is eschatologically indexed as a matter of necessity since, as historical beings, we hurdle toward a future that either is empty or is the future of God, a future that evacuates the very meaning of history or, in judgment, confirms its ineluctable gravity and bivalence.

What I am pragmatically taking to be the other bookend of Benedict's circling from and back to Augustine consists of the reflections on Augustine that make their way into Benedict's popular book *Church Fathers*. The importance of Augustine is already indicated in the number of reflections devoted to him. He gets five; no other patristic figure gets more than two. The reason Augustine is treated thus is not because he is especially venerable, or because of his huge literary production, or because of his overwhelming theological intelligence. All this can be granted. But what is truly significant about Augustine is that he is not so much past as present: Augustine is "a man of today, a friend, a contemporary who speaks to me."[5] What comes through Augustine's writings is the "everlasting timeliness of his faith."[6] What mattered most for Augustine also matters most for Benedict: while this faith is appropriated by Augustine through conversion, as it needs to be appropriated by all of us, this faith, as a gift, belongs proximally to the Church and ultimately to Christ. Benedict makes it a point to avoid unnecessarily inflating Augustine's own faith, as if it were special in kind over and beyond the fact that faith is personal and thus unique. Benedict is neither being deliberately democratic nor showing anxiety with regard to how specialness is likely to play in popular Catholic piety or in high culture contexts inclined to appreciate and laud religious talent. His sole purpose is to make sure that the ground on which Augustine stands, and from which he preaches, prays, ministers, and writes, is the same ground of every Christian.[7] Augustine exemplifies, rather than constitutes an exception to, the rule that there is nothing superior to simple faith. The faith of the theologian does not rise higher than simple faith but rather attends and tends to it. This provides the horizon of interpretation for Augustine's famous formula to which Benedict commits himself without reservation: *credo ut intelligas*. All genuine theology, no matter how conspicuous the level of intellect, and no matter how salient the mastery of intellectual disciplines, is but faith seeking understanding. And if this seeking of understanding is for the individual inquirer, it is even more for the Church. It is easy for Benedict to interpret the *Confessions* in this way, and it is not difficult to follow suit with regard to the very sophisticated *City of God*, which unsurprisingly Benedict believes is Augustine's greatest book, and also with regard to *On Christian Doctrine*, the classical text of both biblical hermeneutics and Christian cultural engagement.[8]

Benedict's point is not simply formal: he means to suggest that if theology can go under the banner of faith seeking understanding, then theology is irreducibly pastoral. The pastoral designation is intended to cover all of Augustine's work and admits of no exception. Nonetheless, there is an interesting rhetorical moment in Benedict's fourth conference on Augustine, when he entertains the prospect that *De Trinitate*, with its conceptual intricacies and its articulation of analogies, might be deemed intellectualist and speculative rather than pastoral. Without conceding the point, Benedict speaks approvingly of how Augustine was prepared to interrupt his reflection on the Trinity in favor of more pastorally useful instruction and writing.[9] I will explore Benedict's telling distinction between pastoral and nonpastoral theology in due course, and comment on what is at stake for him.[10] Here, however, I would like to underscore how Benedict refuses to introduce a hierarchy between Augustine's treatises and catechesis, on the one hand, and his biblical commentary, on the other. Benedict mentions with approval Augustine's *de Catechizandis Rudibus*, and this courtesy could be extended to the *Enchiridion*, which provides a digest of Christian faith.[11] And Benedict does not fail to praise *Enarrationes in Psalmos*, which is not only Augustine's longest biblical commentary but also a text about prayer, its necessity, possibility, and actuality, which is constitutive of the Church itself.[12]

These reflections, both on the texts of Augustine and on Augustine's figuration, throw light back on the books and essays produced in the interregnum between what I am referring to as bookends. It suggests a reason as to why Benedict would move from the more Wissenschaft-oriented Tübingen to the more Church-oriented Regensburg. It gives a clue as to why Benedict would be directly involved in the production of the Catholic catechism. It helps to explain Benedict's preference for laying bare in a nontechnical way the deposit of faith, either in whole, in, for example, *Introduction to Christianity*

(1968),[13] or in part, whether the theological topic to be presented is God, last things, creation, liturgy, or the Christ of Christian faith.[14] Without any animus toward academic theology, and adamant about the positive relation between reason and faith, Benedict is persuaded that theology goes astray if it becomes reductively apologetic and reduces itself to being the handmaid of other disciplines, whether sociology, political theory, or philosophy. Thus Benedict's recurring criticisms of the hegemony of the historical-critical method in biblical interpretation and his argument for the continuing validity of the canonic modality of exegesis.[15] Benedict also makes it evident that he has heard the call of another famous modern Augustinian, Henri de Lubac, who, with his equally famous protégé Hans Urs von Balthasar, advised a "kneeling theology." Theology and prayer go hand in hand, with theology arising from prayer and prayer being a form of theology. Prayer is the dialogue between the Christian and God, made possible by the grace spoken in the Word. Theology either reflects this dialogue or in its failure risks emptiness and distortion. And all prayer is theology insofar as it has the Word as its subject and object.

Together with Augustine's agonistic view of history and his articulation of its eschatological horizon and his sense that theology should speak from and to the Church, there is a third trait in Augustine's theological figuration that gets repeated in Benedict. This trait is that of the controversialist who feels called on to write in response to perceived threats both from within and from without the Church. For Augustine, there were a number of perceived internal threats to the faith of the Church. There was first Manichaeism, which had lodged itself within the Church and, hiding under the umbrella of Paul, supported a dualist anthropology of spirit and matter and an even more egregious dualist theology of coeval good and evil principles. Later in Augustine's life his sense of the tradition and integrity of the Church made him take issue with those who were Arian in their Trinitarian theology, Pelagian in the way they understood the pursuit of holiness, and Donatist in their refusal to recognize the rehabilitated excommunicated. On the external side, Augustine perceived in particular the threat of the coercive power of the state and also the social and political chaos constituted by attacks on the state.

Benedict also responds to very long lists of provocations that arise from within and without the Church. Perceived threats from within the Church can be as general as the loss of a sense of a vital tradition, confusion on the status of the biblical text and how to read it, the lack of a coherent understanding of the Church in general and the papacy in particular, the failure of religious imagination when it comes to the sacraments, and looking to nonecclesial and nontheological sources when it comes to comprehending and negotiating with other religions as well as other Christian confessions—to supply a very abbreviated list. Over a period of almost sixty years of writing, Benedict has addressed all these issues. Interestingly, challenges from without the Church take the form of threats by the empire, which are either explicit or implicit. The empire functions coercively or exercises power in and through a dominant discourse which regulates both religious and nonreligious domains. As is well known, throughout his long career Benedict has spent considerable time criticizing Marxism as an anti-Christian world power, and latterly the modern liberal state, which functions equally hegemonically by stipulating what can and cannot function as public discourse.[16]

The following caveat needs to be entered. While the parallelism between Benedict and Augustine with regard to the two different kinds of challenges works fairly well, there is at the very least this difference: in the case of Benedict, the internal challenges are more closely connected with outside challenges in that, in the case of Marxism but perhaps especially in the case of modern liberal democracy, the ideologies have secreted themselves into the Church. The evidence for the former is, in Benedict's view, a certain style of liberation theology; the evidence for the latter is everywhere, in that the dominant liberal ideology leads to distrust of authority, suspicion with regard to doctrine, questions with regard to the viability and validity of tradition, and bafflement with regard to Christian practices and Christian forms of life.[17] Given the internalization of a dominant ideology, although the ultimate template still remains Augustine, the proximate template is provided by another Augustinian, John Henry Cardinal Newman. For it is hardly controversial to claim that what unites the multigenre and multisubject work of this religious thinker, whom Benedict declared blessed in 2010, is his sense that liberal ideology not only dominates outside explicitly Christian circles, but has very much come to dominate within the Church.[18]

BENEDICT'S AUGUSTINIAN REPETITION: TOPIC FOCUS AND SUBSTANTIVE POSITION

As I indicated at the outset, Benedict's repetition of Augustine goes far beyond a similarity in theological style. It consists, in addition, of topic focus and, above all, substantive theological repetition. To recall, I named five areas where substantive theological overlaps are especially conspicuous: (a) eschatology, (b) the relation of faith and reason, (c) biblical interpretation, (d) the relation of faith and culture, and (e) prayer and liturgy. I will speak to all five substantive overlaps, since it is precisely my point that it is in repeating a defining constellation of substantive positions put forward by Augustine that entitles the commentator on Benedict to label his thought Augustinian. At the same time I want to speak in some detail only about the first two, since there can be found in this volume essays on Benedict's biblical interpretation, on his political thought, and on his understanding of liturgy. Beginning, then, with eschatology, the first thing to be said is that in Benedict, as in the *City of God,* eschatology is twofold: it is at once a core topic area concerned with the four last things, death, judgment, heaven, and hell, and an argument about a structural distinction which if ignored or not paid sufficient attention entirely beggars all of Christian theology, because it leads to a misinterpretation of the narrative of salvation history. This distinction is the distinction between the "kingdom of God" and "the kingdom of man."[19] If both Augustinian contributions are, from Benedict's point of view, equally enduring, it is probably the case that prevention of the collapse of the distinction between the two kingdoms, or in Augustine's language the two "cities," is felt to be the more urgent of the two Augustinian tasks, given the number of texts in which it is discussed and the temporal spread of these texts, which are basically coincident with Benedict's entire literary production. Accordingly, I want to spend considerably more time on this aspect of Benedict's repetition of Augustinian eschatology than the first.

Augustinian Eschatology

Whatever the identified priorities, a brief word on Benedict's presentation of classical eschatology in his well-known *Eschatology*, which is largely Augustinian in kind, is in order. In the original foreword, in line with the essentially Augustinian theological figuration I have spoken about above, Benedict testifies that he intends to address an important dogmatic topic in a popular, as opposed to scientific, form. What he goes on to say is at least as revealing: the theological thinking he presents is self-consciously ecclesial rather than the creative thought of an individual theologian.[20] Benedict is not apologizing: his intent is to question the modern penchant in theology for originality, which often issues in an apologetic style theology that tries too hard to please secular disciplines that have come to enjoy authority. Benedict does not explicitly label the ecclesial eschatology he retrieves "Augustinian," nor is it the case that in his articulation there are no specifically modern elements. If one looks carefully, one can see some ideas that bear a real resemblance to Rahner's theology of death, exercised as it is with the communion between the dead and the period between death and judgment.[21] So Benedict's theology is neither all the way through classical nor, by the same token, Augustinian without remainder. Again, although the biblical emphasis in *Eschatology* hardly puts Benedict in a camp entirely different from the very biblical Augustine, the self-consciousness of his biblical reference, and its dealing with a canonical list of twentieth-century biblical scholars, is decidedly modern.[22] All this, however, functions as qualifier. The overall eschatological contours are, unmistakably, provided by the *City of God*, as this text proved foundational in the Western tradition and was carried through theologically by Bonaventure as well as Aquinas and imaginatively (and theologically) through Dante. The notes that Benedict strikes with respect to the afterlife in Christianity, namely, bodily resurrection, qualitatively deeper participation in God, and unrestricted openness to other persons, and that it is the soul that carries individual identity in the "interim" between individual and general judgment, are all Augustinian. In fact, it is no exaggeration to say that in *Eschatology* there are no discernible departures of a substantive type from what can be found in the *City of God*. There are, however, subtle shifts in tonality and level of certitude. Benedict is, for example, more emphatic than Augustine was in the *City of God* that God is defined by love, more inclined to think of hell as a state of absolute alienation from God and self than as a place of graphic punishment in keeping with divine justice, and considerably less certain than Augustine was about how heavily hell is populated.[23] If, in the end, Benedict himself is the author of these softening modulations of Augustine, it is probably the case that he is influenced in this respect by two other admirers of Augustine, Henri de Lubac and Hans Urs von Balthasar.

If the catechetical side of *Eschatology* recollects an Augustinian-style articulation of the last things, what we might call the more polemical side focuses on the tendency in modern theology essentially to misinterpret the kingdom by confounding the kingdom of God with the kingdom of man. In the introduction to *Eschatology* Benedict expresses a worry about the secularization of eschatology in the modern age—a point he returns to throughout the text. For him, the main agent of secularization at this juncture is Marxism, and he is particularly interested in the ways in which this secularization gets internalized in theological discourse itself. He does not mention liberation theology, but the implication that in its borrowings from Marxism liberation theology tends to be insufficiently guarded is obvious. It is not hard to extrapolate, therefore, to the concerns Benedict expressed about liberation theology as head of the Congregation of the Doctrine of the Faith (CDF). Still, it is obvious that the range of theologies with respect to which questions arise concerning the immanentization of the kingdom of God extends much further than liberation theology. Chapter 3 expressly states that the theology of hope, articulated by his erstwhile Tübingen colleague Jürgen Moltmann, seems to suggest the reduction of the kingdom of God to the kingdom of man.[24] It seems evident to Benedict that the kingdom of God gets interpreted as a social program, which thoroughly emasculates Christian hope by taking away its transcendent vector.[25] In the process, however, it essentially displaces the person of Christ, who is the pivot of salvation history and who is the one who makes our redemption actual and possible and who is the one whom we meet at the end of history. It is in the context of criticism of the modern theology of hope, which, if it has Moltmann as its most influential spokesman, has its origin self-consciously in the Marxist Ernst Bloch, that Benedict makes an appeal to the two accounts of the Temptation scene in the synoptic Gospels, which have everything to do with the confusion of the kingdom of God with the kingdom of man.

Benedict does not tarry with the Temptation scene in *Eschatology*. Nonetheless, its importance cannot be gainsaid. In *Jesus of Nazareth* Benedict provides it with a suitably extended treatment in which he not only makes the general point about the means as well as the ends of the kingdom of God and the kingdom of man but also suggests the classic nineteenth-century appropriation and development of the Temptation story by Vladimir Soloviev and Fyodor Dostoyevski, in which the target is a new form of political apocalypse.[26] Simply in terms of fact, Benedict does not speak in extenso of either figure. Largely this is because, once again, Benedict understands that the essential figuration of the theologian is not necessarily to be that of the erudite or the scientist but the pastor. But it is also the case that in and through Catholic theologians such as de Lubac and Balthasar Soloviev's and Dostoyevski's application of the drama of temptation to the modern world has been effectively assimilated into Catholic thought. In addition, whatever by way of anti-Catholicism is embedded in Russian renarration can effectively be sidelined, for in principle the Temptation scene is the *agon* between two construals of the Christian life that structure history, which were (re)marked by Augustine in the *City of God*, one of which (the kingdom of man) has a genius for counterfeiting the other (the kingdom of God).

From *Eschatology* we turn to a text written three decades later. *Spe Salvi* is Benedict's second encyclical. Benedict expressly comments outside the text on its Augustinianism, which in any event is clearly evident on internal grounds. The encyclical articulates the two dimensions of eschatology that we saw in *Eschatology*, that is, the positive articulation of Christian hope based on the authority of Scripture and tradition and a more critical side in which authentic Christianity can be distinguished from what counterfeits it. In its recollection and performance of a double-sided eschatological discourse, *Spe Salvi*, as well as *Eschatology*, is formally Augustinian. If there is a major difference between the later and the earlier text, in addition to that of their presumptive authority, it has to do with the differing proportions of the positive and the negative.[27] In *Eschatology* the elucidation of a classical (Augustinian) eschatology is dominant, the criticism of modern theologies of hope recessive. Not so in *Spe Salvi*. A large section of the text is devoted to critique. The central site of the critique can be found in the section of the text that goes under the title, "The Transformation of Christian Hope in the Modern Age" (#16–23). Therein Benedict discloses the shift of vector in modern hope from the vertical to the horizontal, a process that in philosophy begins in Kant and ends with Marx. The point that Benedict is making does not belong to an anodyne history of ideas. Benedict is not as ready as Fukuyama and others are to celebrate the death of Marxism, and, as indicated already, he continues to see signs of it in theology.[28] Yet even when Benedict shifts back into an apparently more elucidatory mode (#23–31), the critical note is not lost. In fact, criticism becomes more explicitly Augustinian. In #30–31 Pope Benedict speaks to the tendency to confound the kingdom of God with the kingdom of man. At the conclusion of the text (#44)—just to show how consistent Benedict is on this point—there seems once again to be an echo of the Temptation scene, in that the real and unobtrusive goods of God are substituted for by the more conspicuous and specious goods of the world.

Spe Salvi serves as something like a relative terminus for an Augustinian articulation of the specifically Christian nature of Christian hope and the argument against its simulacra. While largely repeating what we found in *Eschatology* and *Spe Salvi*, both of which hark back to Benedict's reflections on Augustine and Bonaventure in the 1950s, Benedict's writings in the intervening period exhibit one or two telling differences. Consider, for example, *Values in a Time of Upheaval* and *Truth and Tolerance*.[29] Benedict consistently recurs to the kingdom of god and kingdom of man distinction in order to protest their conflation. Unlike Metz, who is as anxious as Benedict to maintain the distinction, Benedict's main target continues to be Marxism, not modern liberal democracy.[30] In a telling comment he advises against giving Marxism a death certificate, and in a passage that might have come equally from Jacques Derrrida or an old guard communist, Benedict suggests that Marxism continues to have "a ghostly existence in the souls of many people, and it has the potential to emerge again and again in new forms."[31] Still, there are a few different cords struck, and Benedict makes sure to note that they further specify rather than qualify his basic Augustinianism. A point made with greater force in these texts is the connection between the city of man and violence.[32] By contrast, the city of God, which the Church may bear but with which it is not identical, is a kingdom of peace. This kingdom, which precisely cannot be brought about by human beings but only in and by the Holy Spirit, testifies to the triune God whose internal relationality models the peace that is the divine intent for human beings.[33] Benedict does not exempt religions from being implicated in violence, even if he tends to exculpate Christianity in principle if not in fact. When it comes to other religions, and especially nonmonotheistic religions, the contemporary thinker with whom Benedict seems to have most in common is René Girard.[34] He sees with Girard the propensity in nonmonotheistic religions toward a sacrificial mechanism that procures a variety of immanent goods, including the identity of the group.[35] More nearly than Girard, however, he associates these nonmonotheistic religions with the political religions critiqued by Augustine in book 6 of the *City of God*.[36]

There remain, however, two crucial eschatological themes, the first perhaps more prominent in Benedict's early work, the other a constant throughout Benedict's writing career and no less conspicuous in *Jesus of Nazareth* than in *Eschatology*. The first concerns the figure of Joachim de Fiore and pneumatic eschatology; the second concerns the positive as opposed to negative description of apocalyptic. I will be brief with respect to the first, and with regard to the second, I will merely lay down something of a foundation, since I will be returning to the topic of apocalyptic when I deal with Benedict's understanding and practice of biblical interpretation and also when I speak to Benedict's Augustinian take on prayer and liturgy. In his book on Bonaventure, Benedict shows himself interested in assessing whether and how Bonaventure's theology of history was influenced by the thought of the Spiritual Franciscans in general and Joachim de Fiore in particular.[37] While, undoubtedly, Benedict's overall view of Bonaventure's teaching on history is positive, he does sense that Bonaventure's sound Trinitarian theology of history is disturbed somewhat by Joachimite elements that seem to suggest some kind of movement in history beyond Christ and thus beyond the Church. Overall, Benedict's judgment is that Bonaventure's constitutive Augustinianism remains intact. This text precedes the publication of Henri de Lubac's great *La postérité spirituelle de Joachim de Fiore,* although by the time he wrote the text on Bonaventure, it is very likely that Benedict knew of de Lubac's views on how Joachim de Fiore is at the root of modern secular forms of apocalyptic. Benedict is also likely to have known of Balthasar's views on Joachim as the source of modern pneumatological and eschatological deformation.[38] Of course, his erstwhile colleague at Tübingen, Jürgen Moltmann, after Ernst Bloch, had made Joachim fashionable as a carrier of a forgotten mode of biblical apocalyptic.[39] Although perhaps concentrated in the earlier phase of Benedict's authorship, reference to Joachim does occur in later texts. In *Church, Ecumenism, and Politics,* in his recurring critique of apocalyptic imagination, more than likely now under the express influence of de Lubac and Balthasar, Benedict refers to Joachim as the ultimate origin of the modern eschatological schemes that are immanentist in basic character.[40] From Benedict's point of view, this means that God has been either displaced/replaced or redefined to depend for his actuality on the world and history. Still, it is probably worth underscoring that Benedict merely echoes a genealogy that is fairly worked out in both de Lubac and Balthasar. Undoubtedly convinced by the broad line of the argument, which in any event is confirmed by Moltmann and Bloch, albeit with an entirely different evaluation, Benedict does not spend much time persuading either Christian believers or their cultured despisers about its truth value.

As we have already seen, Benedict is extremely critical of intrahistorical constructions of the kingdom of God, which necessarily involve a confusion of the kingdom of God with the kingdom of man.

Benedict has no problem considering these schemes, in which this confounding occurs, to be forms of apocalyptic. It would seem, then, that as an Augustinian eschatological thinker, Benedict is constitutively an anti-apocalyptic thinker. Similar to Balthasar, however, this would prove a very premature conclusion.[41] It looks as if the issue is more nearly the contrast between deficient and sufficient forms of apocalyptic, with Christianity proving to be the latter. It would be convenient if Benedict more than implied that Augustine was an apocalyptic thinker when writing his dissertation on the *City of God*, but it would be stretching interpretation to say more. What is interesting is that in *Eschatology*, in the context of decrying secular forms of apocalyptic, Benedict by no means dismisses apocalyptic altogether. He affirms the exclamation of messianic expectation expressed in "Come Lord come" *(maranatha)* but insists that this not be a free radical, as perhaps it tends to be in the modern intellectual world. The prayer—and prayer it is—should be tied to the figure of Christ. And in his survey of the biblical material, Benedict not only admits that the "kingdom of God," which is preached by Jesus, has an apocalyptic background, but also, in the case of the New Testament, that apocalyptic cannot be detached from Christ. According to Benedict, Christ refigures apocalyptic and makes it a function of his person.[42] For Benedict, no less than for Balthasar, the canonical apocalyptic tradition of Daniel and Revelation is illiminable.[43] The Book of Revelation, for example, is a visionary text which, in an unsurpassed way, places the Lamb of God before our eyes, and by doing so develops and completes the Fourth Gospel's disclosure of God as love. Nothing could be more crucial. But Benedict also wants to draw our attention to the Lamb being the criterion by which the empire or state is judged—something that is also implicit in the apocalyptic books of the *City of God* (bks. 20–21).

Now, while this insight about authentic as opposed to inauthentic apocalyptic finds expression from time to time in Benedict's occasional pieces, in his recent *Jesus of Nazareth* it is given something like a complete expression. Taking once again as his focus the symbol of the "kingdom of God," Benedict refuses to marginalize the apocalyptic horizon of the utterance. What has to be decided, then, is not

whether or not this symbol is apocalyptic but to what form of apocalyptic it belongs and how we might describe it. There are three sites of
discussion in volume 1. One of these is the last chapter, in which the
"little apocalypses" of Matthew 25 and Luke 17:24 ff. come in for discussion. Benedict associates the Son of Man who is spoken of here
with the Son of Man in the vastly more panoramic Revelation 17, who
is there the one sacrificed from the foundation of the world and who
blends the glorious depiction of Daniel with the Suffering Servant of
Second Isaiah.[44] Another site of discussion is Benedict's reflection on
the Temptation scenes in Luke and Matthew, to which I have already
referred. Benedict agrees with Soloviev in understanding the Temptation scene as a form of apocalypse in which a false and immanentist
apocalyptic of the kingdom of man is substituted for the kingdom of
God. It is in this context that he brings up Marxism.[45] Interestingly,
however, he does not protect himself against the charge brought forward by Dostoyevski (and implicitly repeated by such thinkers as
Yoder) that the institutional Church has, in fact, succumbed to the
lure of power.[46] Admitting this, he wants to identify otherwise *the*
contemporary challenge of challenges: "The Christian empire or
secular power of the papacy is no longer a temptation today, but the
interpretation of Christianity as a recipe for progress and the proclamation of universal prosperity as the real goal of all religions, including Christianity—this is the modern form of the same temptation."[47]

The interesting thing here is that Marxism is no longer the prevailing option but liberal democracy and perhaps the ideology of capitalism that goes hand in hand with it. The connection between
Benedict's comments here and in *Caritas in Veritate* should be obvious. I have left the third and crucial point until last. It is as important
as it is simple. Christian apocalyptic in the final analysis centers on a
figure. Obviously, it will have much of the apparatus of the apocalyptic genre: there will be emphases on suddenness and lightning flashes,
experiences of overwhelming glory, expectations of an imminent end
to all things, and the reality of judgment otherwise than the world
judges. But Christian apocalyptic refigures the genre of apocalyptic in
light of the figure, Jesus Christ, the Lamb slain from the foundation
of the world, who is the center of history as he is the center of reality,
who is alpha and omega.

The Proper and Improper Relation of Faith and Reason

Even if the theme of eschatology, with its double inflection, is truly key to getting a handle on Benedict's Augustinianism, and even if the apocalyptic motif in Benedict's texts is crucial in that it provides an Augustinian tonality for his entire theology, and which includes his reflections on topics not apparently apocalyptically inflected, such as the relation between faith and reason and the liturgy, there are other areas of substantive retrieval of Augustine to which it is worthwhile attending. When it comes to understanding the relation between faith and reason, it is evident that Benedict follows Augustine fairly closely. The correlative formulas of "faith seeking understanding" and "understanding ordered to faith" crisscross and crosshatch Benedict's entire theological oeuvre. Faith and reason are made for each other, but even more than Augustine, Benedict is alive to the prospect that they will separate and become alien to each other and, as such, will be damaging to the Church. It is this prospect and fact in history that is the real subject of "The Regensburg Address" rather than the somewhat misleading opening that stirred the ire of mullahs.[48] Throughout its history Christianity has shown a tendency toward an exclusionary form of faith correlative to a God defined as pure will—who therefore can and must operate outside the rules of reason and ethics. Benedict points to the theological voluntarism of the late medieval period. The crucial passage is #25. After speaking to the proper synthesis of faith and reason in Augustine and Aquinas (Benedict does not distinguish between the two), he goes on to say, "there arose with Duns Scotus which, in its later developments, led to the claim, that we can only know God's *voluntas ordinate*. Beyond this is the realm of God's freedom, in virtue of which he could have done the opposite of everything he has actually done."[49] Although Scotus is cited here, a careful reading of the passage suggests that Benedict's real target is late medieval nominalism, in which the distinction between the pairs *voluntas absoluta–voluntas ordinate* and *potential absoluta–potentia ordinate* come to be central for theology, which effectively unhinges the connection between intellect and will in God and thus rolls back the identification of God with Logos and, indirectly, the identification of God with

Love. In the above passage, the emphasis falls on "later developments" rather than on Scotus. Scotus is implicated only to the degree to which he established some of the conditions for a set of distinctions characteristic of William of Ockham and nominalism in general. It is of no little interest, however, that Benedict uses the plural rather than singular when it comes to "development." This suggests that the binaries brought into theological circulation by the theological voluntarism of nominalism extended beyond this period. What these theological discourses might be can only be a matter of conjecture. On the basis of Benedict's general interpretation of the Reformation, however, it is not unlikely that he is giving something of a seal of approval to the well-established historiography of Heiko Oberman, to the effect that while the Reformation can in some fundamental respects be regarded a *novum*, it is also true that some of its basic architecture depends on nominalism, and, more specifically, some of its constitutive binaries.[50] Still, even if this inference is legitimate, this should not be taken to mean that it is the Protestant variety of Christianity that is, in the end, responsible for the prizing apart of reason and will and the exaggeration of the latter at the expense of the former. Even if Benedict wishes to highlight the early modern period, in which the separation is authorized, and God effectively ceases to be Logos, he understands well both that the separation is a constant temptation throughout history and that post-Reformation Catholicism is far from exempt. The rule of exclusion was laid down as early as Tertullian, who, in a bravura moment of rhetoric, asked what Athens (philosophy) had to do with Jerusalem (biblical faith). And Tertullian was hardly unique in the early Church in emphasizing God's "good pleasure" in all things. And then there is the phenomenon of Jansenism in the modern Catholic period, whose influence through thinkers such as Arnauld, Saint Cyran, and Quesnel extends far beyond what could have been expected of Jansenius's Augustinus, precisely because the views about God's hidden will were so deeply embedded in a theology so obviously Catholic in its sacramental sense and its sense of holiness.[51]

Equally, in "The Regensburg Address" Benedict points to the hypertrophy of reason, whereby reason has become contracted and its range defined by what can be scientifically known, and thus by its utility.[52] He views this contraction as a cultural and social disaster, one he has been contending with for decades. For Benedict, the only way to go forward is to recover the classic Augustinian view of their intrinsic connection, in which reason ultimately pays homage to a wondrous and wondrously inexhaustible reality, and in which reason takes on the responsibility of clarification of faith, which deepens it and makes it, in the end, more wondrous still. What makes this possible is that in Christianity and the Gospel of John in particular reason is more than reason, word is more than word, since reason is connected with the superabundant reality, which is Love.[53] And it is because of this that God is always reasonable and good and what is not reasonable or good cannot come from God. With the exception of the unique marker of Love, the views articulated in "The Regensburg Address" are entirely consonant with the views articulated by John Paul II in *Fides et Ratio,* in which normatively faith stretches out toward its own transparence, which enriches it, and where reason finds completion in recognition of a depth of reality it cannot fully penetrate, but where factually they have separated, leaving us with the distorting images of both. In the diagnostic sections of *Fides et Ratio* faith disintegrates into fideism and reason into irony, skepticism, and relativism, which rule beforehand against the discovery or givenness of truth.[54]

The split between faith and reason or reason and faith is a recurring theme in Benedict's popular writings. The essays in *Values in a Time of Upheaval* constantly recur to the separation of faith and reason and the unedifying consequences that attend such a separation. Separate from each other, faith and reason become pathologies. Faith not inflected by reason degenerates into fanaticism, and reason, reduced to being instrumental, loses all contact with the depth of reality and mystery which might cull its promethean pretensions.[55] On their own, faith and reason become sicknesses.[56] The pathological construction is fairly typical, in that Benedict understands himself to speak to the healing of each. This is possible, he insists, if and only if faith and reason are brought into conversation with each other. Perhaps Benedict's clearest statement of this view is to be found in a passage in his 2004 essay, "What Keeps the World Together": "I would speak of a necessary correlation between reason and faith, reason and religion, which are called to purify and heal one another. They need each other, and they must acknowledge one another's validity."⁵⁷

One symptom of the pathological character of faith and reason is violence. Benedict agrees in part with the liberal critique of religion that faith can and does lead to violence. As does Newman, he thinks it has to be conceded that there is plenty of evidence in the modern period when Christian faith turned fanatical, and did so without the tincture of reason or reason as wisdom, which protects against violence.⁵⁸ And, as "The Regensburg Address" suggests, he is an interested observer of Islam and especially of its disclaimers that reason cannot be construed as having anything to do with divine commands, which are unimpeachable. But he also makes a point that William Cavanaugh has made with considerable force recently, that is, that a reason intoxicated with its own competence also sponsors violence.⁵⁹ Thus, from Benedict's point of view, both faith and reason become deranged without a healthy relationship between them, and with horrendous consequences for the humanum. As the Christian God is Logos and Love, the Christian vision is always one of peace. As Benedict makes this particular turn, the connection with the Augustine of the *City of God* once again becomes transparent. For that text offers nothing less than a theo-ontology of peace, grounded in the perfect and perfecting relations between the persons of the Trinity.⁶⁰

THE BIBLE AS SCRIPTURE

We have seen already that Benedict is an admirer of *De Doctrina Christiana*, even if he does not articulate what he takes to be the enduring contribution of the text, which is a classic of the craft of biblical interpretation as well as a learned reflection on what it means to consider the Bible as Scripture. Still, there are a number of contributions of this text that became standard elements in the Catholic tradition, of which Benedict is undoubtedly aware. These include the following: (a) the common sense of the Christian tradition guides interpretation of the biblical text; the text arises from tradition and is interpreted by it; (b) while the literal sense of the text is to be given priority, there are other senses also, even if they refer back to the literal sense; and it should be remembered that the literal sense is not reducible to some historical fact *behind* the text; (c) the unity between Old and New Testament is Christ and the Holy Spirit as the executor of unity; and (d) the biblical text is not simply a classic text, which is endlessly interesting, but nothing less than the Word of God or the word of the Word. As such, the biblical text is incommensurable. It is obvious that Benedict supports all four of these characteristic Augustinian elements. It is equally obvious that all four of these elements are challenged by the historical-critical method, if not necessarily in principle, then most definitely in fact. In referring to *Jesus of Nazareth* in passing, some of this was at least hinted at. As Benedict suggests in the foreword to volume 1, (a) the historical-critical method is regarded as a scientific method, whereas whatever the value of traditional ecclesial modes of interpretation they fall short of being scientific and thus lack real validity; (b) the literal sense of the text is not the Word of God that can be applied in multiple situations and in various ways but a situation or fact that lies outside or behind the text; (c) contingently at least, the rise of the historical-critical method has led to the eclipse of canonic exegesis, thereby compromising the unity of the text; and (d) by implication—if not by explicit statement—the Bible does not function as incommensurable. The historical-critical method applies invariantly to all ancient texts, and the accommodations made to the biblical text belong to the same order of accommodation that would be extended to any ancient text, given the required respect for the specificity.

It is true that Benedict's Augustinian commitments are merely implicit in *Jesus of Nazareth*. Indeed, one could say that they are as much—if not more—performed than clearly stated. Nonetheless, *Jesus of Nazareth* can presuppose Benedict's long-standing articulation of what constitutes adequate hermeneutical protocol vis-à-vis the biblical text and clear arguments of where the historical-critical method goes wrong if it does not restrict its claims. Arguably, Benedict's clearest statement of the current crisis of biblical interpretation, his analysis of the overclaims of the historical-critical method, and the presentation of his own (re)constructive position are to be found in his powerful 1989 essay, "Biblical Interpretation in Conflict." I will turn shortly to provide a brief analysis, but before I do, I want to say a brief word about an analysis of the minuses and pluses of the historical-critical method that would be hard to surpass in terms of lucidity, balance, and economy. I am speaking of Benedict's 1983 essay, "Taking Bearings in Christology," which reworks a talk given in 1981 to celebrate the first Council of Constantinople.[61] While this essay is substantively theological, it is also hermeneutical. In an essay structured around seven theses, Thesis 7 gives as balanced an appraisal of the historical-critical method as can be found anywhere in Benedict's work: "The historic-critical method and other modern scientific methods are important for an understanding of Holy Scripture and tradition. Their value, however, depends on the hermeneutical (philosophical) context in which they are applied."[62] Even without further exegesis, this is a suggestive passage. The choice of the terms *Holy Scripture* and *tradition* already suggest that the historical-critical method is to be in the service of a text assumed by a religious community over time to be incommensurable. In the pages that follow, Benedict does not fail to make this point explicit.[63] The historical-critical method is a "tool," not an end in itself.[64] Certainly, the latter was the tendency in the Enlightenment.[65] The note Benedict strikes in his development of Thesis 7 is positive, but it is evident that he thinks that this Enlightenment model represents an ever-present danger both in understanding the historical-critical method and in its application. It has in the past often functioned imperialistically.[66] Nonetheless, he espies a positive trajectory. The historical-critical method has undergone internal critique at the hands of its better practitioners and as the historicity of the method itself came to be recognized and assimilated. Thus there is no need to reject the method outright, thereby repeating the exclusionary posture that that method itself has too often exhibited. What is called for in interpretation is integration, not exclusion.

As already suggested, it is "Biblical Interpretation in Conflict" that contains Benedict's most forceful statement on the problems and opportunities presented by the historical-critical method for a community which over two millennia has read and interpreted the biblical

text, has used it in homilies and liturgies, and has regarded it as providing the bases of its doctrines, practices, and forms of life. This essay
is also, in a quite definite way, a reflection on *Dei Verbum* and its intent
in endorsing the historical-critical method. Although Benedict articulates a way forward that involves paying more than notional respect to the historical-critical method, the note struck is a bit more
exigent and troubled than that found in "Taking Bearings in Christology." Notice of this is provided in the opening paragraph, in which
Soloviev's apocalyptic story about the Antichrist is recalled and in
which the reader is reminded that the Antichrist was a famous exegete
from Tübingen.[67] The essay proceeds to detail each of the four liabili-
ties of the historical-critical method I suggested were implicit in *Jesus
of Nazareth*. First, the historical-critical method has illustrated an im-
perialist tendency to insist on objectivity when it comes to interpreting the biblical text.[68] Benedict does not get into general hermeneutical issues of the kind familiar since Hans-Georg Gadamer, who in
Wahrheit und Method (1961) asked the question whether to demand
an objective interpretation of all texts is not illegitimately to extend a
method appropriate in the natural sciences to that of the historical
sciences. What exercises Benedict is, given background assumptions
of the historical-critical method, whether the biblical text would be
reduced to the level of every other text, and thus ceases to be Scripture.
Indeed, he finds that throughout the history of its application, the
proponents of the historical-critical method have not been attendant
to its biases, which are closely connected with its origins in the Enlightenment critique of confessional Christianity.[69] A constitutive
problem with regard to proponents of the historical-critical method
over the centuries is, ironically, a lack of the sense of history when it
comes to its own foundation.[70] Second, the historical-critical method
is interested in facts to which the biblical text refers and in discovering
the real historical forces behind the text that account for why the biblical writers say the things they do.[71] But this is, on the one hand, to
confound fact and truth and, on the other, to be naive with respect to
the hypothetical and reconstructive nature of the entire interpretive
enterprise.[72] Third, unless modified or corrected—and happily its
history illustrates that both have happened[73]—the historical-critical

method has a tendency to "dissect" the Bible into elements.[74] Thus dissected, there is no real way of constructing unity. Fourth, the three foregoing features of the historical-critical method—at least when it functions outside the constraints of the Church and Church tradition—effectively disbar the biblical text from functioning as Scripture, that is, as the Word of God, and thus as totally incommensurable with every other text, ancient or modern. Of course, there are different ways of insisting on the Bible as the Word of God, and throughout his powerful essay Benedict questions the value of a number of them. Although they occupy very different ends of the Protestant spectrum, Benedict is persuaded that both fundamentalism (103) and Bultmann's biblical hermeneutic remain under the sway of the historical-critical method by being reactions to it. The insistence on the Bible as the Word of God—a position as old as Catholicism itself and gloriously exemplified in the work of Augustine—is the position that is ratified at Vatican II in *Dei Verbum*.[75] The historical-critical method is affirmed in the context that the Word of God is, in the final analysis, revelation, which finds its center and ultimate meaning in Christ.

CHRISTIANITY AND CULTURE

De Doctrina Christiana is the text in which Augustine lays down the incommensurability of the biblical text and establishes for the Western tradition some basic hermeneutical rules that essentially lasted until the Reformation. *De Doctrina Christiana* is also the text in which Augustine insists on the truth of the biblical text, the capacity of the preached text to shape a Christian community, but also to assimilate what is good from the surrounding culture and reject what could not be assimilated. The assimilation, therefore, was critical. This complex hermeneutical stance was expressed in the notion of *spolia Aegyptorum*, which was at once descriptive of a Christian praxis and a mandate to form a Christian culture. To do justice to the role *De Doctrina Christiana* played in the formation of a culture that held in high regard the liberal arts would demand more eloquence and a much more extensive discussion than I can offer here.[76] I will limit myself to a single text, *Truth and Tolerance,* and isolate a number of points in which Benedict supports positions fundamental to *De Doctrina,* and which now not only are challenged, but seem to have been replaced by a consensus in which Augustinian claims are refused a hearing. The first of these is the very claim to truth. It is a modern and contemporary axiom that there is no *res* corresponding to Christian *signa,* whether of the biblical text or of the Christian tradition. While, logically speaking, the inability of Christianity to sustain its validity claims might be specific to it, Christianity, in fact, is just an instance of a new truth or meta-truth: that is, that truth is relative. Relativism, Benedict claims, has become the new orthodoxy.[77] The second point, closely related to the first, concerns claims not simply about the truth of Christianity, but about the uniqueness of Christianity. To claim that Christ is the eschatological disclosure of God becomes, strictly speaking, unsayable: if one religion or philosophy is true, then the same can be said of all or at least many.[78] Benedict well recognizes that in cases such as this, truth is being ascribed by courtesy.[79] For Benedict, as with *De Doctrina,* in Christianity the claim to uniqueness is as ineluctable as the claim to truth. One could say that both are elements of Christian grammar. Benedict is not belligerent. Should it be pointed out that both claims will inevitably be contested and counterclaims made, Benedict, undoubtedly, would agree. That history, according to Benedict, will prove a battleground of claims does not provide sufficient reason to surrender them. In the meantime, other religions and cultures are to be treated with more than tolerance; they are to be treated with love. It may very well be the case that Christianity will only be eschatologically vindicated.[80] Third, inscribed in Christianity's claim to truth and uniqueness is European imperialism.[81] The only available mode of address is redress: since Christianity betrayed pure faith by becoming a specific culture, it cannot impose this cultural tradition in or on a non-European world. No longer, as in Augustine, is Christianity possessed of the ability to critique all non-Christian cultures; it can now only be the object of critique. Acculturation and accommodation have become the new watchwords, and the mandate is to leave indigenous cultures intact. For Benedict, the mandate is at best naive, in that it assumes that indigenous cultures are pristine and immune from history and that one is forbidden ethical analysis. At worst, the mandate is ideological in that while it styles evangelization as imperialistic there is, in the meantime, the phenomenon of globalization and homogenization, which totally destroys indigenous cultures, and political and economic exploitation, which sins against the inhabitants' human dignity.

DOXOLOGICAL IMPERATIVE: CENTRALITY OF PRAYER AND LITURGY

Benedict recognizes the importance of prayer in Augustine, not only in his personal life, but also in the centrality he gave to it in his biblical commentaries and especially the commentary on the Psalms, which, of course, provide the Psalms with a Christological reading that has both a subjective (Christ is the speaker) and an objective (Christ is the content) dimension. For Benedict, prayer is essential to the Bible. In a trenchant statement, he insists, "To delete prayer and dialogue, genuine two-way dialogue, is to delete the whole Bible."[82] Prayer, in fact, is constitutive of Christian faith, and is what distinguishes Christianity from every and any philosophy, as well as from Eastern religions.[83] This dialogue with God is dialogue with an other who is totally other, which is made fully possible for us in and through Christ, whose very being as rendered in act and word is constituted in his relation to the Father.[84] In the introduction to volume 1 of *Jesus of Nazareth* Benedict writes:

> Again and again the Gospels note that Jesus withdrew "to the mountain" to spend nights in prayer "alone" with his Father. These short passages are fundamental to our understanding of Jesus: they lift the veil of mystery just a little; they give us a glimpse into Jesus' filial existence, into the source from which his action, teaching, and suffering sprang. This "praying" of Jesus is the Son conversing with the Father; Jesus' human consciousness and will, his human soul, is taken up into that exchange, and in this way human

"praying" is able to become a participation in his filial communion with the Father.[85]

This guiding summary is filled out throughout both volumes but especially in the chapter on the Lord's Prayer in volume 1.[86] There Benedict notes the defining significance of prayer in the Judaism from which Jesus comes, and its abiding significance for us his followers. Even more, however, Benedict underscores how this prayer reflects Jesus' filial relation to the Father, and thus suggests the Trinitarian horizon for all prayer: if the referent of prayer is the Father, then the Spirit is the enabler and Christ the one who stands in our place.[87] Because prayer has to do with participation, prayer has to do with our call to be holy and not simply to be moral or "good enough."

The Lord's Prayer illustrates a point that Benedict generalizes about Christian prayer—that prayer is essentially an affair of the "we" rather than the "I." Thus, even our private prayer has as its context the ecclesial community. As Benedict intimates in *Feast of Faith*, it is within this community, which teaches one how to pray, that one achieves communion with Christ and thus one's identity.[88] In and through prayer, one renders the Church as an ecclesial being, as well as constitutes oneself as an ecclesial being. There is something at once generically Augustinian and specifically Balthasarian about Benedict's view of prayer as elaborated in the essay that provides the title for the book. It, at once, recalls Augustine's elaboration of the *Totus Christus* in his *Commentary on the Psalms*, in that our praying is inserted into the Church of which Christ is the head and in that our praying in turn is a praying in and through Christ to the Father in the Holy Spirit. And Benedict here as elsewhere keeps in mind the basic thesis, elaborated by Balthasar in his great book on prayer, that, while valid in itself, private prayer is ordered toward communal prayer rather than the other way around.[89]

As is well known, Benedict has not been an admirer of the contemporary flattening of the liturgy. Much of his energy has been spent determining an adequate view of the Eucharist and determining what an adequate reception of Vatican II would look like.[90] That prayer and Eucharist intersect again and again throughout *Feast of Faith* is hardly accidental since, on the one hand, the eucharistic prayer is an entering into the prayer of Jesus himself and, on the other, the content is the sacrifice of Jesus himself, who exemplifies the love that holds nothing back.[91] Benedict self-consciously sides with Augustine on this point.[92] And it is Augustine, but likely channeled through Romano Guardini, who emphasized that liturgy is the practice in which we most nearly perform the dependence that is our relation to God and which points to the eschatological perfection of this relation.[93] In the essays in *Feast of Faith* and *The Spirit of the Liturgy,* the Eucharist is not only memory but also thanksgiving and a prolepsis of the eschaton.[94] The Eucharist, however, renders real the love of God and grounds the future in which the true freedom of the human being, which lies in worship, is realized. Benedict does not shy away from thinking of the Eucharist as having a decisively apocalyptic flavor.[95]

Much more could be said of Benedict's attempt to articulate an adequate understanding of the liturgy and to revive the adorative matrix, threatened as they are by modern conceptions, and in much the same way that the historical-critical method has threatened, in fact if not necessarily in principle, the very notion of Scripture. There is the same scientistic-positivistic esprit, which shows a tendency to reduce the meaning of liturgy to facts that lie behind liturgy's apparent form. For example, the Eucharist is primarily a meal, and the Christian Eucharist is reducible without remainder to the Passover.[96] With respect to the former Benedict avers that

> we must reject that the Christian liturgy originates simply in the Last Supper, there is simply no hiatus between Jesus and the Church. The Lord's gift is not some rigid formula but a living reality. It was open to historical development, and only where this development is accepted can there be continuity with Jesus. Here, as so often, "progressive" reformers exhibit a fundamentally narrow view of Christian beginnings, seeing history piecemeal, whereas the sacramental view of the Church rests upon an inner developmental unity.[97]

When it comes to reducing the Eucharist to the Passover, for Benedict it is evident that this ignores (a) that in the Christian Eucharist the Passover is fundamentally altered by being placed in the context of the first day of the resurrected Lord; and (b) that those who propose such a view have lost all sense of typology, that is, that a saying or action in the context of biblical Judaism points toward a completion in which the new meaning introduced is understood to be the full meaning and truth of the earlier saying or action.[98] This reductive sensibility, which has been thoroughly infected by the Enlightenment, has no time for the mystery that is both attended to and rendered in liturgy.[99] Benedict's reservations here cannot fail to remind of Augustine in the *Confessions*, who if more than grateful for the help provided by philosophy in his weaning from myth also thinks that it is bedeviled by pride. Benedict discovers that much modern thought, which flies under the banner of philosophy, is intolerant of discourses and practices that evoke and render a saving reality but cannot understand it all the way down.[100]

CONCLUSION

In this essay, written in honor of Benedict XVI on his eighty-fifth birthday, I argued that Benedict's theology is constitutively Augustinian. If there were anything valuable in the essay, it is not so much the "Augustinian" ascription itself as the laying out of what the range and level of repetition of the historical Augustine would have to be in order for the ascription to be truly meaningful and not indicate either a point of view or an evaluative stance. This required speaking to a double and reinforcing repetition of style and theological substance. This is to speak to range. The level of repetition had to do in particular with the sheer volume of recall in Benedict's texts of Augustine on the level of substance. I discussed in more or less detail five of the more conspicuous features of an extensive and deep repetition of theological substance: eschatology; the picture of a healthy and, correspondingly, an unhealthy relation between faith and reason; biblical interpretation and the presumptive status of the biblical text; clarity on the relation between Christianity and non-Christian culture; and, finally, the doxological imperative instantiated in the prayer and liturgy of the Church. While I did not have enough space to develop the point, it is important that these features constitute an interlocking set, and are not merely an aggregate. I lavished particular attention on eschatology. While Benedict's treatment of "last things" in *Eschatology* has become something of a classic in the way that *Introduction to Christianity* has, this was not the reason for the preferential treatment. The reason was the interconnection between eschatology, considered as the doctrine of last things, and Benedict's eschatological vision of history, which, as the history of salvation, is also the history of a struggle between the kingdom of God and the kingdom of man in all its ideological vehemence and its implicit and explicit violence. As with Augustine, Benedict believes the *agon* to be in crucial respects structural. This does not mean, however, that the *agon* between the kingdom of God and the kingdom of man cannot under some circumstances become exacerbated. This is how Augustine assesses his own historical situation as he writes the *City of God*. In facing up to the exacerbation, Augustine can use the Book of Revelation as a visionary lens in and through which he can outline and critically assess the dangers to faith and the Church. For Augustine, this is not pessimism but Christian realism. Similarly with Benedict. He diagnoses in the present moment the counterfeiting of the kingdom of God; he espies the split between faith and reason, which truncates both and leads to the pathologies of fanaticism and terrorism, on the one hand, and, on the other, a conscienceless reason that for all its preaching of tolerance is intolerant and prone to violence; he discerns that the biblical text is being reduced to fairy tale and/or historical factoids; he finds all too evident the prejudice that, in all its negotiations with culture, it is Christianity that is required to yield; and he finds that prayer and liturgy, which are two of the central practices of faith, are taken to be anachronistic and that the making of saints, which is the aim of the Church, has become an object of ridicule. There is an apocalyptic imagination at work in Benedict, and it is Augustinian in basic form. But this is not pessimism. Rather, it is simply the hope which holds out that what opposes the Love revealed in the passion, death, and resurrection of Christ cannot prevail.

NOTES

1. In this sense the circle is more nearly a spiral.

2. For the former, see Joseph Ratzinger, *Volk und Haus Gottes in Augustins Lehre von der Kirche* (Munich: Karl Zink Verlag, 1954). The dissertation was completed in 1952. For the latter, see the five conferences on Augustine in Benedict XVI, *Church Fathers: From Clement to Augustine,* trans. L'Osservatore Romano (San Francisco: Ignatius Press, 2008), 167–96. "Catechetical" is a relatively adequate descriptor of these conferences on the Church fathers, since two of the fundamental elements of Catholic belief covered by the Universal Catechism (1992) are living in the faith of which saints are the exemplars and the centrality of prayer. See Ratzinger's reflection on the Universal Catechism in a book he coauthored with Cardinal Christoph Schoenborn, *Introduction to the Catechism of the Catholic Church* (San Francisco: Ignatius Press, 1994), 9–36.

3. See Benedict XVI, *Jesus of Nazareth: From the Baptism in the Jordan to the Transfiguration,* trans. Adrian. J. Walker (New York: Doubleday, 2007); and *Jesus of Nazareth: Part Two: Holy Week: From the Entrance into Jerusalem to the Resurrection,* trans. Vatican Secretariat of State (San Francisco: Ignatius Press, 2011).

4. The Habilitation was completed in 1957. A very abbreviated version of the Habilitation (which was the subject of severe criticism at the Defense) appeared in 1959. See *Die Geschichtstheologie des heiligen Bonaventura* (Munich: Schnell & Steiner, 1959). For a serviceable translation, see *The Theology of History in Saint Bonaventure,* trans. Zachary Hayes (Chicago: Franciscan Herald Press, 1971). See Joseph Ratzinger's *Eschatology, Death and Eternal Life,* trans. Michael Waldstein (Washington, DC: Catholic University of America Press, 1988). This represents a translation of *Eschatologie: Tod und ewiges Leben* (Regensburg: F. Pustel, 1978). The quote is from Benedict XVI, *Church Fathers,* 196. When he makes this statement Benedict has already declared that the first part of *Deus Caritas Est* owes much to Augustine.

5. Benedict XVI, *Church Fathers,* 178.

6. Ibid.

7. On simple faith, see Joseph Ratzinger, *God and the World: Believing and Living in Our Time: A Conversation with Peter Seewald,* trans. Henry Taylor (San Francisco: Ignatius Press, 2002), 71.

8. Benedict XVI, *Church Fathers.* For *Confessions,* see 184–87; for *City of God,* see 186–87; and for *On Christian Doctrine,* see 188.

9. Ibid., 187–88.

10. One of the reasons Benedict prefers Communio theologians such as de Lubac and Balthasar to Rahner is that, in his view, the latter tends to concede too much to the prestige of the scientific method.

11. Benedict XVI, *Church Fathers;* for *de Catechizandis Rudibus,* see 188.

12. Ibid., 189.

13. *Introduction to Christianity,* trans. J. R. Forster (San Francisco: Ignatius Press, 2004). This text corresponds to Augustine's compendious account of faith in the *Enchiridion.*

14. For reflections on God as triune, see *The God of Jesus Christ: Meditations on the Triune God,* trans. Brian McNeil (San Francisco: Ignatius Press, 2008). This translates the much earlier *Der Gott Jesu Christi: Betrachtungen über den Dreieingen Gott* (Munich: Kösel-Verlag, 1976). The basis of the English translation is the new German edition published in 2006. Here Benedict develops his reflections on the triune God offered in *Introduction to Christianity,* which were somewhat schematic. For creation, see *In the Beginning: A Catholic Understanding of the Story of Creation and Fall,* trans. Boniface Ramsey (Grand Rapids, MI: Eerdmans, 1995). For liturgy, see *The Feast of Faith: Approaches to a Theology of the Liturgy,* trans. Graham Harrison (San Francisco: Ignatius Press, 1986); also *The Spirit of the Liturgy,* trans. John Saward (San Francisco: Ignatius Press, 2000). With respect to Christology, in addition to the two-volume *Jesus of Nazareth,* see *Behold the Pierced One: An Approach to a Spiritual Christology,* trans. Graham Harrison (San Francisco: Ignatius Press, 1986). This latter text is meditative or contemplative in nature.

15. See especially the foreword to *Jesus of Nazareth,* I, xi–xxiv, where Benedict expresses his respect for the historical-critical method while still arguing for canonical exegesis. The views expressed in *Jesus of Nazareth* regarding the historical-critical method are of long standing. See, for example, Benedict's essay "Biblical Interpretation in Conflict," in *God's Word: Scripture, Tradition, Office,* trans. Henry Taylor (San Francisco: Ignatius Press, 2008), 91–126. The original essay, "Schriftauslegung im Widerstreit," was published in 1989.

16. The essays, mainly from the past decade but some dating from the 1990s, gathered in *Values in a Time of Upheaval,* trans. Brian McNeil (San Francisco: Ignatius, 2006), give clear indication of both of these tracks. Most of the essays question the marginalization of Christianity by the modern secular state, with special reference to the European situation. That Benedict still regards Marxism as a threat is indicated in the 2002 essay "To Change or Preserve" (11–29). Here Marxism is labeled a false form of apocalyptic or messianism. If the urgency with respect to Marxism is Benedict's own, he can

depend on a labeling that has been around for a considerable time and which is provided different expressions in two of his favorite theologians, Henri de Lubac and Hans Urs von Balthasar.

17. The best-known expression of Benedict's reservations regarding liberation theology is the silencing of Leonardo Boff in 1984.

18. See my "Newman and Anti-Liberalism," *Sacred Heart Review* (Fall 1992): 63–88; also "Newman and the Argument of Holiness," *Newman Studies* 9, no. 1 (Spring 2012): 52–74. Newman makes it plain throughout his sixty-year writing career that rationalism or liberalism in religion is the greatest challenge mainline Christianity faces and, accordingly, has to be resisted. Newman's intellectual biography, *Apologia pro vita sua* (1864), underscores that, at a root level, seeking an answer to rationalism in religion provides the underlying motor in Newman's journey to Rome. When he received the Cardinalate in 1879, Newman summed up his career as one spent fighting the forces of liberalism in religion.

19. Although Benedict understands the contrast between the kingdom of God and the kingdom of man to be biblical in the last instance, there is no contradiction in suggesting that, for him, the classical theological reflection is provided by Augustine, who, after all, is quintessentially a biblical thinker Benedict is in line with a number of twentieth century Catholic theologians, for example, Balthasar and de Lubac, who spoke out against a confusion they identified as the immanentization of transcendence.

20. The North American theologian John E. Thiel has spoken eloquently to the shift in the understanding of the authority of the theologian, which has as its backdrop Romantic notions of individual talent. See his *Imagination and Authority: Theological Authorship in the Modern Tradition* (Minneapolis: Fortress Press, 1991). Thiel argues that while the notion of theological talent gained sway in Protestant circles more quickly than it did in the Catholic Church, it gradually gained a foothold in Catholic circles through a reading of Schleiermacher. Subsequent to the Tübingen school, where, he believes, such a view gets authorized (especially in J. S. Drey), there has existed the potential for tension between theological charisma and the authority of the magisterium. This has been especially the case in the post-Conciliar period.

21. While Rahner is not heavily cited in *Eschatology*, he is mentioned on a number of occasions. As one would expect, the text usually referred to is *Zur Theologie des Todes: Mit einem Exkurs über das Martyrium* (Freiburg: B. Herder, 1958). Benedict also notes how Rahner avails of de Chardin to make the point that at death the soul becomes transcosmic rather than acosmic (Ratzinger, *Eschatology*, 191).

22. Among the better-known biblical scholars with whom Benedict engages are R. Bultmann, J. Greshake, J. Jeremias, A. Schweitzer, and J. Weisse. The list of biblical scholars is dominantly German. A notable exception is the English biblical scholar C. H. Dodd.

23. On Benedict's emphatic emphasis on God's love, note that while in *Eschatology* Benedict affirms the reality of hell on the basis of Scripture and tradition, the section is noticeable for its brevity (Ratzinger, *Eschatology,* 215–18). In fact, Matthew 25, which is so important to Augustine in the *City of God,* is not adduced, and consequently hell is regarded more nearly as the refusal of the offer of divine love than an exercise in retributive justice. Benedict has a number of different concerns in this section. On the one hand, he wishes to put some epistemological limits on what we can know about hell (Augustine seems to know quite a lot), and, on the other hand, he does not want the Christian believer to conceive of hell as an expression of the limit of God's mercy. The latter is a guiding concern of Balthasar, whose notion of Christ's descent into hell seems to be conspicuous in Benedict's very brief discussion. Hell is the consequence of the self's definitive choice to close himself or herself off from God. This view clearly has an Augustinian ancestry. Conspicuously absent from discussion are Augustine's views about the *massa perditionis* and the election of the few. On Benedict's view of hell, note that, for Benedict, who God is can only be revealed in the economy. In *Eschatology* the crucial act in and of salvation history is defined by the cross and even more by Christ's descent to Sheol to rescue the "dead." While there is no reason to suppose that Benedict is in full agreement with Balthasar's entire paschal theology, at the very least he places himself broadly within a Balthasarian horizon in which, while judgment is real and the person can fall out of relation with God, God is more nearly defined by love than by justice or at the very least by a loving justice.

24. Ratzinger, *Eschatology,* 61. See the new foreword to the second edition of *Eschatology* (Washington, DC: Catholic University of America Press, 2008), xvii–xxii.

25. Ratzinger, *Eschatology,* 58, 59.

26. For the discussion of means and ends, see Benedict XVI, *Jesus of Nazareth,* I, 25–45. On the Temptation story, see *Jesus of Nazareth,* I, 35–36. Benedict also refers to Soloviev's short story on the Antichrist in the opening paragraph of his essay "Biblical Interpretation in Conflict," in Ratzinger, *God's Word,* 91. Again, Balthasar and de Lubac are Catholic precursors. For de Lubac, see *The Drama of Atheistic Humanism,* trans. Ann Englund Nash, Edith M. Riley, and Mark Sebanc (San Francisco: Ignatius Press, 1995). The original French text dates from 1944. For de Lubac's discussion of Dos-

toyevski, see 269–394. Soloviev's story on the Antichrist is mentioned at 326 and 334. Benedict has read this text. He mentions it in his essay of 1969 (originally a talk on Bavarian radio), "Faith and Knowledge." See *Faith and the Future* (San Francisco: Ignatius Press, 2009), 13–34, esp. 28 (originally published by Franciscan Herald Press, 1971). Of course, Balthasar had already pointed to the religious importance of Dostoyevski in volume 2 of *Apokalypse der deutschen Seele: Studien zu einer Lehre von Ietzten Haltungen*, 3 vols. (Salzburg: Pustet, 1937–39), even as he complained about Dostoyevski's Panslavism (2.248–51). This worry is repeated in *The Drama of Atheistic Humanism*, 368–69. For Balthasar's most sustained reflection on Soloviev, see *The Glory of the Lord: A Theological Aesthetics*, vol. 3: *Studies in Theological Style: Lay Styles*, trans. Andrew Louth, John Saward, Martin Simon, and Rowan Williams, ed. John Riches (San Francisco: Ignatius Press, 1986), 279–352. The German edition of this volume of *Herrlichkeit* (2.2) dates from 1962. For Soloviev's apocalyptic view of the Antichrist, see 349–51. For general connections with Dostoyevski, see 294–95, 342–44.

27. An encyclical clearly enjoys a different and higher authority than a text written by a theologian, even one with the name of Joseph Ratzinger.

28. See Francis Fukuyama, *The End of History and the Last Man* (London: Free Press, 1992).

29. See, among other texts, Ratzinger, *Values*, 114, 120.

30. Although the main target of Metz's critique is modern bourgeois culture, from time to time he does criticize totalitarian brands of Marxism, as was the wont of Critical Theory, which he confesses influenced him significantly. Thus, there are definite points of overlap as well as difference. More work can be done here. Unfortunately, in one of their main dialogues Metz and Benedict seem to talk past each other. See Joseph Cardinal Ratzinger, Johann Baptist Metz, Jürgen Moltmann, Eveline Goodman-Thau, Tierno Tanier Peters, and Claus Urban, *The End of Time? The Provocation of Talking about God: Proceedings of a Meeting in Ahaus*, trans. Matthew Ashley (Mahwah, NJ: Paulist Press, 2004), esp. 4–53.

31. Ratzinger, *Values*, 17. For Derrida, the annunciation of the end of Marxism is premature. For its continuing subterranean force, see Jacques Derrida, *Specters of Marx: The State of the Debt, the Work of Mourning, and the New International*, trans. Peggy Kamuf (New York: Routledge, 1994).

32. The essays in *Values* touch on the imbrication of violence and secular forms of thought. National Socialism and Marxism are both condemned. But Benedict wishes to make a case that goes beyond ideologies, which might be thought to have a religious basis, to the very notion of the state itself. It is the state in the form of Pontius Pilate that sacrifices Christ for the

good of the whole (58–59). In an interesting appeal to Revelation that is Augustinian in overall orientation, Benedict underscores the eschatological judgment made against the violence of the state. For the violence prosecuted by the secular state, see also Ratzinger, *Introduction,* 250–54.

33. See in particular "Belief in the Triune God and Peace in the World," which is the epilogue to *Values in a Time of Upheaval.* See Ratzinger, *Values,* 161–67. In his essay "Search for Peace" in Ratzinger, *Values,* 101–16, Benedict makes it clear that while Christianity is a religion of peace, it is not in the strict sense pacifist.

34. Benedict speaks in a very Girardian way of the unhappy interconnection of violence and religion when he notes the blood sacrifice that was routine in Aztec religion. See Joseph Ratzinger, *Truth and Tolerance: Christian Belief and World Religions,* trans. Henry Taylor (San Francisco: Ignatius Press, 2004), 74–75.

35. For Benedict's refutation of Assmann, see Ratzinger, *Tolerance,* 210–17.

36. This is a theme regularly struck by John Milbank in *Theology and Social Theory: Beyond Secular Reason* (Oxford: Blackwell, 1990). See in particular 402 and 407 for his critique of Robert Marcus's view that Augustine's theology of history opens up the domain of the secular.

37. Benedict worries in his book on Bonaventure about too much emphasis on Spirit as Spirit is loosened from the Church.

38. The imputation that the apocalypticism of the modern age can be traced back to Joachim is already in play in *Apokalypse der deutschen Seele.*

39. See Jürgen Moltmann, *Theology of Hope: On the Ground and the Implication of a Christian Eschatology,* trans. J. W. Leitch (London: SCM Press, 1967). For a convenient translation of Ernst Bloch's *Das Prinzip Hoffnung,* see *The Principle of Hope,* 3 vols., trans. Neville Plaice, Stephen Plaice, and Paul Knight (Cambridge, MA: MIT Press, 1995).

40. Joseph Ratzinger, *Church, Ecumenism, and Politics: New Endeavors in Ecclesiology,* trans. Michael J. Miller et al. (San Francisco: Ignatius Press, 2008), 211–12.

41. I make the case for Balthasar as an apocalyptic thinker in my forthcoming *Anatomy of Misremembering,* vol. 1: *Balthasar and the Specter of Hegel* (New York: Crossroad, 2012). For a more synoptic expression, see my *Theology and the Spaces of Apocalyptic* (Milwaukee: Marquette University Press, 2009), 44–54.

42. Ratzinger, *Eschatology,* 32.

43. Ibid., 14–15.

44. Benedict XVI, *Jesus of Nazareth,* I, 332.

45. Ibid., 30; also 31, 33.

46. See John Howard Yoder, *The Politics of Jesus: Vicit Agnus Noster* (Grand Rapids, MI: Eerdmans, 1972); also *The Original Revolution: Essays in Christian Pacifism* (Scottsdale, PA: Herald Press, 1971). For a good synoptic account of Yoder's anti-Constantinian position, see Nathan Kerr, *Christ, History, and Apocalyptic: The Politics of Christian Mission* (Eugene, OR: Cascade Books, 2009), 127–60. See also Benedict XVI, *Jesus of Nazareth*, I, 39–40.

47. Benedict XVI, *Jesus of Nazareth*, I, 42–43.

48. See James V. Schall, *The Regensburg Lecture* (South Bend, IN: St. Augustine's Press, 2007). Schall's book includes the lecture ("The Regensburg Address," at 130–48), but the bulk of the book is commentary in which he persuasively argues that the main topic of the lecture is outlining the proper relation between faith and reason and giving an account of their separation throughout history to the mutual detriment of both.

49. Ibid., 137.

50. This thesis essentially characterizes Oberman's career and to some extent generated an entire historiographical school that continues to have influence in the academy. For a representative text, see his *The Harvest of Medieval Theology: Gabriel Biel and Late Medieval Nominalism* (Cambridge, MA: Harvard University Press, 1963). With a view to uncovering Benedict's intentions, the interpretive strategy that would likely yield the best results is to connect #25, which speaks to developments of Scotus, and #32, in which Benedict claims that it is with the Reformation that the program of de-Hellenization is first introduced.

51. Benedict may or may not have read deeply in Jansenism, but from de Lubac's explorations on the theology of grace he has some knowledge of this intrinsically Catholic phenomenon, as well as what is at stake theologically.

52. In "The Regensburg Address," #40–56. The critique of instrumental reason is a constant throughout his work. A good example is provided by Benedict's 1969 essay "Faith and Philosophy," in Ratzinger, *Faith and the Future*, 61–85, where there is an attack against the positivism of Auguste Comte but even more important of Kant's understanding of the limitations of reason that encourage the positivistic mentality.

53. "The Regensburg Address" and *Deus Caritas Est* have to be seen together. The papal encyclical precedes his lecture by a year, but the Johannine designation of God as Love is still intrinsically connected to the other designation of God as Logos, which is the thrust of the lecture. In "The Regensburg Address," see especially #17–24.

54. Benedict confirms just about all of this in his subtle reflections on *Fides et Ratio* in Ratzinger, *Tolerance*, 183–93. He particularly underscores

relativistic forms of thought, which, in the name of democracy, foreclose not only truth, but the very sense of the quest for it. Benedict does not mention either Jacques Derrida or Richard Rorty in his defense of the encyclical against those who judge it to be undemocratic, but he attacks Rorty in his 1992 essay "What Is Truth? The Significance of Religious and Ethical Values in a Pluralist Society," in Ratzinger, *Values*, 53–72, esp. 61. See also Ratzinger, *Values*, 47, where Rorty is compared unfavorably to the Russian dissident A. D. Sakharov. Derrida comes under attack in another essay in the same text, "Tensions and Dangers," in Ratzinger, *Values*, 101–21. Benedict brings out the latent nihilism of Derrida's thought in the following passage (111), which is italicized in the English-language text: *"Reason capable only of recognizing its own self and that which is empirically certain paralyzes and destroys itself."*

55. This is a point made by Newman throughout his *Oxford University Sermons*, which predate his conversion. See, Ratzinger, *Values*, 36, 110.

56. The most explicit asseveration of this is to be found in the essay "Searching for Peace: Tensions and Dangers," in Ratzinger, *Values*, 109–11.

57. Ratzinger, *Values*, 43. For a similar asseveration, see 28.

58. I am thinking here specifically of the eleventh of the fifteen sermons that make up the *Oxford University Sermons* which goes under the title "Love the Safeguard of Faith against Superstition." While Newman insists that faith is not faith unless it goes beyond what is provable, it is true that in certain contexts its "leap" is unregulated by a character that has been formed in and of love. This is not the place to trace out how Newman validates the connection of love and faith and how the connection prevents violence, but the correlation anticipates the connection that Benedict makes in both "The Regensburg Address" and his encyclical *Deus Caritas Est*. See William Cavanaugh, *The Myth of Religious Violence: Secular Ideology and the Roots of Modern Conflict* (New York: Oxford University Press, 2009). See also my comments in a symposium on the book in *Pro Ecclesia* 20, no. 4 (Fall 2011): 342–48, in which I argue that Newman is an ally in the unmasking of the secularist projection. Moreover, when Newman makes the interesting point that the charge of fanaticism with regard to Christian faith continues to be recycled long after anyone kills or is killed because of belief, he anticipates Benedict's indictment of secular reason and its masking of its own propensity to violence.

59. For Benedict's negative comments on National Socialism, see Ratzinger, *Tolerance*, 233–34, 240, 248; also Ratzinger, *Values*, 102–4, 142, 145–46.

60. In this regard, see Benedict's 2004 essay "Belief in the Triune God and Peace in the World," in Ratzinger, *Values*, 161–67. The triune God is the unsurpassable figuration of Shalom.

61. In Ratzinger, *Behold,* 13–46.

62. Ibid., 42.

63. Ibid., 42–46.

64. Ibid., 43.

65. Ibid.

66. Ibid.

67. Ratzinger, *God's Word,* 91.

68. Ibid., 91, 101.

69. Ibid., 91.

70. Ibid., 100.

71. Ibid., 92.

72. Ibid., 92, 95.

73. Corrected in the case of Bultmann and Dibelius, who separate faith entirely from history and effectively sunder the Old from the New Testament. See Ratzinger, *God's Word,* 102–12. Benedict is interested in modifying. This involves a new synthesis which links the historical-critical method, which rightly underscores the importance of the historical Christianity, with tradition and both with a commitment to the revelation to which each is responsible (114–26).

74. Ibid., 92.

75. Ibid., 103.

76. See, for instance, the essays gathered in Duane W. H. Arnold and Pamela Bright, eds., *De Doctrina Christiana: A Classic of Western Culture* (Notre Dame: University of Notre Dame Press, 1995). See especially the very useful bibliography, 245–60.

77. Ratzinger, *Tolerance,* 186; also 79.

78. Ibid., 92, 102–4.

79. Ibid., 102. Throughout *Truth and Tolerance* Benedict argues against the pluralist view of religion which tends to take a Kantian form, regarding all religions as phenomenal expressions of a the noumenal essence of religion, which, as ineffable, is not tied to any particular symbols, doctrines, concepts, practices, or forms of life.

80. If it did not exceed the scope of this essay, it would be interesting to explore the relation between Benedict and Pannenberg on this point.

81. Ratzinger, *Tolerance,* 85 ff.

82. See Ratzinger, *Feast of Faith,* 16.

83. Ibid., 32. Benedict has particularly in mind Greek philosophy, with which Christians dealt from the beginning, both in the writing of the New Testament and in its interpretation; see 17. Whether Benedict would continue to hold the view expressed in this text, that Asiatic religions represent

the main challenge to Christianity, depends at least in part on how we interpret the statement. If the statement has to do with the clash between types of religion, between Christianity as a religion based on prayer and religions that do not have prayer as their basis, then it is not unlikely that Benedict remains committed to a view that was most influentially stated by one of his great teachers, Henri de Lubac. If, however, the issue is that of challenge from other religions, as this challenge is unspecified with regard to type, then it might well be the case that with the emergence of a global Islam—which is a religion of prayer—Benedict would pronounce differently on the challenge; see 24–25.

84. Ibid., 28–29.

85. Benedict XVI, *Jesus of Nazareth*, I, 7.

86. Ibid., 128–68.

87. Ibid., 135.

88. Ratzinger, *Feast of Faith*, 29.

89. Hans Ur von Balthasar, *Prayer*, trans. Graham Harrrison (San Francisco: Ignatius Press, 1986).

90. For Benedict, these essentially amount to the same thing.

91. Ratzinger, *Feast of Faith*, 37.

92. See especially Ratzinger, *Spirit of the Liturgy*, 28. Interestingly, in speaking to the notion of sacrifice, Benedict invokes Augustine, who grasps its purpose, which is that of a transformed world and a divinized humanity.

93. The title of Benedict's book repeats that of Guardini, and in the preface Benedict pays homage to Guardini's *The Spirit of the Liturgy* (1918), which Benedict suggests is at the origin of the liturgical movement.

94. For thanksgiving, see Ratzinger, *Spirit of the Liturgy*, 43, 55; for prolepsis, see 21.

95. In Ratzinger, *Feast of Faith*, 57. Although Benedict's point here is very general, it is in line with Daniélou's more concerted apocalyptic contextualization of the Eucharist.

96. See especially Ratzinger, *Feast of Faith*, 39–50.

97. Ibid., 49.

98. For (a), see Ratzinger, *Feast of Faith*, 45. For (b), see Joseph Ratzinger, "On the Meaning of Sacrament," trans. Kenneth Baker, S.J., *FCS Quarterly* (Spring 2011): 28–35. The original German article, "Zum Begriff des Sakramentes," was delivered as a lecture in 1978 and published in 1979.

99. See Ratzinger, "On the Meaning of Sacrament," 29–31.

100. In line with *Fides et Ratio* Benedict thinks that this modern form of philosophy distorts the very essence of philosophy as the search for wisdom.

The Dynamic of Advent

chapter two

CULTURE AND CONSCIENCE
IN THE THOUGHT OF
JOSEPH RATZINGER/
POPE BENEDICT XVI

PETER CASARELLA

Benedict XVI's opposition to the "dictatorship of relativism" derives from a homily delivered in St. Peter's Basilica on the eve of the conclave at which he was elected pope. Too often the phrase is taken as if it were a blast from a bunker in the U.S. culture wars. It cries out for deeper analysis. Such an analysis would show the then-cardinal's engagement with actual forms of dictatorship, his keen awareness of different forms of relativism, and his profound grasp of the complex language and reality of bearing witness to the truth. The phrase "dictatorship of relativism" aptly captures his concern that the question of truth cannot be shunted to the side or managed solely through the techniques of public relations. Truth has to be considered in its very foundations. The phrase provokes thought, not just for Catholics, but for the whole human family.

The phrase also highlights the deep connection between the question of culture and moral principles. This essay deals with the question of Pope Benedict XVI's theology of culture and the place of moral reasoning in it. He speaks often about the failure of moralism. He means that it is impossible to address moral conflicts by ignoring either the true breadth of reason or the concrete demands being placed on the "living 'we'" of the Christian community.[1] As with "dictatorship of relativism," Pope Benedict's genius lies in his ability to find a concrete configuration that offers a living synthesis. The fruit of his meditation is not an abstract system but, like that of the gospel itself, is a word that performs and an action that speaks.

The thesis that I would like to defend is that the Holy Father prioritizes conscience in a nonmoralistic fashion in his treatment of the relationship of faith and culture. In June 2011, in his address to cultural leaders in Zagreb, he described conscience as "the keystone on which to base a culture and build up the common good." He continued, "It is by forming consciences that the Church makes her most specific and valuable contribution to society."[2] Conscience is accordingly a key to cultural renewal in a way that implies both personal and social transformations.

My argument has three parts. I begin with the basic outlines of Joseph Ratzinger's theology of culture and focus on how he links the foundations of moral reasoning to a phenomenology of culture and interculturality. In the second part, I focus on his theory of conscience and try to show where cultural formation fits into it. I conclude by considering witnessing to the truth. For Pope Benedict, I maintain, the witness to truth is the key to seeing how culture and conscience are necessarily intertwined.

CULTURE: THE DYNAMIC OF ADVENT

In his study of the philosophy of culture, Ratzinger likens the dynamic within culture to the phenomenon of advent. The comment derives from the study of Virgil by Theodor Haecker, who is much esteemed by Ratzinger. Haecker was an ardent opponent of fascism in

Germany who earned fame for his translations of Kierkegaard and Newman. Fr. D. Vincent Twomey, S.V.D., in his fine book on Pope Benedict rightly suggests, in my opinion, its wider applicability to Benedict's theology of culture.[3] Accordingly, the fullest sense of progress within a culture is progress made toward the revelation of a Redeemer. Progress here is defined in unsecular terms. Ratzinger questions notions of social progress that have become untethered from belief in God and ties real progress to a challenging and self-critical process of intercultural dialogue.

For Ratzinger, all cultures are in some fashion religious. Most reach a crisis when agents of social change submit the religious element to critical inquiry. Ratzinger counters the Enlightenment model of criticism, namely, that of gradual emancipation from self-imposed tutelage and the undue influence of religious institutions, without ignoring its potential benefits. The idea that religion and culture are separate spheres, he says, is an invention of relatively modern European vintage. This secularizing norm does not prevail in other cultures and in other periods.[4] Ratzinger defines culture as "the social form of expression, as it has grown up in history, of those experiences and evaluations that have left their mark on a community and have shaped it."[5] Cultural agents are not solely occupied with religious questions, but these questions occupy a central place: "Indeed, the very heart of the great cultures is that they interpret the world by setting in order their relationship to Divinity."[6] Some cultures—Ratzinger terms these entitities "cosmic/static cultures"—do not valorize the historical dimension. The cosmic cultures reveal the universe as a mystery and point out that death and rebirth are paths for human existence. The cultural paths of Judaism and Christianity are, by contrast, historical ones. Without the historical dimension cosmic cultures are not well positioned to deal with change.

Renewal and change are valuable processes in cultural development. The meeting of cultures, Ratzinger states, is "the healing Pasch for a culture, which through an apparent death comes to new life and becomes then for the first time truly itself."[7] The phenomenon of advent presupposes that there are agents of change within the dynamic of a culture who advocate radical change based on the religious wisdom of the community. Ratzinger himself mentions the struggle to achieve racial equality in the United States as an example of a religiously based social transformation.[8] Although this connection is not made explicit, he appears to be speaking in a phenomenological key about the "prophetic radicalism" of the Old Testament.[9] For example, he cites Jonah's prophetism as an example of religious progress since Jonah is able to warn the heathens of Ninevah of God's destruction of their city. "They know in their inmost hearts," writes Ratzinger, "that he exists, the one God, and they recognize the voice of that God in the preaching of the foreign prophet."[10] The modern critiques of religion by Dietrich Bonhoeffer and Karl Barth (and even in a certain way by the atheists Ludwig Feuerbach and Karl Marx) all carry some vestige of this radicalism.[11] In sum, historical cultures are never static but have a great capacity to endure over time because they are constantly subjected to further tests of allegiance to their ultimate source of Being. Cultural progress here is tied to a firm belief in a Creator.

Violence can ensue when cultures come into conflict with one another. Here we encounter what appears at first glance as one of Ratzinger's signature criticisms of contemporary Catholic theology. He relativizes the centrality of "inculturation" as a way of speaking about how cultures come into contact with one another. He prefers to speak about "the meeting of cultures" or "interculturality." His basic concern is again to lay bare the unacknowledged impact of secularism on the interpretation of religious experience:

> For "inculturation" presupposes that, as it were, a culturally naked faith is transferred into a culture that is indifferent from the religious point of view, so that two agents that were hitherto alien to each other meet and now engage in a synthesis together. But this depiction is first of all artificial and unreal, because there is no such thing as a culture-free faith and because—outside of modern technical civilization—there is no such thing as religion-free culture.[12]

In other words, only in a fairly secularized context might one assume that a culture is a fixed body of unreligious beliefs that includes a certain number of separate or at least separable religious beliefs. According to the secularized view as defined by Ratzinger, inculturation would then consist in the adaptation of those elements of the religious beliefs that are not in accord with the other values of that culture. But since religious belief is mutatis mutandis the very foundation of *every* culture, the surgical model of cultural adaptation never works in practice. When one tries to extract all religion from the culture (or vice versa), one is left with a cadaver. The living bond between religion and culture is much more complex and organic.

The advent dynamic is a way to speak about the progression of cultures "toward the Logos of God, who became flesh in Jesus Christ."[13] In that sense, its theological presuppositions are clear. But advent also refers to the capacity of any culture—Christian or non-Christian—to remain open to an *encounter* with another culture without sacrificing *either* its religious foundation *or* the necessary stance of openness. This definition speaks volumes. It is more easily illuminated by broadening one's examination of the thought of Joseph Ratzinger/Pope Benedict XVI. The category of interpersonal encounter is a carefully defined leitmotif in Ratzinger's thinking.[14] Advent is a cross-cultural, interpersonal reality that obtains in some measure before, during, and after the historical advent of Christian faith: "A successful transformation is explained by the potential universality of all cultures made concrete in a given culture's assimilation of the other and its own internal transformation. Such a procedure can even lead to the resolution of the latent alienation of man from truth and himself which a culture may harbor."[15]

Over time historical cultures remain rooted in their beliefs in a transcendent Source but become more purified and more open to challenges to their own potentially universal scope. This openness derives from the fact that all cultures have a common experience with human nature. No culture has a monopoly on human nature, and every culture can learn something new about human nature through its interaction with other cultures. Ratzinger's resolute commitment to intercultural dialogue is nurtured by his confidence in the ability of our contemporaries to recover the lost language of human nature.

CONSCIENCE IN OUR AGE

The link between human nature and the need for dialogue brings us to the question of conscience. This link has been a concern of Joseph Ratzinger since the early stages of his intellectual formation. For example, he tells the story from his days as a young academic of meeting a fellow professor, a skeptic about Christian morality, who claimed that Hitler and members of the Nazi SS would have their actions automatically justified in heaven on account of the inherently subjective nature of an erroneous conscience. "Since they followed their (albeit) mistaken consciences," he reports his colleague as saying, "one would have to recognize their conduct as moral and, as a result, should not doubt their eternal salvation."[16] That troubling experience led him to the Catholic psychologist Albert Görres, who had written about how feelings of guilt are objective constituents of the human constitution. "All men need guilt feelings," stated Görres.[17] Ratzinger is thus concerned that conscience has been treated reductively and rightly worries about the consequences of such a reductiveness: "The identification of conscience with superficial consciousness, the reduction of man to his subjectivity, does not liberate, but enslaves. It makes us totally dependent on the prevailing opinions, and debases these with every passing day."[18] At its root the problem of conscience is not different from that of culture. In both cases, the central issue is the avoidance of the question of truth. An erroneous conscience is self-justifying only in a world in which truth has been shunted to the side.

In his 1991 address, "Conscience and Truth," at the annual workshop of the National Catholic Bioethics Center Ratzinger faces this problem in two ways: in terms of paradigmatic witnesses to the truth of conscience and in terms of a new presentation of the basic structure of conscience. In that address he develops an initial approach "of example and narrative" by rereading two figures, Newman and Socrates.

Ratzinger was introduced to Newman by Theodor Haecker, by his teacher Gottlieb Söhngen, and also by a German writer named Alfred Läpple who returned from an English war prison in 1946 to serve as a prefect to young seminarians and even before the war had started a dissertation on Newman's theology of conscience.[19] The key to the mature Ratzinger's reading of Newman, which he reprised on the occasion of the beatification, is the way in which Newman's understanding of conscience is "diametrically opposed" to a metaphysical division of the world into an objective realm of scientific experiment and a subjective realm of morals. Newman submitted himself and his conscience to the path of obedience to the truth. This path involves siding neither with the modern advocates of scientism nor with the modern advocates of subjectivism. It involves training one's attention on the objective demands of an interior truth. Ratzinger is by his own admission trying to draw out the Augustinian in Newman:[20]

> Conscience for Newman does not mean that the subject is the standard vis-à-vis the claims of authority in a truthless world, a world that lives with a compromise between the claims of the subject and the claims of the social order. Much more than that, conscience signifies the perceptible and demanding presence of the voice of truth in the subject himself. It is the overcoming of mere subjectivity in the encounter of the interiority of man with the truth from *God*. The verse Newman composed in 1833 in Sicily is characteristic: "I loved to choose and see my path; but now lead thou me on!"[21]

Newman heals the rift between subjective and objective truth by appealing to his own neo-Augustinian phenomenology of graced inwardness. Accordingly, we must turn inward to resolve our moral dilemmas, but in that introspective move we confront something other than the mere shell of subjectivity. Ratzinger maintains that conscience is given as "an organ, not an oracle," in the words of Robert Spaemann.[22]

Having established the graced nature of inward moral certitude, it might seem like a step backward to present as the second guide a pagan author such as Socrates. But that is not at all the case for Ratzinger, who draws here heavily from Romano Guardini's *The Death of Socrates*. Ratzinger equates "the final meaning of the Socratic search" with "the profoundest element in the witness of the martyrs." Ratzinger recognizes that the serene acceptance of death by Socrates stands in stark contrast to Jesus' cup of wrath.[23] The figure of Socrates represents not just Stoic resolve, but our capacity as citizens to make an argument for the sake of the *polis*. Socratic reasoning in this view aims at the truth in the face of a Sophist's counterargument that we set the standards for ourselves. Ratzinger recognizes that some Catholic moralists have appropriated Socrates for their own purposes, that is, in order to rationalize the positive content of the biblical message. Socrates nonetheless remains for Ratzinger the nearly universal paradigm of conscientious political martyrdom.[24]

Two distinct dimensions of Ratzinger's general theory of conscience converge in this portrait of Socrates. Socrates is a political liberator because he recognized that truth transcends formal labels such as conservative, reactionary, fundamentalist, progressive, revolutionary.[25] His engagement in argument is not for the sake of displaying his virtuosity as a rhetorician or any other mode of technical mastery. His sacrifice is made for the love of justice and to show the emptiness of judgments made on the basis of "a pure formalism." Socrates represents an unmodern prelude to Kant's categorical imperative. His witness shows the limits of political justice in Periclean Athens (or potentially in any political community), but as public testimony it speaks certainly as persuasively as Kantian universalism to humanity's given capacity to seek truth. If there is a transcultural exemplum of conscience transcending any particularity, it would have to retain the Socratic feature of maintaining a connatural affinity with a truth not of one's own making.

Ratzinger also highlights the tragic and paradoxical character of Socrates' quest.[26] Socrates engages Euthyphro on piety while knowing that he himself is a man condemned for impiety. The judgment that piety cannot be what is pleasing to the gods becomes through Socrate's midwifery a recognition that the gods are at war in a very worldly fashion. The implicit pantheism is firmly established by Socratic interchange but is taken by Ratzinger as a "renunciation" of the radical Mosaic distinction between God and world. Herein lies Socrates' adventlike greatness: he can educate mankind to a worldliness that remains in itself a tragic blessing. He is the pre-Christian prophet of the grandeur and misery of human progress. "What God makes of the

poor broken pieces of our attempts at good, at approaching him, remains his secret, which we ought not to presume to try to work out,"
writes Ratzinger.[27] Both of Ratzinger's guides testify to the value and
limits of the breadth of reason. Conscience is a rational organ whose
form of rationality is inherently self-limiting.

On this basis Ratzinger proceeds to develop a general theory of
conscience. Drawing on the clues provided by Newman and Socrates,
he seeks out ways to build "bridges between subject and object."[28] The
medieval scholastic tradition distinguished between two levels of conscience: *synderesis* and *conscientia.* Saint Bonanventure, for example,
reviews the prevailing distinctions between the two terms and concludes that *synderesis* names the natural potentiality and *conscientia* a
disposition.[29] Ratzinger upholds the general scholastic distinction, although he seems to prefer in his own articulation of *conscientia* the
more finely articulated view of Saint Thomas. The general distinction
Ratzinger himself makes is between an ontological level and a level of
judgment. He can follow Saint Thomas in noting that in the *actus*
of *conscientia,* what he labels "an event in execution," one is bound to
follow one's conscience even if it is erroneous. But he notes that there
is nothing here that leads to a "canonization of subjectivism" (in either
a modern or in a neo-Abelardian sense).[30] Saint Thomas thus invali-
dates the subjectivist claim that the binding character of an erroneous
conscience can unbind the sinner from all guilt. The fault here lies
rather (and here the formulation comes from Ratzinger) "in the neglect of my being[,] [one] that made me deaf to the internal prompt-
ings of the truth."[31]

Ratzinger maintains that "many of the unacceptable theses regarding conscience are the result of neglecting either the difference or
the connection" between the ontological level of conscience and conscience as an act of judgment.[32] On this basic point, his concept of
conscience upholds the scholastic tradition. He then introduces an
innovation, one that he offers to clarify the sometimes imprecise mode
of expression in the standard account. *Synderesis,* he suggests, can be
better expressed by means of the Platonic category *anamnesis,* or what
we might today call "memory of the origin." The Bonaventurian distinction between natural potency and an acquired disposition is thus

replaced by a more Thomistic distinction, one between an *inner on-tology* that is repugnant to evil and attracted to good and an *act* that recognizes the good, bears witness to it, and then makes a judgment based on the particularities of the situation.[33] The ontological foundation of conscience is thus, in his words, "the fact that something like an original memory of the good and true (they are identical) has been implanted in us."[34]

I cannot enter here into a comparison of Ratzinger's new language with the whole of the scholastic tradition, but I would just note that the terminological shift coheres remarkably well with more general features of Ratzinger's thinking about the origins and destiny of the human person. In his *Eschatology, Death, and Eternal Life,* a text he first published in 1977, there is similarly an original theory of a dialogic relationship between the creature made in the image and likeness of God and the divine Trinitarian communion. The theory of immortality of the soul is in this way treated as an original Christian inheritance via a reading of Augustine on *memoria* time.[35] In his 1985 catechesis, *In the Beginning,* Cardinal Ratzinger also recovers the lost doctrine of the original human dependency on God.[36] Seen in this light, the foundation of moral conscience is a preexisting capacity for dialogue with the very source of one's Being, with the openness to Love that is revealed incarnately in the person of the firstborn of all creation. The innate moral sense is akin to Saint Basil's notion regarding "the spark of divine love that had been hidden in us," or, even better, to Saint Augustine when he said, "We could never judge that one thing is better than another, if a basic understanding of the good had not already been instilled in us."[37] This inner sense is the condition for the possibility of acting in good conscience but by itself has no "retrievable contents."[38] Because of its universal scope, the link between a memory of the good implanted in a creature and the creature's responsiveness in and through the activity of conscience is a safeguard against relativism. The givenness of conscience cannot be erased by an erroneous conscience. The givenness of conscience is a form of being a dependent creature that likewise transcends what is given to conscience by a particular culture.

Sometimes an emphasis by theologians on the doctrine of conscience is taken to be individualistic. Ratzinger is rightly concerned to counter this not uncommon objection. His starting point is well grounded in recent Catholic social teaching. The *Compendium of the Social Doctrine of the Church* says that the Church's social doctrine is "theological-moral" because it is found at the crossroads where Christian life and conscience come into contact with the real world.[39] The term *political conscience* is also used in the *Compendium*.[40] Ratzinger has likewise become known as an ardent advocate of the Church's social teaching, especially since the promulgation of *Caritas in Veritate* (2009).[41]

The precise issue here is more specific than just the affirmation of teachings about social justice. The question is, rather, this: How, if at all, does Ratzinger/Pope Benedict connect a coherent vision of society with the general formation of conscience? If we take his 1984 keynote address to the National Catholic Bioethics Center as the point of departure, we see that the formation of conscience is indeed a thoroughly social process. At the same time he circumscribes certain false conceptions of a social conscience. His basic concern remains the rift between objective thinking and subjective morality. Given that conscience must steer clear of both objectivism and subjectivism, Ratzinger then addresses the question of how the will of God and of the community can each serve as sources of morality. His presentation of the role of social processes is dialectical. In general, he follows Spaemann's model that conscience can be likened to the learning of a language since language acquisition also involves a complementarity of internalized and externalized processes.[42] I will highlight three elements in Ratzinger's dialectics of social consciousness. First, a society informed by the truth of the Christian message must break down existing social boundaries and present itself as a new entity in the world. This is the root meaning of catholicity, he notes, and as such continues to have meaning for us even today.[43] This new form of ecclesial solidarity was dramatically represented in the martyrs of the early Church, but that quality of newness cuts across all generations. Catholicism cannot degenerate into a club based on national, ethnic, or ideological allegiances without sacrificing its pledge of allegiance to evangelical newness. Second, the unconditional nature of God's will remains a constant for social formation. The modern turn to the subject may have made it more difficult to articulate a mission from God, but it remains the basis for both authentic moral formation and the self-reflexive process of overcoming ethnocentrism and idolatry. Nominalism (the treatment of the will as antithetical to the demands of reason) and deism (a Christianity that has become blind to the active and unconditional will of God) are but two sides of one coin in this regard.[44] The will of God allows a believer to form her or his conscience in such a way as to not rely exclusively on experience and custom. In a secular landscape, this form of liberation is desperately needed. The will of God awakens conscience to its own transcendent calling. Social consciousness comes into play precisely where the awakening to transcendence is taking place. The community is the "we" that constitutes the proximate source of moral knowledge for individuals in diverse contexts and with diverse compositions. The process of authentically interpreting divine revelation for the sake of communal formation points to the role of the Church. The scaffolding for social consciousness thus consists in recognizing the new place of the Christian community in the world, seeing the analogical import of the communion with the divine will, and promoting processes of inclusive incorporation that incarnate this vision. All formation of conscience is social, even though some forms of social consciousness can be driven by the norms of a secular ideology that distorts our receptivity to God's will. The formation of an individual conscience focused only on private self-improvement would by the same token be a further expansion of the dictatorship of relativism. Ratzinger recognizes that this account is nothing more than an ideal construct and offers in the rest of the 1984 address specifics on the role of bishops and magisterium in its implementation. I have focused on how he articulates the phenomenology of Christian social existence to show that he has coherently expressed the reasonability of a Christian social conscience.

Where does grace fit into Ratzinger's account of conscience? Part of Ratzinger's genius, I submit, is his ability to step back from the standard approaches to a theology of conscience in order to consider anew the dynamics of nature and grace. Before commenting on this question, I would note that the general question here had been a main concern of the young scholar who gave his 1959 Inaugural Lecture in Bonn on the topic "The God of Faith and the God of the Philosophers: A Contribution to the Problem of Natural Theology." I also want to highlight a little-known and still untranslated lecture delivered in 1961 and published in *Miscellanea Medievalia* in 1963. It concerns how Saint Bonaventure sought to clarify the question posed by Henri de Lubac regarding the role of the supernatural in Catholic theology. Whereas de Lubac in his 1946 study, *Surnaturel: Études historiques,* had claimed that the independence of nature from grace originated after Saint Thomas Aquinas with the freeing of the category of the supernatural from the natural desire to see God according to his essence, Ratzinger shows that a similar tendency is already making itself visible in the works of the Seraphic Doctor (what he terms "die beginnende Verselbstständigung der Metaphysik bei Bonaventura," "the beginnings of an autonomy of metaphysics in the work of Bonaventure"). The thesis itself verifies that Ratzinger was no restorationist in his early studies of the tradition. On the contrary, he was in the wake of Henri de Lubac's impetus exploring the roots of the problem of modernity as it was evinced in medieval authors. Regarding Bonaventure's doctrine of conscience, the thirty-four-year-old theologian states:

> "et hoc ius est, quod dictat recta ratio" [and in this case right is what is prescribed according to correct reason]. If one adds to that [statement of Gratian] Bonaventure's statement in his doctrine of conscience, namely, that truth is *naturaliter impressa* [implanted by nature] in the heart of man, there is thus practically speaking an authentically metaphysical doctrine of natural law and correspondingly an authentically metaphysical concept of nature, that in and for itself can give way to an autonomous realm *(Eigenbereich)* of philosophical thinking. . . . The metaphysical concept of nature consequently remains subject to historical, which in terms of our question means theological, illumination.[45]

It would be a mistake to read too much into this early historical research, but the points of connection to what came later are

nonetheless clear. From an early stage Ratzinger was curious about the
possibility and limits of a rational conscience as that tradition developed in the course of the Christian experience through the ages. In
the case of this essay, Ratzinger showed only a passing interest in the
mechanics of conscience. He intimated in 1961 that perhaps even
Bonaventure was willy-nilly a transitional figure on the way to modern
developments. He was already then focused squarely on the problematic separation of an autonomous realm of abstract reason from the
guidance of nature's own claims and from the salvific balm of grace.

Ratzinger believes with the whole of the Catholic tradition that
the Word of God, the gifts of the Holy Spirit, the witness or advice of
others, and the magisterium of the Church all contribute to the formation of conscience.[46] But he is also able to unfold the dynamics of
graced inwardness through an indirect method. In his essay "Conscience and Truth" he cites the conclusion of Aeschylus's *Oresteia* and
a comment made by Hans Urs von Balthasar about the implicit theology of the tragedian: "Calming grace always assists in the establish-
ing of justice, not the old graceless justices of the *Erinyes* period, but
that which is full of grace."[47] Aeschylus provides a clue as to how
natural reason can confront the Socratic paradox regarding the pleth-
ora of gods. Orestes' guilt over matricide is a result of his obedience to
the will of Apollo and the *simultaneous* claim made on his conscience
by the Furies. But the final scene in which the Furies are miraculously
transformed into spirits of reconciliation points toward the advent of
a personal redeemer who can expiate by bearing human suffering.
Once again we witness the centrality of the advent dynamic.

Christian revelation is ultimately about such a freeing of conscience, that is, a new and noninnocent openness to a washing away
of guilt. Revelation surpasses the natural expectations of reason without violating or subtracting from what reason can see on its own accord. In 1975 Ratzinger turns to the pre-Constantinian experience of
claiming the name "Christian" and writes:

> Here the link we found in the Ten Commandments between the
> concept of God and the moral idea is repeated at a most sublime
> and exacting level in the Christian context: the name "Christian"

implies fellowship with Christ, and hence the readiness to take upon oneself martyrdom in the cause of goodness. Christianity is a conspiracy to promote the good; the theological and moral aspects are fused inseparably, both in the word itself and deeper, in the basic concept of what Christian reality is.[48]

By taking the name "Christian," one is already submitting to a moral vision of reality. But that claim does not make the moral experience of being Christian purely deontological. The experience of grace among the followers of Christ is one in which there is a palpable offer of communion with God through a recognition in faith of the power of the cross to heal sins. This can be a real liberation: "the yoke of truth became 'easy' (Matthew 11:30) when the Truth came, loved us, and consumed our guilt in the fire of his love."[49] This is a distinctively Christian idea. Prior to Christianity, Ratzinger writes, purification could involve either the external expiation of animal sacrifices or ritual actions aimed at a more noetic and disembodied flight into the realm of pure Ideas. Nineteenth-century Christianity, he continues, reduced purity to the sexual sphere and thereby reverted to the pre-Christian suspicion of the body. Drawing on Saint John's gospel, Ratzinger sees Christian purification as primarily being incorporated into Christ's body, "being pervaded by his presence."[50]

WITNESSING TO TRUTH

Pope Benedict maintains that a good conscience is directed to the truth. But how can the truth of a good conscience be disseminated in our day, namely, in the wake of relativism's dictatorship? In his "Letter to Artists," Pope Benedict recalls the vital connection between beauty and truth:

Indeed, an essential function of genuine beauty, as emphasized by Plato, is that it gives man a healthy "shock," it draws him out of himself, wrenches him away from resignation and from being content with the humdrum—it even makes him suffer, piercing him like a dart, but in so doing it "reawakens" him, opening afresh the eyes of his heart and mind, giving him wings, carrying him aloft. . . . [Dostoevsky] says this: "Man can live without science, he can live without bread, but without beauty he could no longer live, because there would no longer be anything to do to the world. The whole secret is here, the whole of history is here." . . . Beauty pulls us up short, but in so doing it reminds us of our final destiny, it sets us back on our path, fills us with new hope, gives us the courage to live to the full the unique gift of life.[51]

The overcoming of moralism flows through the path of beauty. This vision extends beyond the artist as such. It applies to the neo-Augustinian form of rhetoric that Joseph Ratzinger forged as a bishop and as bishop of Rome. The fruits of conscience should not be articulated in an abstract, overly technical fashion. "Morality requires not the specialist but the witness," states Ratzinger.[52] Witness in our contemporary idiom can have an overly juridical sense, a narrowing that loses the link to beauty. "Witness" here means a witness to the natural beauty of conscience. The connection to beauty and its contemplation also establishes the fundamental difference between genuine witnessing and modern attempts at a renewed biblical "orthopraxy."[53]

Pope Benedict uses the category of witnessing to the truth in order to paint a broad canvas of how conscience and culture can be renewed in our times. A few examples will suffice to illustrate his vision of the authentic power and beauty of conscience. The first is hardly known outside of German circles, namely, the poet Reinhold Schneider (1903–58). His witness is not easily encapsulated. Balthasar produced two versions of a biography.[54] Resistance fighters in Nazi Germany carried his sonnets to the front lines as a source of hope; he himself openly opposed rearmament after Germany's defeat. Ratzinger's most important essay on this topic, "Das Gewissen in der Zeit" (literally, "Conscience in Time," signifying both "in the tradition that has been handed on to us" and "as a temporal process"), was published when he was a professor in Regensburg and appeared in the German edition of *Communio* in the first year of its existence.[55] It reiterates his well-known skepticism regarding Jesus as a social revolutionary.[56] The heart of the essay is, however, a meditation on the legacy of Schneider and in particular the political import of a free conscience as developed in Schneider's influential novel about Bartolomé de Las Casas. Ratzinger highlights four acts of conscience, three from the historical novel and one based on a contemporary conversation. The first is the testimony of a fictional Indian girl bereft of power and political ambition who in Schneider's work convinces the Spanish conqueror to see for the first time the depth of suffering of the indigenous. The second is the prophetic figure of Las Casas, who petitioned the Spanish Crown with only partial success to recognize Indians as creatures of God and candidates for baptism. The third is the young emperor Charles V. He agrees to meet Las Casas with a copy of *The Imitation of Christ* on his desk and must then and there decide how to wield power in the light of the friar's extraordinary request. The fourth is Charles de Gaulle, a man haunted by the colonialist legacy of Napoleon who in André Malraux's sympathetic account melancholically resigns himself to Algerian independence as a self-limiting choice for the soul of France. In each case Professor Ratzinger's point is that Christians do not gain power by revolutions: "power attains greatness when it lets itself be moved by conscience." He no doubt wrote the essay to provoke those on the Catholic left who had tired of the language of conscience and advocated in its place structural social change. But even here Ratzinger's polemical rejoinder is notable for its balance. Christianity must struggle against totalitarianism (Hitler openly denied the free exercise of conscience, he recalls) and other ideologies that limit the freedom of conscience precisely in order to make space for the free play of justice. The shocking claim of the cross of Christ is that the testimony of a powerless witness can make possible in a radical way the self-imposition of limits on the conscience of the powerful.

Another testimony is the Holy Father's address to the Latin American bishops at Aparecida on May 13, 2007. There he spoke twenty-four years after the publication of the first document from the Congregation of the Doctrine of the Faith on social liberation and made this bold proclamation:

The Church is the advocate of justice and of the poor, precisely because she does not identify with politicians nor with partisan interests. Only by remaining independent can she teach the great criteria and inalienable values, guide consciences and offer a life choice that goes beyond the political sphere. To form consciences, to be the advocate of justice and truth, to educate in individual and political virtues: that is the fundamental vocation of the Church in this area.[57]

This call of conscience is directed toward the transformation of individual, social, economic, and political structures. Conscience is moved by its own co-natural affinity with the truth. The Christian admirer of Socrates rehearses in the same address his critique of ideologies that proffer social utopias in place of an openness to transcendence. Like the dying Socrates the Church must take its distance from and examine critically the courts of opinion that render their judgments based on beliefs in gods who do not save. The purpose of this ecclesial and personal self-distancing from ideology is *not* disengagement or privatization. On the contrary, the taking of a distance allows the disciple of Christ to commit to a new form of life, to focus on the face of Christ in the wounded innocence of the poor. Guided by an informed conscience and nurtured by the sacraments to heed this divine mandate, integral human liberation becomes a new possibility for humanity. In this sense, Benedict's doctrine of conscience strengthens through its renewed moral clarity the preferential option for the poor.

As a kind of coda to this litany of witnesses, I would add the Holy Father's moving and persuasive testimony to two quite different instantiations of the modern *polis,* the German Reichstag[58] and the Cuban people assembled in the Plaza de la Revolución in Havana.[59] In the former address, he offered the "listening heart" of King Solomon as a renewed path for modern juridical reason, as his thoughts regarding that which establishes in our day the foundations of a free state of law (in his native tongue, "einige Gedanken über die Grundlagen des freiheitlichen Rechtsstaats"). Even the environmental movement, he wagered, gives us the opportunity to listen to the language of nature and respond accordingly. Positivist reason is compared to a bunker with no windows. "Is it really pointless to wonder," he asks his fellow Germans, "whether the objective reason that manifests itself in nature does not presuppose a creative reason, a *Creator Spiritus*?" In his Cuban homily, he reiterated: "The personal encounter with the one who is Truth in person compels us to share this treasure with others, especially by our witness." As a final reflection on the Gospel, he offered the example of a patriot and thinker much revered by the Cubans, Fr. Félix Varela.

> Father Varela offers us a path to a true transformation of society: to form virtuous men and women in order to forge a worthy and free nation, for this transformation depends on the spiritual, in as much as "there is no authentic fatherland without virtue" (*Letters to Elpidio*, Letter 6, Madrid 1836, 220). Cuba and the world need change, but this will occur only if each one is in a position to seek the truth and chooses the way of love, sowing reconciliation and fraternity.[60]

The wisdom of Solomonic listening reason and Varela's search for transformative virtue are both testimonies to a truth about human nature that has largely been forgotten in the West. By invoking them in these very distinct and particular contexts, the Holy Father's words remain provocative, timely, and universal.

CONSCIENCE AND CULTURE

I have argued for the interdependence of the doctrine of conscience and the theology of culture in certain writings of Joseph Ratzinger/ Pope Benedict XVI. Conscience is an attribute of human nature that in its universal, quasi-Socratic scope serves as a beacon to all cultures. At the same time, a Christian conscience needs to confront itself and other moral systems in culturally specific situations to guarantee that its truthfulness stands at the service of human nature in all its conflicting variations. Living out this challenge can yield tragic results, as we see in the cases of those who die for their conscience. (I think here of the monks of Tibhirine.) Interculturality in this account is part and parcel of the path, for such a truth-driven encounter is a potent antidote to the dictatorship of relativism.

I conclude with a biblical synthesis. The full interior connection between culture and conscience can be found in Benedict's retrieval of the Pauline notion of *logike latreia* (Rom 12:1, "spiritual worship").[61] Pope Benedict offers as his paraphrase "wordlike" sacrifice, an embodied and thus culturally meaningful offering to God offered as self-expression of the whole of the human person. Paul is exhorting us to see that when Christian living is offered in the one Body and in the one living Christ, then it becomes its own kind of Eucharist for the world.[62]

NOTES

1. On this latter phrase, see Joseph Ratzinger, "Bishops, Theologians, and Morality," in *On Conscience: Two Essays* (San Francisco: Ignatius Press, 2007), 57.

2. Benedict XVI, "Meeting with Representatives of Civil Society, Political, Cultural, and Business World, Diplomatic Corps and Religious Leaders," Zagreb, June 4, 2011, accessed on-line at www.vatican.va/holy_father/benedict_xvi/speeches/2011/june/documents/hf_ben-xvi_spe_20110604_cd-croazia_en.html.

3. Vincent Twomey, S.V.D., *Pope Benedict XVI: The Conscience of Our Age* (San Francisco: Ignatius Press, 2007), 132.

4. Joseph Ratzinger, *Truth and Tolerance: Christian Belief and World Religions,* trans. Henry Taylor (San Francisco: Ignatius Press, 2004), 59.

5. Ibid., 60.

6. Ibid., 61.

7. Ibid., 63.

8. Joseph Ratzinger, "The Church's Teaching—Authority—Faith—Morals," in Heinz Schürmann, Joseph Cardinal Ratzinger, and Hans Urs von Balthasar, *Principles of Christian Morality* (San Francisco: Ignatius Press, 1986), 47.

9. This term is used to refer to an aspect of the Old Testament that is taken up by Jesus. See Benedict XVI, *Jesus of Nazareth: From the Baptism in*

the Jordan to the Transfiguration, trans. Adrian J. Walker (New York: Doubleday, 2007), 122–27. For a thoughtful Muslim contemporary on Christian prophecy as treated by Pope Benedict XVI, see Mona Siddiqui, "'Searching for the Face of the Lord': Hope or Heresy?" in *The Pope and Jesus of Nazareth: Christ, Scripture, and the Church,* ed. Adrian Pabst and Angus Paddison (London: SCM Press, 2009), 247–61.

    10. Ratzinger, *Tolerance,* 99.

    11. Ibid., 65–66.

    12. Ibid., 64.

    13. Ibid., 193–97. This entire discussion is an unfolding of the notion of truth in Pope John Paul II's encyclical *Fides et Ratio,* especially in the light of the accusation that the pope had adopted a fundamentalist view of religion and culture.

    14. I treat this theme in my "Searching for the Face of the Lord in Ratzinger's *Jesus of Nazareth,*" in Pabst and Paddison, *The Pope and Jesus of Nazareth,* 83–93. Emery de Gaál notes that Ratzinger's 1959 inaugural lecture concluded with this citation from Richard of St. Victor: "Quaerite faciem eius semper" (Seek always his countenance). Emery de Gaál, *The Theology of Pope Benedict XVI: The Christocentric Shift* (New York: Palgrave Macmillan, 2010), 76.

    15. Joseph Ratzinger, "Christ, Faith, and the Challenge of Cultures, Address to the Presidents of the Asian Bishops' Conference in Hong Kong," during a March 2–5, 1993, meeting. See also Ratzinger, *Tolerance,* 63, for a nearly identical statement.

    16. Joseph Ratzinger, "Conscience and Truth" (Keynote Address of the Tenth Bishops' Workshop of the National Catholic Bioethics Center, on the general topic "Catholic Conscience: Foundation and Formation"), in Ratzinger, *Conscience,* 21.

    17. A. Görres, "Schuld und Schuldgefühle," in *International Katholische Zeitschrift "Communio"* 13 (1984): 434, as cited in Ratzinger, *Conscience,* 18 n. 3.

    18. Ratzinger, *Conscience,* 21.

    19. Joseph Ratzinger, *Milestones: Memoirs, 1927–1977,* trans. Erasmo Leiva-Merikakis (San Francisco: Ignatius Press, 1998), 43. Tracy Rowland reports, "As Alfred Laepple once remarked, when he and Ratzinger were seminarians, Newman was their hero" (www.abc.net.au/religion/articles/2010/09/16/3013343.htm).

    20. On this point, see Ratzinger, *Conscience,* 24, as well as Cardinal Ratzinger's address on the occasion of the first centenary of the death of

Cardinal John Henry Newman, April 28, 1990, www.vatican.va/roman _curia/congregations/cfaith/documents/rc_con_cfaith_doc_19900428 _ratzinger-newman_en.html.

21. Ratzinger, *Conscience,* 25, citing from Newman's famous poem, "Lead Kindly Light," in Newman, *Verses on Various Occasions* (London: Longmans, 1888). Original emphasis.

22. Joseph Ratzinger, "Bishops, Theologians, and Morality," 61, citing Robert Spaemann, *Moralische Grundbegriffe* (Munich: Beck, 1982), 81.

23. See Joseph Ratzinger, *Eschatology, Death, and Eternal Life,* trans. Michael Waldstein, 2nd ed. (Washington, DC: Catholic University of America Press, 2007), 72–79.

24. For his reservations about how Socratic rationalism can enter into a Catholic context in an uncritical fashion, see Ratzinger, "The Church's Teaching Authority—Faith—Morals," 52 n. 2.

25. Ratzinger, *Conscience,* 28–29.

26. Ratzinger, *Tolerance,* 221–22.

27. Ibid., 207.

28. Ratzinger, *Conscience,* 34.

29. He writes: "'*Synderesis*' names the natural potentiality, as it is naturally adapted [to us], whereas '*conscientia*' names a disposition which is not just natural but also acquired; and that nature is always, in itself, rightly moved, whereas what is acquired may fall under rightness or under deviance. Hence, although *synderesis* always exists rightly, *conscientia* may be right or mistaken." Saint Bonaventure, *Commentary on Peter Lombard's Book of Judgments,* 2.29, as found in Timothy C. Potts, *Conscience in Medieval Philosophy* (Cambridge: Cambridge University Press, 1980), 121.

30. On this see, Ratzinger, *Conscience,* 80 n. 19.

31. Ratzinger, *Conscience,* 38.

32. Ibid., 30.

33. For a modern reformulation of the Bonaventurian doctrine, which takes it as peculiarly Franciscan and ultimately an unconvincing form of modern intuitionism, see Potts, *Conscience in Medieval Philosophy,* 32–44.

34. Ratzinger, *Conscience,* 32.

35. For a commentary that highlights this feature, see de Gaál, *The Theology of Pope Benedict XVI,* 280–84.

36. Joseph Ratzinger, *In the Beginning: A Catholic Understanding of the Story of Creation and the Fall,* trans. Boniface Ramsey (Grand Rapids, MI: Eerdmans, 1995), 79–100.

37. Ratzinger, *Conscience,* 32, citing *De Trinitate,* VIII, 3 (4), PL 42, 949.

38. Ratzinger, *Conscience,* 32.

39. Pontifical Council for Justice and Peace, *Compendium of the Social Doctrine of the Church* (Dublin: Veritas, 2005), #73.

40. Ibid., #531.

41. This issue is examined in depth in this volume in the contribution by Simona Beretta.

42. Ratzinger, "Bishops, Theologians, and Morality," 61–62.

43. This idea is developed even further in Michael Budde, "Ad Extra: Ecclesial Solidarity and Other Allegiances," in Michael L. Budde, *The Borders of Baptism: Identities, Allegiances, and the Church* (Eugene, OR: Cascade Books, 2011), 3–23, but without confronting head-on the problem of relativism.

44. Ratzinger's most famous and forceful rejection of nominalism is found in the address delivered at the University of Regensburg on September 12, 2006.

45. Joseph Ratzinger, "Der Wortgebrauch von Natura und die beginnende Verselbständigung der Metaphysik bei Bonaventura," in *Miscellanea Medievalia* 2, Metaphysik im Mittelalter (Berlin: DeGruyter, 1963), 493.

46. Cf. *The Catechism of the Catholic Church*, #1785.

47. Ratzinger, "Conscience and Truth," 40.

48. Ratzinger, "The Church's Teaching Authority—Faith—Morals," 61.

49. Ratzinger, *Conscience*, 41.

50. Joseph Ratzinger, *Jesus of Nazareth: Part Two: Holy Week: From the Entrance into Jerusalem to the Resurrection*, trans. Vatican Secretariat of State (San Francisco: Ignatius Press, 2011), 60–61.

51. "You are Custodians of the Beauty," address of Pope Benedict XVI, November 22, 2009, www.zenit.org/article-27631?1=english.

52. Ratzinger, "Bishops, Theologians, and Morality," 69.

53. Cf. Ratzinger, *Tolerance*, 94–95, 123–26, 129–30; and Ratzinger, "The Church's Teaching Authority—Faith—Morals," 47–73, on the proper understanding of the relationship of orthopraxy to orthodoxy. This critique is not solely or even principally a rebuke of academic positions. It is also a way to question "the gray pragmatism at work in the everyday life of the Church."

54. Hans Urs von Balthasar, *Reinhold Schneider: Sein Werk und Sein Weg* (Cologne: J. Hegner, 1953) and *Nochmals Reinhold Schneider* (Einsiedeln: Johannes, 1991). The second version was published in English as *Tragedy under Grace: Reinhold Schneider and the Experience of the West*, trans. Brian McNeil (San Francisco: Ignatius Press, 1997).

55. Joseph Ratzinger, "Conscience in Its Time," in Joseph Ratzinger, *Church, Ecumenism and Politics: New Essays in Ecclesiology*, trans. Robert

Nowell and Fridesiwide Sandeman, O.S.B. (New York: Crossroad, 1988), 165–79. The original can be found as "Das Gewissen in der Zeit: Ein Vortrag vor der Reinhold-Schneider Gesellschaft," *Internationale katholische Zeitschrift "Communio"* 1 (1972): 432–42.

56. For example, Ratzinger writes, "The growth of freedom that mankind owes to the martyrs is infinitely greater than that which it could be given by revolutionaries." "Conscience in Its Time," 174.

57. Inaugural Session of the 5th General Conference of the Bishops of Latin America and the Carribean, Address of His Holiness Benedict XVI, Conference Hall, Shrine of Aparecida, Sunday, May 13, 2007, #4.

58. Address of His Holiness Benedict XVI, Reichstag Building, Berlin, September 22, 2011, www.vatican.va/holy_father/benedict_xvi/speeches/2011/september/documents/hf_ben-xvi_spe_20110922_reichstag-berlin_en.html.

59. Homily of His Holiness Benedict XVI, Plaza de la Revolución José Martí, Havana, Wednesday, March 28, 2012, www.vatican.va/holy_father/benedict_xvi/homilies/2012/documents/hf_ben-xvi_hom_20120328_la-habana_en.html.

60. Ibid.

61. The entire verse reads: "I urge you therefore, brothers, by the mercies of God, to offer your bodies as a living sacrifice, holy and pleasing to God, your spiritual worship."

62. Joseph Ratzinger, *Pilgrim Fellowship of Faith: The Church as Communion,* trans. Henry Taylor (San Francisco: Ignatius Press, 2005), 114–18.

chapter three

RESOLVING THE RELATIVITY PARADOX

Pope Benedict XVI and the Challenge of Christological Relativism

EDWARD T. OAKES, S.J.

RELATIVISM AND ITS DISCONTENTS

The issue of relativism has long been a concern of Joseph Ratzinger, not only as a theologian, but also, most famously, as cardinal prefect of the Congregation of the Doctrine of the Faith and of course now as pope, *feliciter regnans*. But to understand why relativism has long worried him, we must first get some idea of what the term means and what its implications are, especially in regard to theological debate.

As an initial foray into getting some clearer idea of this murky issue, let me begin with an anecdote, one to the best of my knowledge first recounted by James Luther Adams in his preface to Ernst Troeltsch's influential defense of a relativistic Christology called, aptly enough, *The Absoluteness of Christianity*. Here is Adams's anecdote:

Sometime during the course of World War II the United States War Department brought together a selected group of cultural anthropologists in order to secure their counsel regarding the management of psychological warfare in [the] face of German National Socialism. After the group had assembled in Washington one of their number asked what the War Department really expected of these men. He explained that in his work the cultural anthropologist for the sake of scientific objectivity presupposes the point of view of cultural relativism, and that therefore he entertains no biases or ethical preferences, in short, that he is not accustomed to making value judgments regarding the various cultures he studies. He went on to say that if the Germans preferred Nazism, they were entitled to that preference, just as democratic Americans are entitled to their own different preference. In either case, he said, the preference is simply an expression of a cultural milieu.[1]

What the bureaucrats housed in the War Department thought of this weird objection to their postwar plans can only be imagined. But I cite the anecdote here for the anticipatory light it throws on Cardinal Ratzinger's famous expression, the "dictatorship of relativism," which he voiced on the day before his election to the papacy and which made headlines throughout the world, not least because of the not unreasonable assumption that he was elected precisely because the cardinals in conclave agreed with him. Here is what he said on that occasion:

> How many winds of doctrine we have known in recent decades, how many ideological currents, how many ways of thinking? The small boat of thought of many Christians has often been tossed about by these waves, thrown from one extreme to the other: from Marxism to liberalism, even to libertinism; from collectivism to radical individualism; from atheism to a vague religious mysticism; from agnosticism to syncretism; and so forth. . . . Having a clear faith, based on the Creed of the Church, is often labeled today as fundamentalism. Whereas relativism, which is

letting oneself be tossed and "swept along by every wind of teaching," looks like the only attitude (acceptable) to today's standards. We are moving toward a dictatorship of relativism, which does not recognize anything as certain and which has as its highest goal one's own ego and one's own desires.[2]

At first glance, this expression "dictatorship of relativism" sounds like an oxymoron, even an unfair slur on relativists. For is it not their whole point that it is *absolute* claims that lead to dictatorship and that only *relativism* can preserve us from the totalitarian temptation? But of course, the value-neutrality of social scientists—so garishly on display in the Adams anecdote—shows that in fact relativism is singularly ill equipped to meet the challenge of aggressive totalitarianism when it becomes an active force in history.

The "dictatorship of relativism," however, means more than just collusion with the world's real dictatorships. It also has a deeper—even paradoxical—meaning, one that I can illustrate in many flashpoints in the culture wars: the fact that there are no true relativists across the board. Closet absolutism always lurks in relativistic rhetoric, which can be seen in any number of examples, not least Cardinal Ratzinger's last line that relativists nowadays recognize only their own ego and its desires as its highest goal, an absolute claim if there ever was one.

Other examples come readily to mind. In his famous book *The Closing of the American Mind,* Allan Bloom recommends asking students in a typical undergraduate classroom what the British should have done during the days of the Raj in India about the practice of suttee, the tradition observed in some Hindu villages of the widow throwing herself on her husband's funeral pyre as a sign of her total identification with him. To the typical relativist, the British should never have been in India in the first place, imposing their values hegemonically on a traditional society, which was only minding its own business. But to countenance the practice would validate the subjugation of women. Then there is the issue of pornography, described by Bloom as, in fact, a clash of absolutes:

The sexual revolution marched under the banner of freedom; feminism under that of equality. Although they went arm in arm for a while, their differences eventually put them at odds with each other, as Tocqueville said freedom and equality would always be. This is manifest in the squabble over pornography, which pits liberated sexual desire against feminist resentment about stereotyping. We are presented with the amusing spectacle of pornography clad in the armor borrowed from the heroic struggle for freedom of speech, and using Miltonic rhetoric, doing battle with feminism, newly draped in the robes of community morality, using arguments associated with conservatives who defend traditional sex roles, and also defying an authoritarian tradition in which it was taboo to suggest any relation between what a person reads and sees and his sexual practices. In the background stand the liberals, wringing their hands in confusion because they wish to favor both sides and cannot.[3]

A similar dynamic can be seen to be at work in the controversy over adoptions by gay couples. In spring 2007 Britain's Parliament passed a law requiring all adoption agencies, including Catholic ones, to allow gay couples to adopt children placed in the care of these agencies. Now at first glance it would seem that a true relativist would treat Catholics like exotic Amazonians: sure, they have odd views about the family, whereby only a married husband and wife are the sole legitimate and appropriate couple suited for raising a child, natural or adopted. How weird those Catholics are, but who are we to judge?

Secularists of course disagree and see no problem with the idea that, as the textbook for grade-schoolers has it, "Heather has two mommies." But what does that have to do with Catholics? After all, anthropologists recognize that different societies are marked by different kinship relations: they freely, and nonjudgmentally, discuss matriarchal societies in prehistory, polygamy in seventh-century Arabia and in nineteenth-century Utah, gay "marriage" in Massachusetts and Holland in contemporary society, and so on, all without judgmentalism or moralism. So why not let Catholics live out their peculiar lifestyle too?

But that's not happening, and the question is why. Hypocrisy surely has something to do with it, although I think the real reason stems from the odd admixture of absolutism and relativism in self-professed relativists. Probably we are all a swirling amalgamation of relativism and absolutism. No relativist, I assume, would defend the right of widows to immolate themselves on their husbands' funeral pyres in present-day, noncolonial India (where suttee is now illegal although still practiced occasionally in out-of-the-way villages); and no self-professed absolutist or deontologist would insist everyone must like opera.

So maybe "we are all absolutists now," even though we are also simultaneously "all multiculturalists too" (to borrow a phrase from Nathan Glazer's famous book by that title). Thus we get the paradox of the liberal credo, which Bloom summarizes this way: "There are no absolutes; freedom is absolute."[4] Again, as we saw with the anecdote from Adams, this credo doubles back on itself and leaves the path open to a very real dictatorship, as Bloom notes here:

> The progressives of the twenties and thirties did not like the Constitutional protection of private property or the restraints on majority will and on living as one pleased. For them, equality had not gone far enough. Stalinists also found the definition of democracy as openness useful. The Constitution clashed too violently with the theory and practice of the Soviet Union. But if democracy means open-mindedness, and respect for other cultures prevents doctrinaire, natural-rights-based condemnation of the Soviet reality, then someday their ways may become ours. I remember a grade-school history textbook, newly printed on fine glossy paper, showing intriguing pictures of collective farms where farmers worked and lived together without the profit motive. (Children cannot understand the issues, but they are easy to propagandize.) This was very different from our way of life, [these textbooks implied,] but we were not to be closed to it, to react to it merely on the basis of our cultural prejudices.[5]

So the confusions left in the wake of relativism, which are of such concern to Pope Benedict, run deep and in fact have a genealogy that can be delineated. Alasdair MacIntyre opened the second chapter of his own famous book *After Virtue* by depicting a scene we can all recognize: debates on just war, abortion, capital punishment, and liberty versus equality in political economy are all disputes taking place in an echo chamber, with everyone essentially hurling absolutes at the other side of the debate (as in the "right to choose" vs. the "right to life"). But since these absolutes are conceptually incommensurable, the shrillest debater gets the last word.[6]

In MacIntyre's analysis, the victory goes to the shrillest because the word *good* has lost its meaning when applied to moral situations. Aristotle was able to take for granted that the word *good* can, with no violation to its meaning, be equally applied to a good saddle, a good horse, a good cavalryman, a good general—and a good person. The adjective properly belongs to all these nouns if each item is doing what it is assigned, or designed, to do. The word *good,* in other words, is inherently teleological, and for that reason eminently adjudicable. *Good* means suitability or functionality vis-à-vis some foreseen end, which can be easily ascertained.

Perhaps, though, Aristotle went too far in his teleological understanding of nature; at least so goes the claim. For with the loss of his teleological understanding of physical motion under the impact of Newtonian mechanics and (more controversially) with the loss of the design argument as applied to living organisms under Darwin's impact, the moral application of the word *good* came under heavy challenge, above all from David Hume (in the wake of Newton) and from Friedrich Nietzsche (in Darwin's wake). Now man no longer seems to have a purpose or function that can be assessed by universally recognized standards. Man is no longer here for a reason. This loss of a teleological anthropology means that, according to MacIntyre, good in moral debate becomes a mere emotive term of personal approval; now all contemporary debate about ethics boils down to a choice between incompatible absolutes.

> If the deontological character of moral judgments is the ghost of
> conceptions of divine law which are quite alien to the metaphysics
> of modernity and if the teleological character is similarly the
> ghost of conceptions of human nature and activity which are
> equally not at home in the modern world, we should expect the
> problem of understanding and of assigning an intelligible status
> to moral judgments both continually to arise and as continually to
> prove inhospitable to philosophical solutions.[7]

In other words, the problem of relativism goes as far back as the origins of modernity itself. Given the heated headlines from the front lines of the culture wars now raging, relativism might seem like a fairly recent phenomenon; but in fact it began with Hume and became a truly exigent problem in the nineteenth century, as the writings of Nietzsche and Troeltsch show. This is why Adams aired his anecdote about the relativism of social scientists during World War II in his introduction to the translation of Troeltsch's book *The Absoluteness of Christianity*, the great classic nineteenth-century text in relativistic Christology.[8]

It will be my thesis in the rest of what follows that Joseph Ratzinger/Pope Benedict has, in his steady way, and over the course of a scholarly career spanning half a century, resolved the many paradoxes of relativism outlined above. He has done so primarily in Christological terms, which is why I think a brief look at Troeltsch's Christology will prove a helpful entrée into Benedict's Christological resolution of the challenge of relativism. For it will be my thesis that the challenge of relativism cannot be met unless it is done first and foremost in Christological terms.

CHRISTOLOGICAL RELATIVISM

In a revealing remark Troeltsch once compared Christocentrism in theology to geocentrism in astronomy, and he regarded both as a violation of the Copernican principle, which asserts that we have no privileged vantage point from earth—that we are, as the expression goes, "not that special, so get over it." According to Troeltsch:

> [Historical contingency] seems to make this conclusion impossible: calling the Christian community the eternal absolute center of salvation for the whole span of humanity. . . . Man's age upon earth amounts to several hundred thousand years or more. His future may come to still more. It is hard to imagine a single point of history along this line—and, as it just so happens, the midpoint of *our* own religious history—as the sole area of life. That would be in religion what geocentrism and anthropocentrism are in cosmology and metaphysics. The whole logic of Christocentrism places it with these other centrisms.[9]

Now for Troeltsch, what most undermines Christocentrism is the historical-critical method, not so much because of the results arising from that method as from its very use, regardless of whether or not the results lead to confidence in the figure of the historical Jesus. This is because historical criticism for him is marked by three key methodological principles: (1) the principle of *criticism,* that no historical document—much less one stemming from the ancient world—can be taken on its own terms as automatically reliable but must be subjected to skeptical treatment;[10] (2) the principle of *analogy,* which says that events of the past must be similar to those of the present if they are to be at all understandable, which calls into question the element of the supernatural in historical narratives;[11] and (3) the principle of *correlation,* that all historical events are caught in a complex cause-effect nexus, meaning that they must be interpreted in terms of antecedents and consequences and so are in some sense not surprising but predictable.[12]

Taken together, these three principles lead to Troeltsch's conclusion that all religions make claims that cannot be admitted except in terms inside each religion, since acceptance of those claims entail—at least in part—membership in that religion. Consequently, rejection of those claims is precisely what marks the outsider to that religion as an outsider, which is why Troeltsch so often quoted Jean-Jacques Rousseau's famous observation that religion is "une affaire de géographie."[13]

No wonder Peter Berger can say that historical scholarship challenges theology to its very roots, for historical criticism depends on a prior and "pervasive sense of the historical character of *all* elements of the tradition.... Put simply, historical scholarship led to a perspective in which even the most sacrosanct elements of religious tradition came to be seen as *human products*."[14] At least according to Berger, the sociology of knowledge intensifies this dilemma by showing how the process of socialization determines not just the language we speak, for example, but also our very beliefs and worldviews: "History posits the problem of relativity as *a fact*, the sociology of knowledge as *a necessity of our condition*."[15]

RATZINGER AND RELATIVISM

As every physician knows, a hopeful prognosis depends on an accurate diagnosis. So how does Joseph Ratzinger diagnose this now burning issue in the Church?

First, like any good physician, he must determine how far relativism has extended its ideology into the body of the Church and to what extent it poses a danger. Perhaps this might surprise the untutored, but Ratzinger does not condemn all forms of relativism *tout court*. Like bacteria in the body, which is both essential to metabolism in some forms and dangerous in others, there is a salubrious kind of relativism and a toxic form. For just as bacteria are necessary for digestion, so too certain forms of relativism can serve as an antidote to absolutism, an acid that eats away at dangerous versions of absolutist dictatorships.

In an important address to the heads of doctrinal commissions for the various bishops' conferences in Latin America in 1996, the future pope pointed out that the greatest challenge for the Catholic Church in the immediate postconciliar years was the claim of liberation theology to represent an authentic translation of the gospel message.

Although the Bavarian cardinal was not entirely critical of liberation theology, he certainly saw a problem with it in those versions that uncritically drew on Marxism, which suddenly faced a crisis when the Communist polities of Eastern Europe fell in 1989.

> The fall of the European governmental systems based on Marxism turned out to be a kind of twilight of the gods for that theology of redeeming political praxis. Precisely in those places where the Marxist librating ideology had been applied consistently, a radical lack of freedom had been produced, the horror of which now appeared out in the open before the eyes of world public opinion. The fact is that when politics are used to bring redemption, they promise too much. When they presume to do God's work, they become not divine but diabolical.[16]

Having recovered from—or at least having come to realize—the damage caused by the Communist illusion, public opinion and political thought reacted by shying away from claims to absolutism, a shift that Cardinal Ratzinger actually applauds, at least provisionally.

> In turn, relativism appears to be the philosophical foundation of democracy. Democracy, in fact, is supposedly built on the basis that no one can presume to know the true way, and it is enriched by the fact that all roads are mutually recognized as fragments of the effort toward that which is better. . . . A system of freedom ought to be essentially a system of positions that are connected with one another because they are relative, as well as being dependent on historical situations open to new developments. Therefore, a liberal society would be a relativist society: only with that condition could it continue to be free and open to the future. *In the area of politics, this concept is considerably right.* There is no one correct political opinion. What is relative—the building up of liberally ordained coexistence between people—cannot be absolute. Thinking in this way was precisely the error of Marxism and the political theologies.[17]

Thus there can be a legitimate pluralism on the mediate question of politics. Even Marxism, when shorn of its temptations to absolutism, has a legitimate relativizing role to play: "There are in fact sick and degenerate forms of religion, which do not edify people but alienate them: the Marxist criticism of religion was not entirely based on delusions."[18] But of course the Bavarian concedes to relativism much more than a modified recognition of a legitimate Marxist critique of religion. Further examples of a legitimate relativism would be issues like how to handle the debt crisis in Europe and the United States, for which there is no obviously available algorithm for solving the problem; and certainly the Church has no special competence in these matters. (I suspect Pope Benedict would agree with those critics of national bishops' conferences who score them for pronouncing on too many issues not directly related to their kind of specific authority.)

But that concession to a legitimate relativism can hardly be the last word. Politics is, after all, concerned with justice. There might be a legitimate pluralism in mediate questions, but ultimate questions are not so easily relativized: "There are injustices," says Ratzinger, "that will never turn into something just . . . while, at the same time, there are just things that can never be unjust." So, the question becomes, as he says, "setting limits" to relativism.[19] This need to set limits is especially exigent in our times; and, indeed, in remarks made the year before his election as Pope Benedict, Cardinal Ratzinger echoed what was said above by Bloom and MacIntyre:

> In recent years I find myself noting how the more relativism becomes the generally accepted way of thinking, the more it tends toward intolerance, thereby becoming a new dogmatism. Political correctness . . . seeks to establish the domain of a single way of thinking and speaking. Its relativism creates the illusion that it has reached greater heights than the loftiest philosophical achievements of the past. . . . Being faithful to traditional values and to the knowledge that upholds them is labeled intolerance, and relativism becomes the required norm. I think it is vital that we oppose this imposition of a new pseudo-Enlightenment,

which threatens freedom of thought as well as freedom of religion. In Sweden, a preacher who had presented the biblical teachings on the question of homosexuality received a prison sentence. This is just one sign of the gains that have been made by relativism as a kind of new "denomination" that places restrictions on religious convictions and seeks to subordinate all religions to the super-dogma of relativism.[20]

THE PRIMACY OF CHRISTOLOGY

The first place where relativism must be kept at bay for the cardinal—and it is crucial that this is the first item on his list—is in Christology.[21] For him, any type of relativism in Christology will inevitably lead to its attenuation. In his book *Introduction to Christianity* Ratzinger compares the situation in theology to the folktale told by the brothers Grimm about "lucky Hans" who traded a lump of gold he stumbled upon for, in turn, a horse, a cow, a goose, and finally a whetstone, which he then threw away as a valueless encumbrance. Such is the consequence of relativism in Christology, he says.

> The worried Christian of today is often bothered by questions like these: has our theology in the last few years not taken in many ways a similar path? Has it not gradually watered down the demands of faith, which had been found all too demanding, always only so little that nothing important seemed to be lost, yet always so much that it was soon possible to venture on to the next step? And will poor Hans, the Christian who trustfully let himself be led from exchange to exchange, from interpretation to interpretation, not really soon hold in his hand, instead of the gold with which he began, only a whetstone, which he can be confidently recommended to throw away?[22]

But as we saw above, there is no relativist who is not also a closet absolutist. Indeed, as Ratzinger shrewdly notes (and this, despite

their formal differences), the loud cries for a relativistic Christology now occupy the same ideological space once taken by liberation
theologians—and some of the latter have moved seamlessly into becoming advocates of the former.

> The so-called pluralist theology of religion has been developing
> progressively since the 1950s. Nonetheless, only now has it come
> to the center of the Christian conscience. In some ways this con-
> quest occupies today—with regard to the force of its problematic
> aspect and its presence in the different areas of culture—the place
> occupied by the theology of liberation in the preceding decade.
> Moreover, it joins in many ways with it and tries to give it a new,
> updated form.[23]

This swift segue from a Marxist-tinged theology to a relativizing one
is, to be sure, not without its ironies, since one of the objections raised
against Christocentrism by the pluralists is that it leads to fanaticism
and particularism—themselves the besetting sins of Communists. Still,
the relativizers are not without their absolutes (no surprise there,
since, as we saw above, everyone is an absolutist about something),
and never more so than in their *command* to dissolve absolutist claims
on behalf of Christ.

> The relativist dissolution of Christology, and even more of eccle-
> siology, thus becomes a central *commandment* of religion. To re-
> turn to Hick's thinking, faith in the divinity of one concrete
> person, as he tells us, leads to fanaticism and particularism, to the
> dissociation between faith and love, and it is precisely this which
> must be overcome.[24]

The same contradiction lurks in their call to dialogue. Of course
dialogue is an important value in relation to the plurality of religions
and has long had, moreover, an honored place in both philosophy and
theology, as we know from Plato and from the art of the medieval
disputation. I am reminded in this context of an observation from
Josef Pieper:

Thomas succeeds not only in presenting the opponent's divergent
or flatly opposed opinion, together with the underlying line of
reasoning, but also, many times, in presenting it better, more
clearly, and more convincingly than the opponent himself might
be able to do. In this procedure there emerges an element profoundly characteristic of St. Thomas's intellectual style, the spirit
of the *disputatio,* of disciplined opposition; the spirit of genuine
discussion which remains a dialogue even while it is a dispute.[25]

But nowadays the call to dialogue in the relativist creed operates in a
different ecology and has become an ultimate value. Both Plato and
the medievals assumed without further ado that dialogue always
aimed at the truth. Indeed, Thomas could be so fair to his opponent
and so serene in presenting opposing views precisely because he was
so confident that dialogue was but the initiating moment leading to
the terminating goal of truth. But once the relativist gives up the notion of truth as an ideal and sees it only as the hegemonic imposition
of an opponent's will to power, then dialogue becomes an end in itself.
In fact—and ironically—it becomes an absolute. So Cardinal Ratzinger comes to this conclusion:

> The notion of *dialogue*—which has maintained a position of sig-
> nificant importance in the Platonic and Christian traditions—
> changes meaning and becomes both the quintessence of the
> relativist creed and the antithesis of conversion and mission. In
> the relativist meaning, to *dialogue* means to put one's own posi-
> tion, that is, one's faith, on the same level as the convictions of
> others, without recognizing in principle more truth in it than that
> which is attributed to the opinions of the others. Only if I sup-
> pose in principle that the other can be as right or more right than
> I am, can an authentic dialogue take place.
>
> According to this concept, dialogue must be an exchange be-
> tween positions that have fundamentally the same rank and
> therefore are mutually relative. Only in this way will the maxi-
> mum cooperation and integration between the different religions
> be achieved.[26]

Note again the irony of the hidden absolutism lurking here in the insistence that dialogue is the ultimate value before which all other claims must be sacrificed. But leaving aside this internal self-contradiction of the relativists, how is someone like Troeltsch—who freely admitted that his critique of an absolutist Christocentrism was merely probable—to be answered? How do we answer Rousseau's observation that religion is geographically specific, tied to specific cultures not easily transferable to other cultures that operate under different presuppositions? How can the genuine value of dialogue be preserved while also maintaining the Church's consistently held view that Christ is the single and universal savior of the human race?

Here again, we find a move by the future pope that might surprise both his admirers and his critics. He rejects the Enlightenment claim that reason can serve as the Great Adjudicator. Indeed, he seems to agree with the postmodernists in at least this point (which they hammer away at consistently)—that reason is always historically situated. "For human reason is not autonomous in the absolute," says the cardinal. "It is always found in a historical context. The historical context disfigures its vision.... Therefore, it also needs historical assistance to help it cross over its historical barriers."[27]

Remarkably, Ratzinger also concedes that this Enlightenment claim for the absolute validity of universal reason was the besetting error of neo-scholasticism. In a passage that shows he was no unthinking revanchist, the future pope openly asserts, "I am of the opinion that the neo-Scholastic rationalism failed because—with reason totally independent from faith—it tried to reconstruct the *praeambula fidei* with pure rational certainty. All attempts that presume to do the same will have the same result. Yes, Karl Barth was right to reject philosophy as a foundation of the faith independent from the faith."[28]

While Ratzinger is by no means a Barthian across the board, he does insist with Barth that Christology must establish its own norms for rationality; for taken in terms of worldly logic, the doctrine of Christ will always be couched in the logic of paradox. This is because reason is a universal endowment both in that being Aristotle defines precisely as a rational animal and in that human faculty that gives access to the inherent rationality of a rationally structured universe.[29]

But Christianity proclaims something revolutionary about that universal Logos, that it is entirely incarnate in but one man, Jesus Christ: "For in him the fullness of the godhead was pleased to dwell" (Col 1:19), the acceptance of which claim leads to the overthrow of worldly logic.

> It is only in the second section of the Creed that we come up against the real difficulty . . . about Christianity: the profession of faith that the man Jesus, an individual executed in Palestine about the year 30, the *Christus* (anointed, chosen) of God, indeed God's own Son, is the central and decisive point of all human history. It seems both presumptuous and foolish to assert that one single figure who is bound to disappear farther and farther into the mists of the past is the authoritative center of all history. Although faith in the *logos,* the meaningfulness of being, corresponds perfectly with a tendency in the human reason, this second article of the Creed proclaims the absolutely staggering alliance of *logos* and *sarx,* of meaning and a single historical figure. *The meaning that sustains all being has become flesh;* that is, it has entered history and become one individual in it; it is no longer simply what encompasses and sustains history but is a point *in* it.[30]

To accept this claim entails an important methodological consideration, one that must overthrow the usual philosophical approach to reality, which seeks out universal patterns, whereas Christianity absolutizes one moment in history.

> Accordingly the meaning of all being is first of all no longer to be found in the sweep of mind that rises above the individual, the limited, into the universal; it is no longer simply given in the world of ideas, which transcends the individual and is reflected in it only in a fragmentary fashion; it is to be found in the midst of time, in the countenance of one man.[31]

These assertions by no means make Ratzinger a fideist, still less an irrationalist. Indeed, in his commentary on the first section of the creed ("I believe in God") Ratzinger stressed a key motif that runs through all his writings: the harmony between faith and reason, between the God of faith and the God of the philosophers, and the dangers to the faith when they are divorced. Nonetheless, and even with that point conceded, a union of faith and history is for him ultimately based on the union of word and flesh, which of course is much harder for the human intellect to grasp and then to accept.

> Perhaps it is already clear at this point that even in the paradox of word and flesh we are faced with something meaningful and in accordance with the *logos*. Yet at first this article of faith represents a stumbling block for human thinking. In this have we not fallen victim to an absolutely staggering kind of positivism? Can we cling at all to the straw of one single historical event? Can we dare to base our whole existence, indeed the whole of history, on the straw of one happening in the great sea of history?[32]

Yes, we can; but it is crucial to point out that in doing so, we are overturning our normal approach to reality, a point regularly stressed by Saint Paul, who not only said, "No one can say Jesus is Lord except by the Holy Spirit" (1 Cor 12:3), but also, and more daringly,

> The word of the cross is folly to those who are perishing, but to us who are being saved it is the power of God. For it is written: "I will destroy the wisdom of the wise, and the cleverness of the clever I will thwart." Where is the wise man? Where is the scribe? Where is the debater of this age? Has not God made foolish the wisdom of the world? For since, in the wisdom of God, the world did not know God through wisdom, it pleased God through the folly of what we preach to save those who believe. For Jews demand signs and Greeks seek wisdom, but we preach Christ crucified, a stumbling block to Jews and folly to Gentiles; but to those who are called, both Jews and Greeks, Christ is the power of

God and the wisdom of God. For the foolishness of God is wiser than men, and the weakness of God is stronger than men. (1 Cor 1:18–25)

In other words, the claims made on behalf of Jesus are so unprecedented that acceptance of them requires the overthrow of worldly norms of rationality, very much including Troeltsch's three methodological norms for genuine historical scholarship: (1) skeptical attitude toward the veracity of documents, (2) analogy with past events, (3) insertion of all events in a continuum of cause-effect. Of course Pope Benedict does not deny the validity of historical criticism applied to the New Testament, for the very good reason that Jesus is a figure in history. In fact, one cannot but be struck by the serene use he makes of the results of historical scholarship in his work, including his two volumes on the historical Jesus, *Jesus of Nazareth*, which includes some high praise for Notre Dame's own John Meier.[33] Still, even when legitimate, historical criticism can only be propaedeutic. Moreover, when applied using a naturalistic methodology, it inevitably falsifies. As the future pope says with lapidary flair about naturalistic historical criticism: "It is not the exegesis that proves the philosophy, but the philosophy that generates the exegesis. If I know *a priori* (to speak like Kant) that Jesus cannot be God and that miracles, mysteries, and sacraments are three forms of superstition, then I cannot discover what cannot be a fact in the sacred books. I can only describe why and how such affirmations were arrived at and how they were gradually formed."[34]

Ratzinger even has a way to prove this point negatively: by looking at the wild swings of historical scholarship on Jesus over the course of two centuries. These swings began in the first half of the nineteenth century with the positivists, who could only see the bare facts of history, facing the Hegelians, who could see only the universal meaning that those facts illustrate or exemplify: "The dilemma of the two courses—on the one hand, that of transposing or reducing Christology to history and, on the other, that of escaping history completely and abandoning it, as irrelevant to faith—could be quite accurately summarized in the two alternatives by which modern theology is vexed: Jesus or Christ?"[35]

For his own schematic purposes, Ratzinger takes Harnack and Bultmann as the two representatives of each fork of the dilemma: Harnack wanted to strip Christianity of any philosophical overlay to reach the Jesus of history, but his failure led, perhaps inevitably, to Bultmann's insistence that the only historically important fact about Jesus is that he existed and died on the cross; everything else comes from faith in the preached Christ. In each case, the move seemed liberating. In Harnack's case, the liberation was from religious division: "Where faith in the Son had divided people—Christians from non-Christians, Christians of different denominations from one another knowledge of the Father can unite."[36] In Bultmann's case, faith is now immune to the ups and downs of historical research, which is endlessly revising its conclusions based on new evidence or new considerations of old evidence.

But as the later history of theology proved, neither approach worked: as Albert Schweitzer later showed, Harnack saw only his own bourgeois image in Jesus, while Bultmann tied the believer not to Jesus but to a verbal event coming from the pulpit. For the future pope, this shuttlecock movement from Jesus to Christ and back to Jesus again (Bultmann's own students came to reject his radical skepticism and launched the so-called Second Quest for the historical Jesus) can itself be illuminating for Christology: "I believe that [this example of Harnack and Bultmann] can become a very useful pointer to something," says the Bavarian theologian, "namely, to the fact that the one (Jesus) cannot exist without the other (Christ), that, on the contrary, one is bound to be continually pushed from one to the other because in reality Jesus only subsists as the Christ and the Christ only subsists in the shape of Jesus."[37]

There is obviously not space enough here to discuss in detail the pope's twofold appreciation-cum-critique of the historical-critical method, which would, inter alia, require a close study and analysis of his two recent books on the historical Jesus. What remains to round out this picture of the pope's response to relativism is one more point he stresses regularly but often goes unnoticed in most versions of the theology of interreligious dialogue: the impermissibility, even on a phenomenological level, of regarding the religions of the world as denoting one univocal genus that can be taken as granted without further ado, under which are subsumed all the specific religions. Just as no one speaks "language" but only *a* language, so, too, man does not belong to "religion" but only to *a* religion. This case would also embrace worldviews, in the generic sense: ideologies are religions too, anthropologically speaking.

But religions, like languages, are specific and have specific teachings, especially about the meaning and reality of what Christians call salvation. The use of the word *salvation* is problematic for some religions: they all must presuppose at least some plight of man to which salvation is the response of hope and betterment. Again, the relativist must claim that all religions lead equally to salvation. To say otherwise would be the very definition of intolerance.

> The question of how men can be saved still tends to be put in the classical manner. And then the theory has been generally accepted that the religions are paths of salvation.... One obtains salvation through all the religions, that has become the current view. This answer corresponds not only to the idea of tolerance and of respect for others, which so thrusts itself upon us these days. It also corresponds to the modern idea of God: God cannot reject people just because they know nothing of Christianity and happen to have grown up in other religions. He will accept their worship and religion just as he does ours.[38]

While initially plausible, such a way of looking at things, according to Benedict, must lead to relativism: "For what each of these religions demands of people is, not just different from, but contrary to what is demanded by others." (One thinks of the different definitions of martyrdom in Christianity and Islam here.) But still they all lead to salvation! "Things that contradict one another," Benedict says, "are seen as leading to the same goal—in other words, that we are once more facing the question of relativism.... Truth is replaced by good intentions;

religion remains in the subjective realm, because we cannot know what is objectively good and true."[39]

Such a position obviously leads to intolerable antinomies. In Plato's *Euthyphro* Socrates asks the important question whether something is pious because the gods happen to say it is or because the gods too recognize its inherent piety. He goes on to point out that a murderer hauled into court never argues that he did the murder but should be let off because—in his case only—murder is permissible; on the contrary, he argues that murder is wrong and unlawful but that in this case he has been wrongly charged because he didn't commit the murder. Good, in other words, is a value inherent to itself, which fact suddenly puts the question of salvation in a whole new light.

> When people talk about the significance of religions for salvation, it is quite astonishing that they for the most part think only that all of them make eternal life possible; and when they think like that, the concept of eternal life is neutralized, since everyone gets there in any case. But that sells the question of salvation short, in most inappropriate fashion. Heaven begins on earth. . . . We have to ask what heaven is and how it comes upon earth. Future salvation must make its mark in a way of life that makes a person "human" here and thus capable of relating to God. That in turn means that when we are concerned with the question of salvation, we must look beyond religions themselves and that this involves *standards of right living that one cannot just relativize at will.* . . . That means that salvation does not lie in religions as such, but it is connected to them, inasmuch as, and to the extent that, they lead man toward the *one* good, toward the search for God, for truth, and for love. The question of salvation therefore always carries within it an element of the criticism of religion, just as, contrariwise, it can build a positive relationship to religions. It has in any case to do with the unity of the good, with the unity of what is true—with the unity of God and man.[40]

Without this perspective, it becomes quite impossible to critique religions and ideologies, since they are all leading willy-nilly to the

same inevitable goal of a saving union with God. But with this perspective, new vistas open out for a prophetic critique of all religions,
Christianity very much included: "There are in fact sick and degenerate forms of religion, which do not edify people but alienate them:
the Marxist criticism of religion was not entirely based on delusions.
And even religions whose moral value we must recognize, and which
are on their way toward the truth, may become diseased here and
there." After discussing certain disturbing features of non-Christian
religions, the future pope then points to Christianity's failings when
measured against the Socratic standard: "And there are of course, as
we all know but too well, diseased forms of Christianity—such as
when the crusaders, on capturing the holy city of Jerusalem, where
Christ died for all men, for their part indulged in a bloodbath of Mos-
lems and Jews."[41]

The point the cardinal is making here is not to grovel as if Christianity is uniquely iniquitous or still less to score points against other
religions. Rather, he is saying that whenever we repent of these
failings—or even when we are merely pointing them out *as* abuses—
we are denying the relativist premise.

> What this means is that religion demands the making of distinc-
> tions, distinctions between different forms of religion and distinc-
> tions within a religion itself, so as to find the way to its higher
> points. By treating all content as comparably valid and with the
> idea that all religions are different and yet actually the same, you
> get nowhere. Relativism is dangerous in quite particular ways: for
> the shape of human existence at an individual level and in society.
> The renunciation of truth does not heal man. How much evil has
> been done in history in the name of good opinions and good in-
> tentions is something no one can overlook.[42]

As to the question of salvation in its ultimate, eschatological
sense, of course revelation does not vouchsafe us an answer. Nor is this
the place to discuss the pope's many writings on eschatology, including of course his remarkable encyclical on that theme, *Spe Salvi,* with
its stress on solidarity—that we are all united in prayer with the Heav-

enly City, the Church Triumphant, that no one is saved alone.[43] But I would like to conclude with this consoling passage from his book on the Eucharist, that premier sacrament of solidarity:

> We cannot start to set limits on God's behalf; the very heart of the faith has been lost to anyone who supposes that it is only worthwhile, if it is, so to say, made worthwhile by the damnation of others. Such a way of thinking, which finds the punishment of other people necessary, springs from not having inwardly accepted the faith; from loving only oneself and not God the Creator, to whom his creatures belong. That way of thinking would be like the attitude of those people who could not bear the workers who came last being paid a denarius like the rest; like the attitude of people who feel properly rewarded only if others have received less. This would be the attitude of the son who stayed at home, who could not bear the reconciling kindness of his father. It would be a hardening of our hearts, in which it would become clear that we were only looking out for ourselves and not looking for God; in which it would be clear that we did not love our faith, but merely bore it like a burden. . . . It is a basic element of the biblical message that the Lord died for all—being jealous of salvation is not Christian.[44]

NOTES

1. James Luther Adams, Introduction to Ernst Troeltsch, *The Absoluteness of Christianity and the History of Religions*, trans. David Reid (Richmond, VA: John Knox Press, [1902] 1971), 7.

2. Joseph Cardinal Ratzinger, "Homily at the Mass for the Election of the Roman Pontiff," April 18, 2005, in *The Essential Pope Benedict XVI: His Central Writings and Speeches*, ed. John F. Thornton and Susan B. Varenne (New York: HarperSanFrancisco, 2007), 22.

3. Allan Bloom, *The Closing of the American Mind: How Higher Education Has Failed Democracy and Impoverished the Souls of Today's Students* (New York: Simon and Schuster, 1987), 98.

4. Ibid., 28.

5. Ibid., 32–33.

6. "It is precisely because there is in our society no established way of deciding between these [rival] claims that moral argument appears to be necessarily interminable. From our rival conclusions we can argue back to our rival premises, but when we do arrive at our premises argument ceases and the invocation of one premise against another becomes a matter of pure assertion and counter-assertion. Hence perhaps the slightly shrill tone of so much moral debate." Alasdair MacIntyre, *After Virtue: A Study in Moral Theory,* 3rd ed. (Notre Dame: University of Notre Dame Press, 2007), 8. I don't think MacIntyre would use the phrase "slightly shrill" anymore; indeed the din is downright cacophonous of late.

7. MacIntyre, *After Virtue,* 111.

8. As Adams makes explicit here: "Troeltsch would have seen in the colloquy in Washington a sign of a major revolution that has affected all spheres of life—the arts, law, and religion as well as the sciences. In his view this revolution has come about as a consequence of the appearance of a new historical consciousness that recognizes the contingent and singular character of the events of history." "Introduction," 8.

9. Ernst Troeltsch, "The Significance of the Historical Existence of Jesus for Faith," in *Ernst Troeltsch: Writings on Theology and Religion,* trans. Robert Morgan and Michael Pye (Atlanta: John Knox Press, 1971), 192–209; here, 189; emphasis added and translation slightly amended. Troeltsch even has an answer to the objection I raised above that there is always a lurking absolutism in relativistic claims: if someone asks how a radical historicist and relativist like himself can get the wherewithal to make such an "absolutist" statement as the one quoted above, he would grant the point, since all historical judgments (including his own) are always statements of probability: "Of course nothing certain can be said here; but it [Christocentrism] is not probable" (189).

10. This applies even to eyewitness accounts, like Julius Caesar's *Gallic Wars,* for his account had the ulterior purpose of advancing his political career in Rome.

11. This is why, when events are lacking analogies, skeptics arise who doubt the event itself: the more unprecedented the event, the more widespread the skepticism. Hence such phenomena as denial of the Holocaust, or the so-called Truthers who claim that the federal government planted explosives in the Twin Towers on 9/11, or (to be sure, in a minor key) those who claim that William Shakespeare, the glover's son from Stratford, did not write the plays attributed to him. These phenomena lack *analogies.*

12. Hegel indulges in this habit throughout his works; and in his philosophy history takes on an air of inevitability, leaving no room for contingency, which prompted Arthur Schopenhauer to make his famous wisecrack that Hegel provided an ontological argument for every event in history except Herr Krug's pen.

13. Thomas Hobbes got at the same point when he said that when someone claims he met God in a dream, the outsider can legitimately transpose that claim into saying the man had a dream of God, without in any way impugning the honesty of the dreamer.

14. Peter Berger, *A Rumor of Angels: Modern Society and the Rediscovery of the Supernatural* (New York: Doubleday, 1990), 34–35; Berger's emphasis.

15. Ibid., 42; Berger's emphases.

16. Joseph Ratzinger, "Relativism: The Central Problem for Faith Today. Address to the Presidents of the Doctrinal Commissions of the Bishops' Conferences of Latin America, Delivered in Guadalajara, Mexico, May 1996," in Thornton and Varenne, *Essential Pope Benedict*, 227–40; here, 228. A revised version of this talk was also published as "The New Questions That Arose in the Nineties: The Position of Faith and Theology Today," in Joseph Cardinal Ratzinger, *Truth and Tolerance: Christian Belief and World Religions*, trans. Henry Taylor (San Francisco: Ignatius Press, 2004), 115–13. I shall throughout be quoting from the original address.

17. Ratzinger, "Relativism," 229; emphasis added.

18. Ratzinger, *Tolerance*, 204.

19. Ratzinger, "Relativism," 229.

20. Joseph Ratzinger and Marcello Pera, *Without Roots: The West, Relativism, Christianity, Islam,* trans. Michael F. Moore (New York: Basic Books, 2006), 128.

21. It is the thesis of Emery de Gaál, *The Theology of Pope Benedict XVI* (New York: Palgrave Macmillan, 2010), that Pope Benedict has sought to resolve all theological disputes in both the pre- and postconciliar Church, from the nature-grace relationship and the nature of the liturgy to the challenge of historical criticism and relativism, in Christological terms.

22. Joseph Ratzinger, *Introduction to Christianity*, trans. J. R. Foster (San Francisco: Ignatius Press, 2004), 31.

23. Ratzinger, "Relativism," 229.

24. Ibid., 231; emphasis added.

25. Josef Pieper, *Guide to Thomas Aquinas*, trans. Richard and Clara Winston (San Francisco: Ignatius Press, 1991), 77–78.

26. Ratzinger, "Relativism," 231.

27. Ibid., 239.

28. Ibid. Needless to say, this assertion has not gone unnoticed by some neo-Thomists of a more traditional bent, nor has it been much appreciated. Thus Steven Long, addressing this very passage: "Of course human reason is always in some historical context or another, but this is no particular reason why—even if all these contexts suffer various typical distortions—that reason cannot see further than such distortions. . . . Further, no ground whatsoever is given for the judgment that 'the neoscholastic rationalism that was trying to reconstruct the *praeambula fidei,* the approach to faith, with pure rational certainty, by means of rational argument that was strictly independent of any faith, has failed.'. . . The same point applies to what follows [in the quotation] when [Ratzinger] writes that 'Karl Barth was right when he rejected philosophy as a basis for faith that is independent of faith itself: for in that case, our faith would in the end be based on changing philosophical theories.' For if a theory is *true* then, despite the fact that there is change in our understanding of it, and even should we come erroneously to think it false, *reality remains the same.*" Steven A. Long, *Natura Pura: On the Recovery of Nature in the Doctrine of Grace* (New York: Fordham University Press, 2010), 215; Long's emphasis.

29. Isaac Newton's law of gravity is, of course, mathematically, a ratio— not accidentally also the Latin word for "reason." No wonder, then, that later historians retrospectively call Newton's century the "Age of Reason," even though that century also witnessed the Thirty Years' War and such outbreaks of irrationality as the persecution of alleged witches.

30. Ratzinger, *Introduction,* 193; Latin and Greek terms italicized by Ratzinger (or at least the translator); other emphases added.

31. Ibid., 193–94.

32. Ibid., 194. Also: "Such a notion, which even in itself is an adventurous one and seemed equally improbable to both ancient and Asiatic thought, is rendered still more difficult in the intellectual climate of modern times" (194).

33. "Excellent studies are already available concerning chronological and topographical questions to do with the life of Jesus. I refer especially . . . to the exhaustive study by John P. Meier, *A Marginal Jew.*" Benedict XVI, *Jesus of Nazareth: Part Two: Holy Week: From the Entrance into Jerusalem to the Resurrection* (San Francisco: Ignatius Press, 2011), xv. Later the pope adds: "From the immense quantity of literature on the dating of the Last Supper and of Jesus' death, I would like to single out the treatment of the subject, outstanding both in its thoroughness and its accuracy, found in the first volume of John P. Meier's *A Marginal Jew*" (302).

34. Ratzinger, "Relativism," 237.

35. Ratzinger, *Introduction*, 198.

36. Ibid., 193, paraphrasing Harnack.

37. Ibid., 201.

38. Ratzinger, *Tolerance*, 202–3.

39. Ibid., 203.

40. Ibid., 205; emphasis added.

41. All quotations from this paragraph are from Ratzinger, *Tolerance*, 204.

42. Ibid. One is reminded in this context of a remark from the (atheist) novelist Anatole France to the effect no greater evil has been done than by those who think man is inherently good.

43. Nor can I discuss the pope's liturgical theology as an important resource for his critique of liberalism; on this, see Geoffrey Wainwright, "A Remedy for Relativism: The Cosmic, Historical, and Eschatological Dimensions of the Liturgy According to the Theologian Joseph Ratzinger," *Nova et Vetera*, Engl. ed., 5, no. 2 (2007): 175–200; reprinted in Geoffrey Wainwright, *Embracing Purpose: Essays on God, the World, and the Church* (Peterborough: Epworth, 2007), 265–90.

44. Joseph Ratzinger, *God Is Near Us: The Eucharist, the Heart of Life*, trans. Henry Taylor (San Francisco: Ignatius Press, 2003), 35–36.

chapter four

A DEPTH OF OTHERNESS

Buddhism and Benedict's Theology of Religions

ROBERT M. GIMELLO

In 1951, fourteen years before the publication of *Nostra Aetate,* the Second Vatican Council's great summons to the mutually entailed enterprises of theology of religions and interreligious dialogue, Henri de Lubac, later to be recognized as a guiding light of the Council, published a learned account of the Christian West's slow, hesitant discovery of Buddhism. He prefaced his study with the following observation:

> The West that is groping its way, little by little and in various ways, toward the discovery of Buddhism, is, broadly speaking, the Christian West. More than the growth in the understanding of Buddhism, we consider here the succession of reactions to it over the course of centuries. For us, therefore, the history of this discovery is not an entirely secular undertaking. It touches not only on the history of civilization and humanism, but still more on the history of religions. It involves the history of Christian missions,

of apologetics, of great spiritual conflicts. It is one line—among many, certainly—that delineates the face of this Europe where we live, one component the explanation of which contributes to our explanation of ourselves. Far from complete, it has just entered, we believe, its most crucial phase. It now forces the Christian intellect to grapple with a reflection that cannot be ignored without cost.[1]

Today, more than six decades after Père de Lubac wrote these words, we are still early in the "crucial phase" of Christianity's encounter with Buddhism, and the demand that Buddhism makes upon Christianity's reflective attention is now, if anything, even more urgent, the danger of harm should Christianity neglect Buddhism even greater, than seemed to be the case in the middle of the past century.

Cardinal de Lubac, one must note, was an admirer of Buddhism—a critical and discriminating admirer, to be sure, but an admirer nonetheless.[2] He was even willing, in the conclusion of his 1951 study, to quote a rather ardent, but not unqualified, encomium of the Buddha from Romano Guardini's *The Lord*:

[There is only one man whom we might be inclined to compare with Jesus: the Buddha.] This man is a great mystery. He lived in an awful, almost superhuman freedom, yet his kindness was powerful as a cosmic force. Perhaps Buddha will be the last religious genius to be explained by Christianity. As yet no one has really uncovered his Christian significance. Perhaps Christ had not only one precursor, John, last of the prophets, but three: John the Baptist for the Chosen People, Socrates from the heart of antiquity, and Buddha, who spoke the ultimate word in Eastern religious cognition. Buddha is free; but his freedom is not that of Christ. Possibly Buddha's freedom is only the ultimate and supremely liberating knowledge of the vanity of this fallen world. Christ's freedom is based not on negative cognition, but on the love of God; his whole attitude is permeated with God's earnest will to heal the world.[3]

To this, however, de Lubac adds still further qualification:

> If we may, as Guardini suggests, seek an analogy for Buddhism in the Old Testament, it is decidedly not in the prayer of the Psalms or the prophecy of Isaiah that we must expect to find it, nor in any of the preparations for nor actual foreshadowing of the Gospels; such an analogy is to be found only in Ecclesiastes (without implying, of course, any similarity in doctrine). On its face, the reality of Buddhism is profoundly ambiguous. We will not claim, with Bergson, merely that it rests on "an incomplete mysticism" because "it has not comprehended the efficacy of human action," and that it "lacks warmth." This characterization clearly captures Buddhism's absence of charity, which follows from the absence of faith and hope. However, we will conceive of it still more as an immense, drastic, and subtle *pars purificans,* a negative preparation achieved by means of emptiness, with the terrible danger that this emptiness will remain so enamored of itself that the message of Easter will not resound with triumphant notes in the Buddhist soul.[4]

Both de Lubac and Guardini, two major influences in Joseph Ratzinger's theology, anticipated in their views of Buddhism the Second Vatican Council's injunction to pay respectful, charitable heed to other religions. They both found in the *buddhadharma* what *Nostra Aetate* would later tell us to look for, even to expect, in traditions other than Christianity, namely, evidence of truth and holiness. De Lubac was especially eloquent on the subject when he wrote, for example, that "one senses in Buddhism that quivering of the spiritual being in contact with the mysterious and the sacred"[5] and when he declared, "Apart from the unique reality in which we worship the trace and the very presence of God, Buddhism is without doubt the greatest spiritual reality in history."[6] But for neither man did affirmative assessment, even awe, of Buddhism lead to an attenuation of faith in the primacy and the definitive character of the salvation offered by Christ. Indeed, it had quite the opposite effect, of reinforcing and deepening that faith and of indemnifying it against the strange intolerance of the modern world's increasingly doctrinaire and aggressive relativism. This is why de Lubac could speak not only of the greatness of Buddhism's "tremendous adventure" but also of its ultimate "failure" vis-à-vis Christianity—of "the foundering of this gigantic raft on which half of humanity embarked for Deliverance."[7]

Joseph Ratzinger himself seems not to have been much concerned, in the earliest phase of his career, with the question of Christianity's proper relation with non-Christian religions (other than Judaism). He appears to have been drawn to that question only somewhat later when he found it necessary to defend the great accomplishments of Vatican II from the abuse and distortions to which they were so quickly subjected in the decades immediately following the Council's conclusion. Those were heady times for the Church, and for some, those who found it hard to segregate the excitement rightly generated by the Council from the turbulence in the secular culture of the era, the wake of the Council became a time of disorientation and intemperance. During the Council, Ratzinger, then in his mid-thirties, had served as *peritus* to Cardinal Frings of Cologne and is believed to have been the author of the cardinal's more consequential interventions in the cause of curial reform. Such contributions to ecclesiastical liberalization or decentralization, together with his theological sympathies and affiliations with the movement of theological *ressourcement*, had earned for Ratzinger an early reputation as a reformer, indeed as one of those responsible for the formation of what would later come to be called the "Spirit of Vatican II." Upon the conclusion of the Council Ratzinger was appointed to the chair of Dogmatic Theology at the University of Tübingen. What he witnessed there in the late sixties— when latter-day Jacobins and their intellectual fellow travelers occupied the halls of academe as well as the streets of the great cities in Europe and America—caused him deep dismay and showed him that the promise of Vatican II to invigorate the Church was under threat by some who took it to be a warrant for drastic, denaturing change (and by others who rejected the Council as having already effected such change). Ratzinger moved to Regensburg in 1968, the West's year of paroxysm, but the anxiety he had begun to feel while still at Tübingen grew over the next two decades into the full-blown conviction that something had gone very wrong. "I am convinced," he said, "that the damage that we have incurred in these twenty years is due, not to the 'true' Council, but to the unleashing *within* the Church of latent polemical and centrifugal forces; and *outside* the Church it is due to the confrontation with a cultural revolution in the West."[8] There were many particular causes for Ratzinger's disquiet, but one of them, and not the least, was the alliance he saw being so quickly forged between those theologians most eagerly advocating dialogue with other religions and those in the wider cultural world who defined dialogue as conversation with the other only on the condition that one suspend, treat as merely provisional, or perhaps even relinquish, one's own beliefs. The accepted and enforced protocol of such "dialogue" was the rule that no one party to it could lay claim to objective truth. In this way what Ratzinger would later identify as the "dictatorship of relativism" peremptorily invaded and claimed exclusive sovereignty over the space of dialogue. After he became in 1981 Cardinal Prefect of the Congregation for the Doctrine of the Faith, deep concern with the intolerance implicit in this strange notion of dialogue would inform his thinking about Christianity's relation to other religions and would influence his official decisions concerning a number of theologians of religion whose work, under the aegis of such an understanding of dialogue, seemed to entail the treatment of Christian doctrine as "true" only in a "relative" sense.

Buddhism was often especially at issue in Ratzinger's reflections on the nature of dialogue for the "Buddhist-Christian dialogue" was flourishing and was held by many, both theologians and contemplatives, to be in various ways particularly promising. Many were eager to proclaim Buddhism as another gift of the Spirit, as a necessary complement to Christianity, as a font for theological renewal of a tradition too long stifled by its adherence to outmoded and parochially Western categories of thought, and as an opportunity to revive and magnify spiritual disciplines that had been allowed to wither in the Western Church at least since the sixteenth century. Such is the background, then, to the informal and formal pronouncements Cardinal Prefect Ratzinger would make on the subject of Buddhism over the course of the 1980s and 1990s. Famous (or infamous) among the former was a remark made to a French journalist in 1997. Asked by the journalist if he "believed that Catholics were in danger of losing their souls in dialogue with other religions, like Buddhism," the cardinal prefect replied:

> Dialogue among religions is necessary in a world growing ever more unified. But the danger is that the dialogue may become superficial. For the relativism that has taken hold of minds today encourages a sort of moral and intellectual anarchism that pushes men no longer to accept unique truth. To affirm such truth has become a mark of intolerance. But a true dialogue is no empty exercise; it has a purpose: the shared quest for the truth. A Christian cannot renounce his knowledge of the truth, revealed to him in Jesus Christ, the only Son of God. If Buddhism beguiles, it does so by appearing to offer the opportunity to touch the infinite, to grasp a bliss without real religious obligation—a spiritual narcissism of sorts. In the 1950s, someone accurately predicted that the challenge to the Church in the twentieth century would not be Marxism, but Buddhism.[9]

The *"autoerotisme spirituel"* to which Ratzinger referred was widely, perhaps sometimes willfully and maliciously, misinterpreted in the popular media. What he was actually suggesting was that a craving for salvation as self-absorption and self-gratification—for transcendence as liberation from the demands of any truth or value outside of oneself—has been the governing impulse for many Christians drawn to Buddhism. This, of course, is not at all what Buddhism actually offers, as Ratzinger well understands, but it is what it can appear *(apparaît)* to offer, what many in the West have hoped or desired to find as they have turned to it, without studying it seriously, simply because it has seemed to be an intriguing and congenial alternative to more demanding kinds of religion from which they had become alienated. We see in these remarks not so much a denigration of Buddhism as another condemnation of the solipsism that lurks in the relativism of any *"dialogue superficiel"* and that can conceal in the cloak of one's own desires the true, demanding otherness of the other.

And yet Cardinal Ratzinger did not hesitate to identify Buddhism—even and especially when it is properly understood and respected rather than used merely as a screen on which to project Western desires—as a "challenge" *(défi)* to the Church, a challenge perhaps greater than that presented by any other non-Christian religion or ideology. Our task is to understand why he saw it as such.

But a brief detour is in order at this point, a diversion from Catholic theology to the secular domain of the academic study of Buddhism. The same years that saw the rapid growth of interest in theological and contemplative engagement with Buddhism also witnessed an explosion of scholarship on Buddhist thought, practice, history, and philology, and the theological/contemplative interest in Buddhism was often outpaced by these new scholarly developments. Let me offer one example, from my own field of Buddhist Studies, the study of Buddhism in China. The career of the *buddhadharma* in the "Middle Kingdom" offers for study not only a wealth of Buddhist thought and spirituality but also a unique historical example of Buddhism in dialogue. In its transmission from India, the culture of its birth, to China, its most challenging field of propagation, Buddhism had to cross wide and deep chasms of religious, cultural, and other differences. I would argue that there are no two civilizations in human history less alike, more consequentially different from one another, than those of India and China (this despite the Western habit of consigning both to the culturally arbitrary, fictitious category "Asia" or "the Orient"). Yet as Buddhism moved from the former to the latter it managed to become a truly Chinese religion, without becoming any the less Buddhist, and it did so while making China a truly Buddhist culture that was no less Chinese for having become also Buddhist. Modern scholarship has come to appreciate that Buddhism surely changed as it took root in China, and that its ability to change is what made its transplantation possible by enabling Chinese to accept it. Yet the change that Buddhism underwent in China has proved, on close examination, never, or at most only seldom, to have been at the expense of fidelity to its own core Buddhist principles and values. Rather than attenuate or adulterate Buddhism's identity as Buddhism, rather than dilute it in the solvent of a relativism *avant la lettre,* rather than assume its subordination to mere historical contingency, Buddhism's sinification has been shown actually to have tempered, strengthened, and amplified that identity. Buddhism's change in China, the change wrought especially by its encounter with Chinese religious traditions, was most often, in fact, just the kind of change that (to revert once again to theology) John Henry Newman discovered in his early studies of the history of Christian doctrine: change as a function of a faith's vitality rather than change as deracination and denaturing. That is to say, it was change as healthy and responsive growth, the kind of change that reveals the fecundity without which faith would be moribund and soon defunct.

I would suggest, therefore, that the sinification of Buddhism, which was also the Buddhist transformation of China, was actually a case of what theologians and others today call "inculturation"—and an especially successful such case at that. I would also suggest that it may serve as a salutary example of the complex dynamics of what we today call "interreligious dialogue," particularly of the kind of genuine, as opposed to superficial, "dialogue" that can be allied with the enterprise of "proclamation." Buddhism's advent and growth in China was, after all, a process by which Buddhists came, for example, better to understand, appreciate, and profit from the ethical seriousness and cosmological reverence of Confucianism and the vitalism of Daoism while Confucians and Daoist came better to know Buddhism and, by virtue of their encounters with the *dharma*, to deepen their self-understanding and to incorporate into their own thought and practice some of the epistemological and phenomenological sophistication and contemplative expertise of Buddhism. Of course, the centuries-long "dialogue" among these traditions did not preclude dispute, nor was it entirely immune to acrimony and hostilities, but neither did it always entail, or fail to move beyond, such conflict. Sometimes it led to conversions, sometimes to recognitions of things shared, sometimes to mutual rejections and suppressions, sometimes to little more than uneasy détentes, some surprisingly small number of times to mere syncretism, but most often, and steadily over the long term, it led to deeper mutual understanding and mutual enrichment.

All this I mention as prelude to further discussion of Joseph Ratzinger's theology of religion because I believe that Buddhism makes at least two kinds of just claim on Catholic theological attention. First and most obviously it demands attention—philological and hermeneutically expert, well-informed critical attention—because, as *Nostra Aetate* suggests, one may find in it, if one looks carefully and not merely wishfully, not the full measure of truth and holiness that only Christ and his Church offer but many things that are both true and holy, many traces, if you will, of the incognito presence of the Spirit. But Buddhism also deserves a kind of second-order attention as a historical example of what fruitful yet faithful interreligious engagement can be and how it can proceed. I would suggest that the study of Buddhist views of Chinese religions, of other Chinese religions' views of Buddhism, and of the complex interactions among these several traditions actually validates Joseph Ratzinger's instructions on how Catholic theology should engage Buddhism and other non-Christian religions. The ill-informed, tendentious, and invidious characterizations of Benedict's theology of religions, which sadly are common in the theological academy and which abound in the popular media, hold it to be reactionary, excessively defensive, uncharitable, insensitive, blind to the value of the other, oblivious of the unbounded reach of the Spirit or the universal presence of the Logos, and (of course) subversive of the ethos of Vatican II. I hope to show, to the contrary, that in his insistence on the fundamental differences between Christianity and Buddhism Benedict XVI has actually been paying generous twofold tribute to Buddhism—first by acknowledging its genuine otherness and refraining from hasty, ultimately condescending assumptions of similarity, and second by following, even if unintentionally, the model of fidelity cum creativity that Buddhism itself has offered in its own historical engagement with the indigenous religions of China and of the other cultures it penetrated. If I am right about this I will only have confirmed insights earlier expressed by Joseph Ratzinger himself, as when he observed:

> Belonging to two cultural entities is impossible in general, *although of course Buddhism represents an exception, in the way it is able to combine itself with other cultural entities as an inner dimension of them,* so to speak.[10]

Or when he wrote:

> Each particular culture not only lives out its own experience of
> God, the world, and man but on its path it necessarily encounters
> other cultural agencies and has to react to their quite different ex-
> periences. This results, depending always on the degree to which
> the cultural agent may be closed or open, inwardly narrow or
> broad in outlook, in that culture's own perceptions and values
> being deepened and purified. *That may lead to a profound reshaping
> of that culture's previous form, yet this does not necessarily involve any
> kind of violation or alienation.*[11]

So much for the excursus into buddhology and sinology. Let us re-
sume our principal discussion with a quotation from the early Ratzinger, from an essay he wrote in 1963, even before the conclusion of
Vatican II and the publication of *Nostra Aetate*, for a Festschrift in
honor of Karl Rahner.[12]

> If we put before the man of today Christianity's conception of
> other religions . . . then he will not for the most part be particu-
> larly impressed. He will easily conclude that the recognition of
> other religions as having a provisional and preparatory character
> is a sign of arrogance. Christianity's rejection of these other reli-
> gions, on the other hand, will seem to him an expression of the
> partisan and disputatious attitude of the various religions, each of
> which tries to assert itself at the expense of the others and is so
> incredibly blind as to be unable to see that in reality they are all
> one and the same. The dominant impression of most people of
> today is that all religions, with a varied multiplicity of forms and
> manifestations, in the end are and mean one and the same thing;
> which is something everyone can see, except for them. The man
> of today will for the most part scarcely respond with an abrupt No
> to a particular religion's claim to be true; he will simply relativize
> that claim by saying, "There are many religions." And behind his
> response will probably be the opinion, in some form or other, that

beneath varying forms they are in essence all the same; each person has his own.

If we were to try to extract, from a current intellectual view of that kind, a couple of characteristic opinions, then we might well say: *the concept of religion held by "the man of today"* (if you will permit me to continue to use this fictional means of particularizing) *is static; he usually does not foresee any development from one religion to another; rather, he expects each person to remain in his own and to experience it with an awareness that is, in its basic spiritual core, identical with all others.*[13]

Apart from demonstrating an amazing foresight in anticipating criticisms of his position that are still being monotonously repeated even today, a half century after this article was penned, these remarks highlight an important but often ignored feature of relativist or soi-disant "pluralist" views of the relations among religions, namely, that such views rule out, or blind themselves to, the possibility of significant religious change, not only change as conversion wrought by, say, the reputedly aggressive intervention of mission, but even change as growth from within or as responsiveness to altering external conditions. The effect of the widely held assumptions that Ratzinger here describes is to make of the various religions things "frozen" or "preserved in amber" for the more or less idle, arm's-length, perhaps dilettantesque contemplation of observers or participant observers who expect to find in them nothing important that they do not already know.

And yet, Ratzinger notes, the pluralist view that all religions share a common core, harbored in diverse but unchanging outward configurations, perhaps even more than inclusivist views that hold other religions to be implicit in one's own, has enormous modern appeal. Thus, over and against prophecies of a single universal "religion of the spirit" to be eventually revealed as underlying all particular religions (as envisioned, to use Ratzinger's own example, by a Sarvepalli Radhakrishnan), he notes that "the Christian theologian looks like a dogmatic stick-in-the-mud, who cannot get away from his know-it-all attitude, whether he expresses it in the swaggering manner of apologists in past times or whether in the friendly manner of contemporary theologians who acknowledge to the other person to what extent he is already a Christian without being aware of it."[14]

Buddhism, Ratzinger might have said (but did not actually say), is especially appealing to the pluralist in this regard insofar as it is seen to be able to wield at will what strikes many as a conceptual "magic wand" in the form of the poorly understood Buddhist meta-doctrine of *upāya* (expedient device, convenient fiction). According to this teaching as it is widely understood, doctrinal differences may be explained away or ignored as having only subjective, pragmatic, and transactional force rather than invariant claim to any objective truth. Particular doctrinal formulations may be useful for certain persons or in certain times and circumstances—this is freely admitted—but they may, or should, be relinquished or replaced when the persons or the situations change. The need to relinquish them once they have served whatever purpose they are thought to suit is famously illustrated by the simile of the raft. Doctrines, like rafts, are useful and may even be necessary equipment for fording rivers, but once one has reached "the other shore" they are not to be clung to and carried always about lest they become mere burdens impeding further progress. Also relevant here is the common understanding of the classical Buddhist gnoseo-logical teaching of two kinds or orders of truth, the one ultimate *(paramārtha satya)* and the other conventional *(saṃvṛti satya)*, coupled with the classic hermeneutical distinction between teachings of "definitive meaning" *(nitārtha)*, which are final and explicit, and those of only "provisional meaning" *(neyārtha)*, which stand always in need of further interpretation. Teachings of provisional meaning are usually understood to convey only conventional, circumstantial, functional truths and to do so usually in cataphatic terms, whereas teachings of definitive meaning are held to disclose ultimate truth and to do so either by way of relentless apophasis (what the Chinese Buddhist tradition calls "the way of the hundred negations") or by some *via eminentiae* that denies in the very act of affirming. If definitive and invariant truth, the truth of things as they really and ultimately are, is always and only expressed or precipitated by negation or silence, then any doctrinal affirmation may be declared efficacious only relative to its proper context. It is not hard to see how such notions of truth and meaning might prove irresistible to theological pluralists or relativists who stumble upon them. Of course I have only sketched in the most superficial way the distinctions between *paramārtha satya* and *nitārtha*, on the one hand, and *saṃvṛti satya* and *neyārtha*, on the other. If one were to probe more deeply into the Buddhist understanding of these categories—to depths greater than most Christian theologians who exploit them are prepared to delve—one would find that they are themselves matters of strenuous dispute within Buddhism and are not usually deployed in ways that support doctrinal relativism. Indeed, one of their most common uses in East Asia is to establish hierarchical systems of doctrinal classification (Chinese: *panjiao zhidu*) in which certain renditions of the Buddha's teaching are held to be strictly and invariantly inferior or superior to others. But those who look to Buddhism for release from what they consider to be dogmatism do not welcome evidence of what might seem to be Buddhist dogmatism. There is also the problem, apparent to those viewing Buddhism from without, of explaining how doctrines that may be judged only provisionally true can be efficacious even in their own limited contexts. Must there not be some sort or degree of correspondence between a provisionally true doctrine and an objective truth if that doctrine is to have even the limited efficacy it is deemed to have? How else is a provisional truth to be distinguished from mere error? After all, a Buddhist may judge the claim that "the world is like a mirage" to be only relatively, not absolutely true, but were he to say that "the world is like a mighty fortress" he would be judged to be absolutely wrong, guilty of out-and-out error. What difference can there be, then, between two such similes—the one judged provisionally true, the other judged invariably false—apart from the measure of their correspondence to the fact of the matter?

In any case, it was Ratzinger's insights into the incoherence and nullifying effects of pluralist relativism and its grounding of religion in mere subjectivity that prepared him to respond astutely to the many post–Vatican II misconstruals of *Nostra Aetate* and related conciliar teachings. As the Church began to reflect on the implications of the famous assertion that it "rejects nothing that is true and holy" in other religions, Ratzinger was ready and able to explain that this pronouncement was actually an invitation to scrutinize other religions, open-mindedly but also critically, so as to determine just what in them is true and holy, and what is not. He saw clearly that it was not an insistence that everything in them is true and holy, nor that they are all as blessed by the care of the Spirit and the presence of the Logos as is Christianity, nor that they are all paths coequal with Christianity in their salvific efficacy, nor that Christianity somehow needs their wisdom and virtue to complete itself. To be sure, he did see in the study of other religions, and in dialogue with them, opportunities for salutary and faithful growth in Christianity, perhaps not unlike the salutary opportunities that had been presented to earliest Christianity by pagan philosophy, but he also saw real dangers in the failure to appreciate those aspects of other religions that are simply incompatible with Christian belief and the Christian life, or are deficient unto Christian ends, aspects overlooked in undisciplined haste to form liberating bonds with the other. Here are some examples, only briefly noted:

- Consider the Buddhist denial of a soul versus the Christian belief that each human person is a distinct embodied immortal soul made in the image and likeness of God. This is a hard antinomy, not to be circumvented by tendentious muffling of the truly radical denotation of the doctrine of *anātman* (no-self). *Anātman*, as a negative locution, can be, and usually is, held by Buddhists to be absolutely, not only relatively or provisionally, true.
- Consider the Buddhist belief in rebirth *ab aeterno* and possibly *in aeternum* versus the Christian belief in a single earthly life for each person, preceded by nonexistence and followed by an eternity in heaven (eternity in God's presence) or hell (eternal alienation from God). Some Buddhist modernists treat the doctrine of rebirth as only an *als ob* claim, but most Buddhists take it quite seriously and literally.
- Consider the Buddhist denial of a transcendent creator God and its disposition to hold Christ to be, at most, simply a wise and benevolent teacher of goodness and justice versus the Christian belief that Christ is no mere wise man but a person who is one with

the creator of all that is. This too is an opposition that cannot be easily explained away, not even with animadversions against onto-theology as a distortion of biblical faith.

- Consider the Buddhist claim, made not by all Buddhists but by many, that we and the seemingly external world are actually illusions or figments of mind, and consider this versus the realism of the Christian tradition and Christianity's respect for the objective, independent reality of a material world made all the more real by the Incarnation. Could a Christian, for example, ever assent to the *Diamond Cutter (Vajracchedikā) Sūtra*'s claim that all confected or composite things, and all persons, are ultimately "like a dream or a magician's trick"?

- Consider the Christian belief that ultimate truth *(aletheia, veritas)* is a divine person ("I am the Way and the Truth and the Life"— Jn 14:6) versus the Buddhist view that ultimate truth *(pāramārtha-satya)* is the entirely impersonal absence of all substantiality or of any ground of existence—not the "disclosure" (again, *aletheia*) of a presence, but the discovery of an absence.

- Consider the essentially introspective orientation of Buddhist meditation versus the Christian practice of prayer as communication with a divine other. It is true, of course, that Christian spirituality admits of, even treasures, deep interiority, but what the Christian encounters in prayerful introspection is the intimate presence of Christ, whereas the Buddhist encounters emptiness *(śūnyatā)*, or perhaps one's own inherent Buddha-nature *(buddhagotra, tathāgatagarbha)*, which in turn is said to be itself emptiness.

- Consider the subtle but deep differences between things Christian and things Buddhist that superficially may seem akin to each other but actually, on deeper investigation, prove not to be so—for example, the Christian doctrine of Christ's loving and sacrificial self-emptying, his pouring forth of himself *(kenōsis)* for the sake of mankind, versus the Buddhist claim that all things and beings are "empty" of substance or own-being *(svabhāva-śūnya)*. Modern Japanese Buddhists (e.g., Nishitani Keiji, Abe Masao, Ueda Shizuteru) and their process theology conversation partners (e.g.,

John Cobb) hold that the doctrine of Christ's self-emptying is Christianity's halting and imperfect acknowledgment of the deeper Buddhist truth of emptiness or "absolute nothingness," but is there really anything more to this than a trivial lexical resemblance? Is Christ's singular sacrificial humbling of himself in "pouring out" his divinity so as to become human really at all like the "dependent origination" *(pratītyasamutpāda)* of all things?

- In a similar vein, consider the largely Yogācāra doctrine of the "three bodies" *(trikāya)* of a Buddha, or the Huayan (Flower Ornament) tradition's teaching of the triunity of the Buddha Vairocana with the great bodhisattvas Mañjuśrī and Samantabhadra—these versus the central Christian doctrine of the Trinity. It has been alleged that they are similar, and one can certainly see similarities in the terminology used in expounding these teachings—for example, the near-synonymity of the Chinese Buddhist terms *yuanrong* (perfect interpenetration) and *wuai* (mutual nonobstruction) with Trinitarian terms like perichoresis or circuminsession (coinherence). However, the "manifest body" *(nirmāṇakāya)* and the "visionary body" *(saṃbhogakāya)* of a Buddha prove on close examination to be mere apparitions of the ultimate and formless "truth body" *(dharmakāya),* and this Buddhist theory must be judged to be a kind of Docetism. And although the three "holy ones" of Huayan are said to coinhere so that each somehow includes, and is included in, the others their relationship is actually such that their oneness is held to be ultimately more real than their threeness.

None of these sharp antinomies is dissolved by *Nostra Aetate's* acknowledgment that truth and holiness may be found in Buddhism, nor has Vatican II commanded us, against all the obvious odds, to finds ways to resolve them. Our cardinal-then-pope has been resolutely concerned for decades to make this clear.

He has also been ever alert to instances in which advocacy of Christianity's equivalence with other religions like Buddhism can be a pretext and an arsenal for mere theological dissent, dissent born not so much of genuine admiration for the other religions as of willful

disaffection from orthodoxy or submission to philosophical obscu-
rantism. Buddhism, for example, offers an impressive array of notions
and arguments that might be exploited by someone intent to hold—in
the manner of a Roger Haight, for example—that Christ is not a hy-
postasis of the triune God but only a "symbol of God." And those no
longer able to credit the singularity of Christ, or the full-throated
claim that Jesus is God incarnate, or the belief that the salvation he
offers is definitive, can find it impossible to resist the pull of Buddhist
apophasis, which strikes them as proleptically postmodern and which
they are quick to sever from the rest of the Buddhist tradition so that
they may put it to their own purposes. Witness this from Joseph
O'Leary, a professed "interreligious theologian," a harsh and doctrinaire critic of "onto-theology," and an ardent but highly selective admirer of Buddhism:

> In its sense of the absolute, its dismantling of idols, its conception
> of a gracious ultimacy embodied in compassionate bodhisattvas,
> Buddhism has plenty to tell us about the divine and about grace.
> This vast continent of spiritual insight cannot be measured by the
> yardsticks of a summary dogmatism or rationalism. Buddhism
> instills the awareness that all religious language and dogma has
> the status of 'skillful means' serving a purpose that transcends
> them. In its teaching of 'detachment from views,' it frees theology
> from the tendency to become trapped in obsessive tracks of
> thought. It shows up the clumsiness of our dogmatic terminology
> of nature, substance, person, hypostasis in regard to Christ; the
> Buddhist categories of dependent co-arising and emptiness are
> more suited to bring out the meaning of Christ (see John Keenan
> on this). Yet amid all its deconstructive impact, Buddhism re-
> mains constantly in touch with bedrock reality and constantly
> brings our mind back to this.[15]

Or this:

> In Buddhism, the experience of emptiness belongs to this level of
> lived encounter. It is an encounter with ultimate saving reality
> analogous to the Christian encounter with the risen Christ. The

encounter between these encounters can happen at the level of contemplation, but it should also happen at the everyday level of faith, through a sharing of languages, which for the Christian means an attempt to speak of Christ in Buddhist terms. Of course there is no point in doing this unless the Christian accepts that the Buddhist experience is an encounter with the absolutely real, just as a Buddhist could not draw on Christian language unless he believed it to speak from the realm of ultimacy.[16]

The unargued asseveration that an encounter with emptiness is analogous to an encounter with the risen Christ is preposterous on its face—unless, of course, one has already reduced the death and resurrection of the Son of God to the status of a mere *upāya* (as though to Christ's question, "Who do you say that I am?" one were to reply, "You are the 'event' which it is convenient for me, for a time and in my present historical situation, to treat as an expression of 'gracious ultimacy'"). Nor does such a misappropriation even do justice to the *agon* of Buddhism's efforts to understand the full implications of its own doctrine of emptiness. In Mahāyāna scriptures too numerous to list the discovery of emptiness, of the fact that all things are unarisen *(anutpattika),* is seen not as an encounter with "gracious ultimacy" but as a moment of sheer terror or vertigo which the bodhisattva must learn to survive and tolerate by cultivating the heroic spiritual courage that Buddhists call the "perfection of forbearance" *(kṣāntipāramitā).* It is in part for this reason that some Buddhist traditions, Huayan and Tiantai, for example, hold emptiness to be not itself the ultimate but only a propaedeutic, a "rinsing of the mind" in preparation for an encounter with the "fullness *(paripūrṇa)* of the marvelous qualities of Buddhahood" (among which qualities, by the way, one will not find the quality of being both fully human and fully divine). It is just O'Leary's kind of misappropriation of Buddhism, such wrenching of Buddhist ideas out of their proper context so as to put them in thrall to the task of drastically altering the Christian message, that prompted Cardinal Ratzinger to publish in 2000 the famous and controversial document, *Dominus Iesus,* which declares (and we know, from reading O'Leary and so many others, that it had to declare):

The Church's constant missionary proclamation is endangered today by relativistic theories which seek to justify religious pluralism, not only *de facto* but also *de iure* (or in principle). As a consequence, it is held that certain truths have been superseded; for example, the definitive and complete character of the revelation of Jesus Christ, the nature of Christian faith as compared with that of belief in other religions, the inspired nature of the books of Sacred Scripture, the personal unity between the Eternal Word and Jesus of Nazareth, the unity of the economy of the Incarnate Word and the Holy Spirit, the unicity and salvific universality of the mystery of Jesus Christ, the universal salvific mediation of the Church, the inseparability—while recognizing the distinction—of the kingdom of God, the kingdom of Christ, and the Church, and the subsistence of the one Church of Christ in the Catholic Church.[17]

Central to *Dominus Iesus* is its distinction between the "theological faith" of Christianity and "belief" as found in other religions. The latter it defines as "that sum of experience and thought that constitutes the human treasury of wisdom and religious aspiration, which man in his search for truth has conceived and acted upon in his relationship to God and the Absolute."[18] What *Dominus Iesus* necessarily speaks to is the question of how we can judge, for example, and by what criteria Joseph O'Leary and others could possibly have determined, that the Buddhist "experience of emptiness belongs to this level of lived encounter . . . with ultimate saving reality" and is thus "analogous to the Christian encounter with the risen Christ." Usually the criteria, if any, offered for such judgments are assertoric but presented as though they were apodictic. They amount commonly to the claim that Buddhism and other non-Christian religions *must needs* be in some fundamental sense revelatory of the truth and thus salvific, and in a measure comparable to Christianity, for to hold otherwise would be to deny the universal operation of the Spirit said to be "moving in all Hearts" (again, O'Leary). But, as *Dominus Iesus* points out, the religions are the sum of *human* experience, *human* treasuries of wisdom, the product of *human* aspirations, and we cannot always be certain that the *human* efforts that generated the religions had always been guaranteed by the Spirit. *Human* finitude and the possibility of *human* error must be taken also into account, and we have no choice but this: to examine the religions expertly, so that we may understand them as their adherents do, and then to determine by explicitly Christian criteria what there is in them that is creditable to the guidance of the Spirit and what may be the product rather of *human* fallibility. Other religions like Buddhism, of course, are not "heresies." They are not willful departures from, or deliberate renunciations of, Christian faith. Nevertheless the question presses itself upon us: by what criteria, for example, could one judge Buddhism to be truly revelatory and salvific while judging, say, Gnosticism to be false and heretical. Is not Gnosticism also one of "the religions" (still very much alive today, by the way, albeit in multiple new guises), and must we not therefore accord to it the same measure of respect and trust that we are urged to accord Buddhism? Should we not look to its many differences from orthodox Christianity, as well as to Buddhist *śūnyatā* and *upāya*, for new and "liberating" conceptions of Trinity and Incarnation, new ways of sloughing off the outmoded Greek ontological categories that underlie the Chalcedonian creed? (And is this not, after all, precisely what Elaine Pagels and other latter-day Gnostics are nowadays recommending?)

The conference from which this volume emerged was named after Benedict's encyclical *God Is Love.* Let us conclude, then, with an application of Benedict's guiding principles for the theology of religion to the theme of love and to the question of whether anything quite like Christian love is to be found in Buddhism, our prime example of "another religion." It is often held that love is in fact one of the more obvious points of convergence between Buddhism and Christianity. Searching for "love" in Buddhism, one usually looks to either *karuṇā* (lit., "compassion" or "pity"), or *maitrī* (lit., "benevolence" or "friendliness"), or *dāna* (generosity, altruism; lit., "giving," cognate with Latin *donare*), or perhaps some amalgam of all three. *Karuṇā* in particular is emphasized in Mahāyāna Buddhism as the principal virtue of the

Buddhist human ideal, the "bodhisattva" (O'Leary's "gracious embodiment of ultimacy"), the being who dedicates himself to saving all sentient beings even at the heroic cost of indefinitely postponing his own
liberation. And *dāna* (altruism) is the first in serial order of the bodhisattva's six or ten perfections *(pāramitā).* But what exactly is *karuṇā,*
or compassion? It is commonly defined in Buddhism as empathy with
the suffering of others—usually *"all* others" *(sarva sattva)* rather than
just some particular other or others. One is inevitably reminded of
certain modern secular ideologies that espouse "love of all mankind"
but disregard the sufferings and needs of particular human beings. (It
is not the case, of course, that Buddhists are callous and indifferent in
this way—usually quite the contrary—but there is something notably
abstract, aloof, or angelic about their ideal of universal compassion.)
As a virtue to be cultivated, rather than as only an ideal to be imagined,
karuṇā is depicted in the Buddhist canon chiefly as an affective disposition that has a powerful transformative effect on those who arouse
it, its arousal being a *metanoia*—the arousal of the aspiration for the
awakening of all suffering sentient beings *(bodhicittôtpāda)*—that in-
stigates and sustains the new religious life. *Karuṇā* can, but need not
always, motivate or yield concrete action on behalf of others. But even
when it does not generate actual compassionate behavior and is just a
spiritual disposition, an intense wish, or a strong sentiment of solidarity, it is believed able mysteriously to effect transformation in others
and in the world at large. Thus, it can be profoundly enacted or "pro-
jected" even while one is engrossed in quiescent meditation *(dhyāna*
or *zazen)* or absorbed in meditative ecstasy *(samādhi).* Indeed, it can
itself be a meditative exercise insofar as it is one of the "four divine
or sublime abodes" *(brahmavihāra)* or "boundless states" *(apramāṇa)*
of the classical Buddhist meditation manuals. It is true that Buddhist
literature, canonical and paracanonical, abounds in examples of ex-
travagantly heroic compassionate action, but that action is almost always couched in myth (tales of bodhisattvas serving their own flesh to
hungry tigresses, etc.) and is seldom illustrated in events from actual
Buddhist history or biography.[19] Also, strangely little attention is paid
in expositions of *karuṇā* to its beneficiaries, who are usually anonymous, generic, and as fictive as the mythical bodhisattvas who care for

them. Moreover, it is commonly maintained that the merit accruing
to the agent of compassion far exceeds its benefit to the patient or recipient. Most important to the Buddhist understanding of compassion, however, is its entailment of the metaphysical doctrines of no-self
(anātman) and emptiness *(śūnyatā)*. Put simply, but not inaccurately I
think, Mahāyāna Buddhists who cultivate compassion also strive to
understand that the beings whom they pity and whom they would save
do not actually exist as determinate personal entities; that they are literally insubstantial, evanescent, unstable, illusory congeries of fleeting
subpersonal events. This is no mere metaphor, no overstatement for
rhetorical effect of a figure of speech. It is rather to be taken most seriously. The suffering beings who are the foci of the bodhisattva's compassion (if, indeed, we can even call them beings, and sūtras say that
really we cannot) have no independent, fixed identities, and, lacking
such identities, they have neither intrinsic worth nor claim of their
own on the bodhisattva's pity. They are pitied, so to speak, not for their
own sakes but as instantiations of the impersonal truth of pervasive
suffering. The bodhisattva's compassion is therefore also a kind of dis-
passion, a remarkably abstract sort of pity. This is not to say, of course,
that Mahāyāna Buddhists cannot be kind, generous, amiable people;
they often are. I, for one, know this because I have so often been myself the beneficiary of their kindness and friendship. Think also of the
Dalai Lama. Anyone who has ever met him or attended one of his
teachings or watched one of his interviews knows that he is a very
warm, genial, even happy person; he radiates kindness. There can be
no doubt that he has true Buddhist compassion for us all, but not because each of us is such a being as deserves his compassion. Rather it
is because his wisdom compels it. His bodhisattva's compassion for us
is more serene and impassable than fervid. It is an empathy more
philosophical than affective, a pity so modulated or restrained by equa-
nimity as to be compatible even with what seems in his case to be a
naturally ebullient personality. Mahāyāna Buddhists constantly submit
their pity to the chastening, the desiccation of *prajñā,* that penetrating
and withering deconstructive analysis of experience that discloses the
emptiness of all persons and things. This makes of *karuṇā,* I think,
a kind of benevolent sadness tempered by stoicism. One is perhaps

reminded of the Japanese appreciation of the lovely evanescence of cherry blossoms, flowers held to be most poignantly beautiful just as they begin to fade. Such is the calm, steady gaze of the compassionate bodhisattva. Of Christ it was said "et lacrimatus est Iesus," but even the famous bodhisattva Sadāprarudita of the *Perfection of Wisdom in Eight Thousand Lines (Aṣṭasāhasrikāprajñāpāramitā)* and other sūtras, whose very name means "the ever wailing one," cries not when confronted by the suffering of sentient beings but only when frustrated in his pursuit of the perfection of wisdom. All this suggests that Buddhist *karuṇā* is something fundamentally different from Christian *caritas,* at least if we understand Christian *caritas* or *agape* to be love of the other owing to the intrinsic worth of the other, and if we understand that worth to consist precisely in the presence of Christ in the other. *Karuṇā* differs from *caritas* also, and even more fundamentally, insofar as God's love is not something he does or feels. Rather, as Benedict has reminded us, it is what he *is* (*Deus Caritas Est*). Nowhere in Buddhism is it ever said, or could it ever be said, that the Buddha or a bodhisattva *"is" karuṇā.*

These differences between the Christian "theological virtue" of love and the Buddhist "perfection" *(pāramitā)* of compassion are examples, only a few from among many that might be noted, of what may be disclosed in the truly discriminate attention that other religions deserve. But such scrutiny can also reveal, not only true affinities or shared values and insights, but also elements of the other religion that can contribute to the growth of Christianity and help Christianity more deeply to plumb its own depths. As but one Buddhist example of the latter let me cite the remarkable epistemological sophistication and acuity of Buddhism. In expounding his first and second "noble truths" the Buddha identified the cause of suffering *(duḥkha),* the pervasive dissatisfaction and unease of the human condition, as "craving" *(tṛṣṇā)* rooted in ignorance *(avidyā).* Discernment of the subtle and complex relations between desire and the failure to know is a hallmark of the Buddhist tradition and one of its great strengths. Christian theology might well profit by study of Buddhism's knowledge of the inveteracy of cognitive concupiscence, its insights into the capacity of the mind, since beginningless time (anādikāliko), to fabricate desired falsehood. Error and falsehood are for Buddhism not mere absences of knowledge; rather they are active forces powerful enough to construct whole worlds of suffering. Owing to the fundamental claim that all things are empty and arise or happen only as undulations in the ocean of interdependence, Buddhists seldom say of anything that it "exists" (asti). They adamantly resist the tendency to ontologize. However, the Madhyāntavibhāga (Discrimination of the Middle from the Extremes), a foundational text of the Yogācāra or "Representation-Only" school of Buddhist thought, proclaims, in deliberately provocative terms, that "the imagination of the unreal (abhūtaparikalpa) does exist." And it argues further that recognition of the existence of constructive ignorance, as much as the perception of emptiness, is absolutely necessary if one is to know things as they really are. Furthermore, it was awareness—indeed, deep wariness—of the powerful alliance of desire with error, which defines us as sentient beings, that led Buddhism so often to appeal to reason (tarka) as well as to meditation as a prophylactic against error. All this, along with Buddhism's astute, fine-grained analysis of the psychology of error, the intricate ways in which the conscious and unconscious mind constructs falsehood, is available to Christian theology, and to take advantage of such riches would not invite the kind of threat to Christianity's integrity that is presented by superficial identifications of kenōsis with śūnyatā or other forced exercises in relativist pluralism.

Let me conclude by returning briefly to the second-order point I made at the outset, about Buddhism's ability to change and adapt to alien cultures without compromising its distinctive core identity. For here we have yet another encouraging model for faithful engagement with different religions. Chinese recognized not long after Buddhism entered their culture that Buddhist compassion differs as much from, say, Confucian "humaneness" (ren) as we find it to differ from Christian caritas, ren being also a kind of love of the other in response to the intrinsic worth of the other, of which the other could never be seen to be "empty." Buddhism was surely tempted, in its commitment to inculturation or sinification, or called upon by its Confucian hosts, to alter its notion of compassion, to modulate or forsake the demand that compassion be exercised only under the rule of emptiness, for such alteration would surely have made of *karuṇā* something more similar to Confucian *ren* and thus more acceptable to the Chinese. However, Buddhism resisted both the temptation and the call, just as it resisted the strong pressures in China's family-centered culture to abandon clerical celibacy and just as in so many other ways it refrained from compromising or diluting its distinctive identity. Yet Buddhism survived, even flourished, in China, and China came to be the richer for Buddhism's resistance to the temptation of facile self-abnegation. I think that Benedict, in *Dominus Iesus* and other of his teachings on the subject of other religions, is advocating that Christianity do the same thing, not only for its own sake, but also for the sake of Buddhism, Hinduism, Islam, and all the other religions. The success of Buddhism in China shows that this is both possible and desirable. Indeed, it is necessary.

NOTES

1. "Cet Occident qui, peu à peu, par des voies diverses, découvre à tâtons le bouddhisme, c'est, à parler en gros, l'Occident chrétien. Plus que les progrès de sa science, nous observons en cet ouvrage, au cours des siècles, la suite de ses réactions. L'histoire d'une telle découverte n'est donc pas pour nous celle d'une aventure toute profane. Elle ne touche pas seulement à l'histoire de la civilisation et de l'humanisme. Elle touche à l'histoire des religions, doublement. Elle touche à l'histoire des missions chrétiennes, à celle de l'apologétique, à celle des grands conflits spirituels. Elle est l'une de lignes— il est vrai, parmi beaucoup d'autres—qui cernent le visage de cette Europe où nous vivions; l'une des composantes qui, en l'expliquant, contribuent à nous expliquer à nous-mêmes. Loin d'être achevée, elle vient d'entrer, croyons nous, dans sa phase essentielle. Elle impose à l'intelligence chrétienne une réflexion qui ne saurait être éludée sans dommage." *La rencontre du bouddhisme et de l'Occident* (Paris: Aubier, 1952), reprinted as vol. 22 of *Cardinal Henri de Lubac: Œuvres complètes* (Paris: Cerf, 2000), "Avant-Propos," no page, following VIII. For valuable reflections on this book and its significance from a perspective more than fifty years after its publication, see *L'Intelligence de La Rencontre du bouddhisme: Actes du colloque du 11 octobre 2000 à la Fondation Singer-Polignac,* Études Lubaciennes II, ed. Paul Magnin (Paris: Cerf, 2001).

2. As evidence of the discriminate character of his appreciation of Buddhism, one may note de Lubac's special interest in Pure Land Buddhism, which he called *Amidisme*. It was in this tradition, based on faith in the saving power of the transcendent yet also immanent Buddha Amitābha, and not in the Zen that has fascinated so many other Christian theologians, that he found greatest affinity, but not identity, with Christianity. See his *Aspects du Bouddhisme: Amida* (Paris: Éditions de Seuil, 1954). See also David Grummet, "De Lubac, Christ and the Buddha," *New Blackfriars* 89, no. 1020 (2008): 502–24; also David Grummet and Thomas Plant, "De Lubac, Pure Land Buddhism, and Roman Catholicism," *Journal of Religion* 92, no. 1 (January 2012): 58–83.

3. *La rencontre*, 284 (note that de Lubac omits the opening sentence of this paragraph). I have quoted here from the new edition of Elinor Casten dyk Briefs's English translation of *Der Herr*, "with a new introduction by Joseph Cardinal Ratzinger." Romano Guardini, *The Lord* (Washington, DC: Regnery, 1996), 355. It is well known that this once, and still, very popular book by Guardini exerted a strong influence on the theology of the young Joseph Ratzinger, who has recently identified it as an early inspiration for his own, also very popular, two-volume *Jesus of Nazareth*.

4. "S'il était permis, comme Guardini nous y invite, de chercher au bouddhisme un analogue dans l'Ancien Testament, ce n'est évidemment point à la prière des Psaumes ou à la prophétie d'Isaïe que nous devrions songer; ce n'est à aucune des préparations ou de préfigurations positives de l'Évangile: c'est uniquement à l'Ecclésiaste (sans qu'il soit question, bien entendu, de comparer les doctrines). Pris à son apparition, le fait bouddhique est profondément ambigu. Nous ne dirons pas seulement avec Bergson qu'il demeure «un mysticisme incomplèt» parce qu'il «n'a pas vu l'efficacité de l'action humaine» et qu'il a «manqué de chaleur». Ainsi sans doute est bien notée en lui l'absence de charité, qui suit l'absence de foi et d'espérance. Cependant nous le concevrons plutôt comme une immense, drastique et subtile *pars purificans*, une préparation négative par la vide, avec le terrible danger que ce vide ne demeure épris de lui-même, — tant que le Message de Pâcques n'aura pas retenti dans l'âme bouddhique avec des accents triomphants." *La rencontre*, 284–85. It is worth noting that in his characterization of Buddhism as a *"pars purificans"* and as vulnerable to the danger of self-absorption in emptiness (*vide*) de Lubac seems to allude to Saint Augustine as understood by Blondel. See Maurice Blondel, "Saint Augustin, l'unité originale et la vie permanente de sa doctrine philosophique," *Revue de Métaphysique et de Morale* 37, no. 4 (1930): 439.

5. See "The Notion of Good and Evil in Buddhism and Especially in Amidism," a lecture given in Paris in 1954 at the conference "Ethnologie et chrétienté," published in Henri de Lubac, *Theological Fragments,* trans. Rebecca Howell Balinski (San Francisco: Ignatius Press, 1989), 334.

6. "Mis à part le fait unique où nous adorons la trace et la presence même de Dieu, le bouddhisme est sans doute le plus grand fait spiritual de l'histoire." *Aspects de Bouddhisme* (Paris: Éditions du Seuil, 1951), 8. Note that these words do not appear in the English translation of the work (*Aspects of Buddhism,* trans. George Lamb [New York: Sheed and Ward, 1954]), for which, it seems, a new foreword was written.

7. *Aspects of Buddhism,* 52.

8. Joseph Cardinal Ratzinger and Vittorio Messori, *The Ratzinger Report: An Exclusive Interview on the State of the Church,* trans. Salvator Attanasio and Graham Harrison (San Francisco: Ignatius Press, 1985), 30. Emphasis in original.

9. "Le dialogue entre les religions est nécessaire dans un monde qui tend à s'unifier. Mais le danger est que s'instaure un dialogue superficiel. Car le relativisme qui s'est emparé aujourd'hui des esprits développe une sorte d'anarchisme moral et intellectuel qui conduit les hommes à ne plus accepter de vérité unique. Affirmer sa vérité passe désormais pour une marque d'intolérance. Or un vrai dialogue n'est pas un mouvement dans le vide. Il a un but: la recherche commune de la vérité. Un chrétien ne peut pas renoncer à sa connaissance de la vérité, révélée pour lui en Jésus-Christ, fils unique de Dieu. Si le bouddhisme séduit, c'est parce qu'il apparaît comme une possibilité de toucher à l'infini, à la félicité sans avoir d'obligations religieuses concrètes. Un autoérotisme spirituel, en quelque sorte. Quelqu'un avait justement prédit, dans les années 1950, que le défi de l'Eglise au XXe siècle serait non pas le marxisme, mais le bouddhisme." Michel Cool, "Le Testament du Panzerkardinal," *L'Express,* March 20, 1997, 70.

10. From an address first given in Salzburg in 1992 and again, with minor changes, at a 1993 meeting in Hong Kong of the Roman Congregation for the Doctrine of the Faith with the Commission for the Faith of the Asian Bishops' Conference. Published under the title "Faith, Religion, and Culture," in *Truth and Tolerance: Christian Belief and World Religions,* trans. Henry Taylor (San Francisco: Ignatius, 2004), 55–79; see 63. Emphasis mine.

11. Ibid., 68. Emphasis mine.

12. "Einheit und Vielfalt der Religionen: Der Ort des christlichen Glaubens in der Religionsgeschichte," in *Gott in Welt: Festgabe für Karl Rahner sum 60. Geburtstag,* ed. H. Vorgrimler (Freiburg: Herder, 1964), 2:287–305. Ratzinger's article was reprinted in a couple of later German col-

lections of his works, e.g., *Vom Wiederauffinden der Mitte: Grundorientierungen* (Freiburg: Herder, 1964), 60–82, and was published, in an English translation by Henry Taylor, under the title "The Unity and Diversity of Religions: The Place of Christianity in the History of Religions," in the anthology *Truth and Tolerance*, 15–44.

13. "Unity and Diversity," 22–23. Emphasis mine.

14. Ibid., 24. No doubt the "friendly contemporary theologian" to whom Ratzinger was here playfully referring was Rahner himself, to whom the essay was dedicated—he, that is, of the then-new theory of the "anonymous Christian." And had he wished he could have cited others besides Radhakrishnan as persuasive prophets of religious convergence: John Hick, of course, but also Huston Smith, Frithjof Schuon, and many others.

15. O'Leary is here, on his webpage (http://josephsoleary.typepad.com/my_weblog/christology/), responding to questions raised about his book *Religious Pluralism and Christian Truth* (Edinburgh: Edinburgh University Press, 1996). The John Keenan referred to here is the author of several books propounding a Mahāyāna Buddhist reformulation of Christian doctrine, one grounded especially in the emptiness and mind-only teachings of the Yogācāra tradition. See, for example, his *The Meaning of Christ: A Mahāyāna Theology* (Maryknoll, NY: Orbis Books, 1989) or *The Wisdom of James: Parallels with Mahāyāna Buddhism* (Westminster, MD: Newman Press, 2005).

16. Joseph S. O'Leary, "Dogma and Religious Pluralism," *Australian eJournal of Theology* 4 (February 2005): 6.

17. *Dominus Iesus*, 14.

18. Ibid., 7.

19. One must, of course, note some important contemporary exceptions to the traditional rule. There is, for example, the work of the Taiwanese nun Cheng-yen (Zhengyan) and her Buddhist Compassion Relief Foundation (Tzu-chi Kong-te Hui/Ziji Gongde Hui), as well as numerous other charitable organizations operating throughout the world. The Venerable Cheng-yen, it is worth noting, is an exemplar of a rather new phenomenon in Buddhism known as "humanistic Buddhism" (Chinese: *jen-chien fo-chiao/renjian fojiao*), which history shows bears the clear imprint of Christian influence, and it is not insignificant that she is sometimes called "the Buddhist Mother Teresa" in the Taiwan media. Closely related to "humanistic Buddhism" is what is called "engaged Buddhism," with its strong emphasis on social service and political activism. This is to be found in Asia, to be sure—in the work in Thailand, for example, of the activist Sulak Shivaraksa—but it is especially associated with Western Buddhism and is in many ways at odds with traditional Asian Buddhism.

chapter five

REFLECTIONS ON *INTRODUCTION TO CHRISTIANITY*

LAWRENCE S. CUNNINGHAM

The only begotten Son of God, as the uncreated Word,
is the book of wisdom.

—Saint Bonaventure, *The Tree of Life*

It may be the case that, as the Italians would say, the story is *ben trovato,* but some reports have indicated that Pope Paul VI was so impressed with Joseph Ratzinger's *Introduction to Christianity* that it was among his reasons for naming Ratzinger archbishop of Munich. I cannot verify the truth of that claim, but it is clear that the book has been very popular since its original publication almost five decades ago.

Joseph Ratzinger tells us in his introduction to his book how it came to be written and what model had inspired it.[1] The book began as a series of lectures given to the general academic body of the University of Tübingen in summer 1967. Ratzinger said that he wanted to do for his audience what Karl Adam had done many decades earlier in his famous *Spirit of Catholicism,* that is, recapitulate the core faith of the Christian tradition. Since his lectures were for the entire academic community, it is clear that he was speaking to both believers and nonbelievers. In that sense at least he intended to give a fair account of the Christian faith that would have the ring of both catechesis and apology.

That Ratzinger mentions Adam's *The Spirit of Catholicism* is not surprising. Adam had given a series of lectures in the 1923 summer term at Tübingen to a mixed audience of several hundred persons. Those lectures (with some additions) were published a year later under the title *Das Wesen des Katholizimus* and subsequently translated into English as *The Spirit of Catholicism.* One surmises that Adam had in mind—and perhaps unapologetically tongue in cheek—the famous work of Adolf von Harnack, published a generation earlier under the title *The Essence [Wesen] of Christianity.*[2] Ratzinger's lectures, in short, had an intellectual history.[3]

If Adam looked back to Harnack, albeit sardonically, then, as I argue here, Ratzinger was looking in another direction—to his own world, a world that seemed to be tired of Christianity in general and Catholicism in particular, even after the seeming "breakthrough" of the Second Vatican Council. His lectures, after all, were given in 1967, only two years after the conclusion of Vatican II with its by then trailing euphoria and only one year before the upheavals of 1968 that marked a burning moment in the West. The one point that it is absolutely crucial to understand is this: 1967 was not an auspicious year to restate old truths, both because the Catholic world was enamored of the *novum* and because the gathering revolutionary spirit emerging in 1968 was sick of the past. The future pope would see firsthand the full wrath of that spirit in Tübingen the year his book was published.

We might note in passing that when Ratzinger published his essays he did not use a universalizing word like *essence* in the book's title;

144 Lawrence S. Cunningham

instead he employed the word *introduction (Einführung)*. This tiny point is made because his intention is to say a first word about the Christian faith but also, as I argue below, to draw his audience into a sympathetic understanding of the Christian faith, not simply provide a sympathetic superficial account of Christianity's main doctrinal points. It has always seemed to me that Ratzinger understood his vocation as a theologian not as a disinterested but learned purveyor of facts but rather as someone who was a pilgrim of faith inviting others to join that journey.

The framework for his book was the Apostles' Creed. By using the template of the creed, Ratzinger was following an ancient practice. Anyone conversant with the history of Christian theology knows that using the creed as a foundation for an exposition of the faith has been a time-honored practice in Christianity. As a genre, the creedal formulation has liturgical roots going back to the third century, when the triple form of questioning of those to be baptized provided the basis for catechesis. Indeed, catechisms from the early modern period on used the creed as an exposition of faith; that usage is at least as old as Martin Luther's little catechism and as contemporary as the *Catechism of the Catholic Church*. As part of the initiation rites the creed was handed to those to be baptized (the *Traditio Symboli*) with the expectation that it would be memorized and handed back. It was this memorized creed on which the bishop would base his instruction. "The creed," Augustine said in *sermo* 213, "is the rule of faith, succinctly worded so as to instruct the mind without overburdening the memory. It is expressed in just a few word but much instruction may be drawn from it. It is spoken of as a 'symbol,' a sort of password by which Christians can recognize one another."[4] Earlier in his career the same Augustine, not yet a bishop, reflected on the creed at a conference of provincial clergy in which he characterized it as "[as] short a form as so great a matter permits." For beginners, who "have not yet been strengthened by diligent and spiritual study and understanding of the divine scriptures," must, in those few words, "accept them in faith" *(De Fide et Symbolo)*.[5]

Much of the commentary on the creed in the ancient Church was made in the context of the liturgical rites of initiation. That was appropriate, given that the creed was in time inserted in the eucharistic liturgy and is thus as much a prayerful invocation as it is a statement of faith. To recite the creed was to affirm that one was a believer and a person of faith. Not coincidentally, the ecumenical councils of both Nicaea and Constantinople in the fourth century affirmed a creed (quite possibly adapted from the liturgical creed used in Jerusalem) not only to express their orthodox faith but also as a rule (canon) to articulate those who were faithful members of the Catholic faith. To recite the creed was to possess the right of attendance at the eucharistic table. It is in that sense that the creed is a "symbol." It is given back as a token of belief.

The British theologian Nicholas Lash has rightly pointed out that it is to mistake the grammar of the creed if it is thought of as a list of what one is to believe. Rather, Lash says, "to say the creed is to say, not many things, but one thing. To say the creed is to confess, beyond all conflict and confusion, our trust in the One who makes and heals the world and who makes all things one. It is not possible to make additions to the creed because, in using it, we have but one word to say in recognition, praise and wonder: 'Yes' and 'Amen.'"[6] The pope, I would argue, would agree with that judgment.

This brief excursus on the historical roots of the creed is intended only to make explicit a point, namely, that the creed has its origin in the liturgy, that it can be understood as a form of prayer, and that its further articulation in the councils was, as its other term signifies, a rule or canon by which the essentials of faith are made transparent and against which deviations were measured. Historically, the audience for the exposition of the creed was the believing community. Its tone was catechetical and not apologetic. Furthermore, the articulation of the creed is both an act of worship and a statement of revealed truth.

Now, it is one thing to enunciate the articles of the creed and another to ask what those articles mean. Thus, we can say, "I believe in Jesus Christ," but what does that mean? To instruct the believer is to answer that and similar questions. That further question, What does that mean? is, of course, a shorthand illustration of the famous Anselmian definition of theology as "faith seeking understanding." In other words, the creed articulates belief, and reflection on that articulation constitutes what would become known as "theology."

Joseph Ratzinger tells us, as I have already noted, that his book began as a series of lectures delivered in summer 1967 to the academic community of the University of Tübingen. His audience, then, was not the newly baptized or even those presumptively Christian. Thus Ratzinger's first audience at the university was that of an educated group that we may assume was ready to hear an intelligent exposition of the historic Christian faith even if not everyone present shared its affirmations. His book must therefore be understood as both a proclamation of the faith and, however tacitly, an apologia for the faith. While he was explicitly ecumenical in his exposition of the historic faith of the creed, as he notes in his 1969 preface to the work, he was also acutely aware that his work was situated in a world where the claims of the Christian faith were at best opaque. It is worth remembering that he begins his lectures by recalling Søren Kierkegaard's parable of the clown who cries out for help for a burning village, to the amusement of a crowd that thinks the clown is merely joking. The clown speaks the truth, but the audience mistakes the truth for a jest. One wonders whether the apocalyptic implications of that parable are to be pursued or not.

Knowing who is being addressed is not a trivial piece of information; indeed, one could argue that Ratzinger is so acutely aware of the "clownliness" of his task that he spends over one hundred pages before he begins to comment on the first article of the creed, and in that initial comment he begins, almost tentatively, with the rubric "Prolegomena to the subject of God." What Ratzinger was doing in 1967, however, was not without precedent. Using the spare affirmations of the creed as a launching pad, his intention was to affirm the faith based on its core platform. It is worthwhile to remember that a year after World War II ended the renowned Reformed theologian Karl Barth was invited back from his academic home and residence in Basel to lecture in Germany. He gave this series of lectures near the rubble of the University of Bonn.

Barth could well have lectured on the terrible events that had concluded just a year and some months before he accepted the invitation. But his topic was the fundamental canon of the faith, the creed. These lectures based on the Apostles' Creed were later published in English under the title *Dogmatics in Outline*. Barth's foreword to the book is poignant: "The audience consisted partly of theologians but the larger part was of students from the other faculties. Most people in the Germany of today have in their own way and in their own place endured and survived much, almost beyond all measure. I note the same in my Bonn lads. . . . For me the situation will remain unforgettable."[7]

One could say, then, that Ratzinger's lectures on the creed were both traditional, in that such an exposition has a long history, and provocative, in that it desires to comment on a creed before an audience that might at best be puzzled by its ancient language and at worst be in a state of rejection in the face of its claims. It is under those presuppositions that I wish to make some observations about Ratzinger's text. There is little need to paraphrase what he has written since the contents are well known by the educated, so I will satisfy myself with some observations about his way of proceeding and some reflections on those observations.

SOME OBSERVATIONS

Looking back on the elapse of thirty years since *Introduction to Christianity* saw light, Ratzinger says that were he to write the book today he would have spent more time on "interreligious discussions" but thinks he was not mistaken about the "fundamental approach": "I put the question of God and the question of Christ in the very center which then leads to a 'narrative Christology' and demonstrates that the place for faith is in the Church."[8] That affirmation of confidence gives us a clue as to how to proceed: the question of God and the God of Jesus Christ, to borrow a title from the later work of Cardinal Kasper. Although Ratzinger touches on all the elements of the creed in his lectures, it is nonetheless the case that his basic thrust is to speak about God, and God's definitive revelation of God's self in the Word made flesh, a hallmark of his theology. In fact, his comments on the part of the creed that begins with faith in the Holy Spirit are not pursued in any depth.

That Ratzinger would start with the question of God should not surprise anyone who knows anything about the humanistic leanings of his audience. After all, one need only recite the litany of names in the German intellectual tradition, familiar to everyone who graduated from the German *Gymnasium* and university. This was an audience that understood the kind of question proffered by Goethe's Faust: of those who would be tempted to slot religion into Kant's practical reason; who trembled before Lessing's ditch; who felt the lash of Nietzsche's excoriating tongue; and so on. In other words, the *Gottesfrage* was imbibed by his Tübingen audience with its intellectual mother's milk. Furthermore, that same audience had still-vivid memories of the catastrophic collapse of National Socialism little more than a decade earlier. The questions that haunted Dietrich Bonhoeffer less than two decades earlier while in a Gestapo prison could not be ignored.

How did Ratzinger frame his discussion of God? His general approach affirmed an ancient theme in Catholic thought: one could fruitfully discuss the God Question within the framework of philosophy, but somehow that discussion took on thick meaning only when it was seen in the light of revelation. Like Pascal, it was not the question of the "god of the philosophers" but the God of Abraham, Isaac, and Jacob. Ratzinger was committed to both faith and reason— to the *fides et ratio* robustly defended decades later by John Paul II. What Ratzinger most insistently desired was that no cleavage be entertained between the god of the philosophers and the God of Abraham. He shrewdly observed that such a rupture, in order to enter into what he called "the purely religious," was a path taken by Schleiermacher and, he added, "paradoxically enough, in a certain sense[,] . . . Schleiermacher's great critic and opponent Karl Barth."[9] He had no desire to abandon the path of reason in favor of faith alone.

Earlier in these reflections I noted that there is an ancestry behind Ratzinger's lectures that has its roots, first, in Karl Adam, and, perhaps, second, in an allusion to Adolf von Harnack. In the present discussion of Ratzinger's reflections on faith and reason there is another genealogy that is more specifically Catholic in its intellectual character: the debate over the precise relationship between faith and reason. That long debate's parameters have been economically summarized in the title of a recent book by the British Dominican Aidan Nichols: *Conversation of Faith and Reason: Modern Catholic Thought from Hermes to Benedict XVI.*[10]

It was Ratzinger's conviction that the biblical portrait, drawing generously not only on the prophetic literature but also on the Wisdom tradition, gave sustenance to the bond that held together the human capacity to know God while accepting, as pure gift, God's self-disclosure as pure gift. Nichols has summarized this position of Ratzinger quite nicely: "The self-communicative fullness of being (a philosophical description) is identical with the self donation of the God of love. Plotting key moments of this convergent identity (absolute Being, unsurpassable love) will involve reference to the Wisdom literature, Second Isaiah, and the Gospel of John where Jesus uses for himself the divine formula, 'I am' or 'I am he.'"[11] In other words, the God about whom Ratzinger speaks is not some abstract concept but One who lives and pours forth intelligibly as the Logos both behind creation and through history.

It is for that reason, drawing on the sapiential wisdom of that strain of the Old Testament, that Ratzinger understands how the intelligibility of the Logos mediated through creation enhances the purely philosophical approach to God as understood in the modern sense as not only insufficient but not life giving. Ratzinger insists that the philosophical god is self-centered, contemplating itself, whereas the God of faith, integrated through human reason, is defined by the category of relationship. Furthermore, the philosophical god is pure thought, whereas the God of faith is also love.[12] It is from that starting point that Ratzinger will draw out the implications of the revelatory foundation that structures the entire creed, namely, that God is triune.

It is at that point that Ratzinger, pondering the opening affirmations of the creed, introduces a striking paradox into his discussion. He notes that "power" language is studded throughout the early part of the creed: "Father Almighty, maker of heaven and earth," and so on. Ratzinger then adds: "What 'almighty' and 'Lord of all' might mean only becomes clear from a Christian point of view in the crib and the cross. It is only here, where the God is who is recognized as Lord of all, and has voluntarily chosen the final degree of powerlessness by delivering himself up to his weakest creature, that the Christian concept of the almightiness of God can be truly formulated."[13] *Power* and *kenōsis* are not contradictory terms in the Ratzingerian vocabulary.

Here I need to reiterate an ancient theological truth concerning the Christian claim, namely, the paradoxical character of the Christian kerygma: the immense, all-powerful, all-seeing, all-knowing God is both absolutely transcendent and profoundly immanent. This tension is the reason the creed can shift so seamlessly from the majestic affirmation of God and Logos into that historical moment when a living human "suffered under Pontius Pilate." To hold that paradox in tension is of foundational importance, and to lose it, especially in Christology but also in theology more generally speaking, is to fall into the opposite but still lethal errors: overstate the transcendent, and the worse error becomes Gnosticism; overstate the immanent, and Jesus, at best, is simply a humanistic "man for others."

The intense paradoxical emphasis of Christian revelation, especially in the field of Christology, has recently been reemphasized by Fr. Edward Oakes, himself a perceptive commentator on Benedict's theology. Indeed, early in his most recent work Oakes cites Ratzinger's reflection on the title "Jesus of Nazareth, King of the Jews" to underscore the profound paradox at the heart of Christology: "This execution notice, the death sentence of history, became with paradoxical unity the 'profession of faith,' the real starting point and taproot of the Christian faith, which holds Jesus to be the Christ: *as* the crucified criminal, this Jesus is the Christ the King. His crucifixion is his coronation; his kingship is his surrender of himself to men, the identification of word, mission, and existence in the yielding up of this very existence."[14]

Ratzinger's entire approach to the mystery of Christ attempts to hold in creative tension the truth of the Eternal Logos and the Logos made flesh. To do that he wishes both to resist the temptation to reduce the person of Jesus to naked history free of philosophical reflection (Harnack) and its polar opposite, which is to lose the historical

Jesus into the philosophical embrace of existential choice devoid of history (Bultmann). Ratzinger, in fact, both in his *Introduction* and in his later thinking, does affirm the historical-critical study of the Scriptures. As he affirms in his study of Jesus, this method is an indispensable dimension of exegesis for a fundamental reason: "For it is of the very essence of biblical faith to be about real historical events."[15] That being said, he also insists on what he calls the "deeper value" by which history becomes inscribed by authors who wrote not in their own name but as members of a living community. The authors write, in short, in the context of "faith-history."[16]

What needs emphasis here is the creative tension, the paradox, if you will, of the source of Ratzinger's Christology: the naked fact(s) of history as mediated by a living witness that reaches beyond history as witnessed in faith. To dissolve that tension is to end either in historical positivism or in an ahistorical Gnosticism. It is for that precise reason that in his *Introduction to Christianity* the modern dilemma for theology is presented as a choice between Jesus or Christ.[17] But, as Ratzinger understands, to choose one is to evacuate the other. The choice between the Jesus of history and the Christ of faith is a false choice if understood as choosing one over the other. In other words, Ratzinger will not make that choice; he will hold the two in tension precisely because the Apostles' Creed (the basis of his lectures) affirms in the same profession of faith both the consubstantial Word and the one who was born of the Virgin Mary, suffered, died, and was buried.

A CONCLUDING NOTE

To hold fundamental theological poles in creative tension—that God is three in one; that Jesus is human and divine; that history derives from eternity and returns to it—is an ancient truth much loved by Ratzinger's own mentors, Saint Augustine of Hippo and Saint Bonaventure. This *coincidentia oppositorum* is a hallmark of Ratzinger's *Introduction to Christianity* and, it can be argued, a leitmotif that runs from his early work down to his mature thinking, both as a prelate in the Vatican and in his taking up of the ministry of Peter. Elsewhere

I have argued that the Petrine office is essentially one of conservation in the sense that it is the office charged with the maintenance of the apostolic preaching.[18] While the pope must be alert to the "signs of the times," those signs must be tested against the Deposit of Faith. To conserve is not to embalm or to render the faith and its expressions into a museum piece. What the young Ratzinger taught and what Benedict XVI exemplifies is that at the heart of the Christian faith is a profoundly puzzling paradox: The Word became flesh. That Word (Logos) is implicated fully in the unfolding of creation, in the mysterious history of the Children of Israel, in the Incarnation, in the dynamic of Trinitarian mystery, but also in human rationality and its unfolding in the human story. Looking back on his own early book introducing Christianity to his Tübingen audience, the pope reiterated what runs like a red thread through all his work: "The God who is *logos* guarantees the intelligibility of the world, the intelligibility of our existence, the aptitude of reason to know God and the reasonableness of God, even though his understanding infinitely surpasses ours and to us may so often appear to be darkness."[19]

In Ratzinger's brief observation one sees the refined thinking of someone who can look back on his early work and still frame his convictions by a subtle but genuine balance between intelligibility and that apophasis that he calls the divine darkness, in a tradition that goes back at least to Saint Gregory of Nyssa but with roots in Scripture itself. When reading Ratzinger, I am constantly reminded of someone who deeply influenced him: Blessed John Henry Newman. Let me then end with a line or two from that great theologian. In his reflections on "revealed religion" in the *Grammar of Assent,* Newman reflects on the spread of Christianity in a brief refutation of the Enlightenment historian Edward Gibbon. Newman writes, "It was the Thought of Christ, not a corporate body or a doctrine, which inspired that zeal which the historian so poorly comprehends; and it was the Thought of Christ which gave a life to the promise of that eternity, which without Him, would be, in any soul, nothing short of an intolerable burden."[20]

At the heart of Ratzinger's understanding of the Christian faith is Newman's "Thought of Christ," which is to say, the Logos who became flesh for us.

NOTES

1. I have relied on the 2004 revised edition of *Introduction to Christianity* with a new preface (trans. Michael J. Miller) of then-Cardinal Ratzinger: *Introduction to Christianity*, trans. J. R. Foster (San Francisco: Communio/Ignatius Press, 2004). All subsequent references are to this edition.

2. See Karl Adam, *The Spirit of Catholicism*, introd. Robert Krieg, C.S.C. (New York: Crossroad Herder, 1997).

3. Of course, I could follow this ancestry farther back into the period of the great Tübingen Catholic scholars of the nineteenth century, such as Drey and Mohler, who attempted to give comprehensive accounts of Catholicism.

4. *Sermo* 213.2, translated by William Harmless. *Augustine in His Own Words*, ed. William Harmless, S.J. (Washington, DC: Catholic University of America Press, 2010), 147.

5. On the historical development of the Christian creeds, see J. N. D. Kelly, *Early Christian Creeds*, rev. ed. (New York: Harper, 1972); Henri de Lubac, *The Christian Faith: An Essay on the Structure of the Apostles' Creed*, trans. Richard Arnandez (San Francisco: Ignatius Press, 1986); Nicholas Ayo, *Creed as Symbol* (Notre Dame: University of Notre Dame Press, 1989); and the magisterial collection *Creeds and Confessions of the Christian Faith*, 3 vols., ed. Jaroslav Pelikan and Valerie Hotchkiss (New Haven: Yale University Press, 2003). Ratzinger himself has a brief excursus on the development of the Apostles' Creed in *Introduction*, 82–102. For other contemporary commentaries on the creed, see, inter alia, Nicholas Lash, *Believing Three Ways in One: A Reading of the Apostles' Creed* (Notre Dame: University of Notre Dame Press, 1993); Christopher R. Seitz, ed., *Nicene Christianity: The Future for a New Ecumenism* (Grand Rapids, MI: Brazos, 2002); and Luke Timothy Johnson, *The Creed: What Christians Believe and Why It Matters* (New York: Image/Doubleday, 2003).

6. Lash, *Believing Three Ways*, 16.

7. Karl Barth, *Dogmatics in Outline: With a New Foreword by the Author*, trans. G. T. Thompson (New York: Harper Torchbooks, 1959), 7.

8. Ratzinger, *Introduction*, 29.

9. Ibid., 139.

10. Aidan Nichols, *Conversation of Faith and Reason: Modern Catholic Thought from Hermes to Benedict XVI* (Chicago: Hillenbrand Books, 2011).

11. Ibid., 198.

12. Ratzinger, *Introduction,* 147–48.

13. Ibid., 149–50.

14. Ibid., 206. Edward T. Oakes, *Infinity Dwindles to Infancy: A Catholic and Evangelical Christology* (Grand Rapids, MI: Eerdmans, 2011), 19. The title of Oakes's book is from the poetry of Gerard Manley Hopkins, nicely encapsulating the paradox that is the theme of the entire book.

15. Benedict XVI, *Jesus of Nazareth: From the Baptism in the Jordan to the Transfiguration,* trans. Adrian J. Walker (New York: Doubleday, 2007), xv.

16. Ibid., xx.

17. Ratzinger, *Introduction,* 196 ff.

18. Lawrence S. Cunningham, *Introduction to Catholicism* (New York: Cambridge University Press, 2009).

19. See preface to the new edition of *Introduction to Christianity.*

20. John Henry Newman, *An Essay in Aid of a Grammar of Assent* (Notre Dame: University of Notre Dame Press, 1979), 359.

Caritas in Veritate

chapter six

GOD'S SAVING JUSTICE

Faith, Reason, and Reconciliation in the
Political Thought of Pope Benedict XVI

DANIEL PHILPOTT

In both substance and sensibility, Pope Benedict XVI's writings on politics portray the modern world as an "age of upheaval," to borrow from the title of a book he published just before he became pope.[1] Having lived through Nazi Germany, he carries a textured sense of the twentieth century as a time of totalitarianism, mass atrocity, and general political crisis. In more recent decades, he believes, an age of globalization and technological progress has become one in which disintegrating moral certainties are threatening the foundations of political orders based on human rights, the rule of law, and freedom. Such is the "dictatorship of relativism" of which he spoke.[2]

What explains the age of upheaval, according to Benedict? At the center of his account is an idea that, I propose, also stands at the center of his corpus of writings on politics: the synthesis of faith and reason. The decline of this synthesis Benedict associates closely with the past century's upheavals. The best hope for recovering this synthesis—and thus the foundations for a just and free society—lies in a revival of the Christian faith, especially the Catholic faith, where he believes this synthesis is found most strongly.

Benedict's case for the synthesis of faith and reason is powerful and pressing. A just response to past political evils, though, requires more than a recovery of sound belief. Mass injustices, whether the totalitarian atrocities of the past century, ethnic conflict, civil war, genocide, religious terrorism, or abortion in modern and modernizing societies, do not exhaust their evil once they have been committed but rather leave behind wounds to persons, communities, and societies. They leave in their wake death, injury, economic loss, trauma, and despair that can persist over ensuing generations, as well as collectively held emotions like hatred, vengeance, and fear that propel cycles of violence. What is also needed, then, is a response that can bring a measure of healing and transformation to these wounds. In the Christian faith this response can be found in God's reconciliation of humanity to himself through the death and resurrection of Jesus Christ. Divine reconciliation then creates the possibility and illuminates the practice of reconciliation among humans in the political and social realm. Reconciliation resonates in the thought of Benedict. He indeed wrote about reconciliation both before and after he became pope.

In this essay I wish to argue that these strands in Benedict's political thought—the need for a renewed synthesis of faith and reason, a revival of belief, and reconciliation, an active, transformational response to past evil—can be woven together to fashion a Catholic response to large-scale political evils of the kind that have characterized the past century. First I want to chart the contours of Benedict's thought on faith and reason. Reconciliation, though, requires more treatment. In the second section of the essay, drawing from Benedict's writings on reconciliation, I develop the idea of reconciliation further as a Christian notion of justice, peace, and mercy and offer some ideas for its enactment in politics. Reconciliation, I argue, not only complements the synthesis of faith and reason but reflects and embodies it as well.

THE SYNTHESIS OF FAITH AND REASON

When, in his "Regensburg Address" of September 12, 2006, Benedict quoted a Byzantine emperor who drew a connection between violence and the disseverance of faith and reason in Islam, he ignited a now-famous brouhaha with the Muslim world, one that began with riots and even the killing of a nun and then evolved into a global dialogue over faith and reason.[3] The irony of the episode is that Benedict had devoted the vast majority of this address to the breakdown of the synthesis of faith and reason *in the West*. Originally, he argued, the New Testament had achieved a "profound encounter" of Hebrew faith and Hellenistic reason. But over the centuries, in Western thought, this woven cord became unraveled through several intellectual mutations: medieval nominalism, the Protestant Reformation, the Enlightenment, and the relativism of the present day.

The importance of the synthesis of faith and reason, its unraveling in the West, and the dangers of this unraveling for society and politics are themes to which Benedict returns again and again in his writings and speeches. What are the dangers for politics? In his public dialogue of January 2004 with Jürgen Habermas, Europe's most famous secular philosopher, Ratzinger argued that a free state—a constitutional democracy with human rights and civil liberties—depends crucially on prepolitical moral foundations, namely, Christianity's classic synthesis of faith and reason.[4] In contemporaneous addresses, most distinctively at Subiaco, Italy, on April 1, 2005, Ratzinger laments Europe's rejection of this synthesis, symbolized saliently by the European Union's explicit omission of Christianity from its account of the historical roots of Europe's values in the preamble of its proposed European Constitution.[5] The political result, according to Benedict, is that the state, no longer grounded in anything outside of itself, poses as the source of its own morality.[6] Such a state cannot be theologically neutral. If it is democratic, it will reflect the opinion of the majority, whatever that happens to be. More ominously, a state that abandons the God of faith and reason is likely to descend into destruction and violence.

In several of his writings and speeches, Benedict explains in more detail what reason and faith each have to contribute to political orders and what political pathologies result when one of these twins is orphaned from the other.[7] Let us take each in turn.

REASON, BUT WITHIN THE LIMITS OF RELIGION

"The Catholic tradition maintains that the objective norms governing right action are accessible to reason, prescinding from the content of revelation," Benedict told British leaders when he addressed them in Westminster Hall in September 2010.[8] Natural law was likewise the central theme of his address to the German Bundestag in September 2011.[9] In both addresses he asserted that natural law is the essential basis of justice and fundamental civil and human rights. Majority opinion, the consensus of a people, or the legal fiat of governing institutions cannot provide such a foundation.[10]

But Benedict has cautioned many times against a reason that is detached from the creative reason of the *logos,* or God. The role of religion, he explained in his Westminster Hall address, is not to supply norms for political life or to propose specific solutions. Rather, it is to "purify," "shed light on," guide, and correct reason, preventing it from becoming distorted, applied partially, or otherwise falling into egregious error. Distorted and misguided, reason has given rise to social evils like the slave trade and the totalitarian movements of the twentieth century. Religion, then, is like a mooring that tethers reason to justice.[11]

What happens to reason when it becomes unmoored? The philosopher Alvin Plantinga has argued that in the contemporary Western intellectual milieu, Christian theism has two major rivals. First there is naturalism, which holds that the universe is entirely material, consisting solely of physical causes. The other is creative anti-realism, which holds that the world is created and shaped by human beings who impose concepts and categories on it.[12] Plantinga's alternative worldviews correspond remarkably well to Benedict's alternative fates

of reason once it is detached from God. First, there is the predomi-
nance of technical reason, the manipulation of the natural world. Second, there is the reason of limitless freedom.

Although Benedict's genealogy of the splaying of faith and reason
contains many mile markers, above all he identifies the Enlightenment as the fork in the road where these two wayward paths originate.
To be sure, he does not reject the Enlightenment wholesale, often
crediting it for advancing institutions and norms like the rule of law,
civil liberties, and human rights, including religious freedom.[13] But he
is skeptical that Enlightenment philosophy can ground these norms
or even ground itself. Exceptional in world history, the Enlightenment developed a secular rationality. Having no external criterion,
however, such rationality cannot establish its own validity. Benedict is
highly skeptical of a pure reason that aspires to be self-sufficient.[14]

Technical reason, one of the Enlightenment's strands, holds that
only what can be proved through experiments can be considered rational. While technical reason can be credited for great scientific
progress, when it is considered the sole or even primary form of reason, it "entails a mutilation of man," as Ratzinger charged at Subiaco.
When a technological, instrumental, and manipulative rationality
predominates, human life loses its sacredness and morality loses its
meaning. The upshot is a loss of a transcendent, universal criterion by
which to render ethical judgment on any technological development,
whether it is the atomic bomb or advancements in biotechnology.[15]

The other strand of Enlightenment thought is a freedom that is
liberated from tradition, authority, and institutions, including, of
course, God and the Church. In his book *Truth and Tolerance* Ratzinger described the freedom of the Jacobins as a rebellion against
truth altogether. But freedom without truth, he counters, is no freedom at all. If freedom does not correspond to nature it will collapse
under the weight of incoherence and the irresolvable claims made
in its name. Ultimately, a freedom of absolute autonomy and self-
definition is impossible for it lacks grounds that can establish or defend it against alternatives. So, it paves the way for the dictatorship of
relativism.[16]

RELIGION, BUT NOT WITHOUT REASON

What, for Benedict, is the role of religious faith in politics? Very small, it might at first seem, beyond the limited albeit important task of correcting reason and preventing it from veering off into the distortions by which it fails to offer sound criteria for justice. Faith serves as a mooring. In his most recent encyclical, *Charity in Truth,* however, Benedict calls for Christian faith to play a more ambitious role in the political order: contributing love.

Love (or charity), Benedict argues in this encyclical, encompasses and does not contradict justice, which is traditionally among the foremost of political virtues. Here, Benedict follows the classical Western definition of justice as the will to render another his due. In the modern West, "due" has come to mean rights. To do justice is to give "recognition and respect for the legitimate rights of individuals and peoples," he says. But if love includes justice, it also exceeds it, he argues, involving mercy, forgiveness, generosity, and—the virtue that Benedict stresses most—gratuitousness, all of which exceed what people have a right to, merit, or deserve. Such love is the love of God in the Bible, revealed and shared through Jesus Christ. Benedict's striking claim is that political, economic, and social life must be informed by gratuitousness and other gifts of love if it is going to flourish. Economic development, for instance, requires more than the logic of exchange and contracts that characterize the market but also the gratuitousness that generates the trust and solidarity on which exchanges depend for their success. Even justice itself depends on the love that exceeds justice, Benedict argues.[17] Because Benedict believes that Christian love is crucial for sustaining political and social life, religion turns out to be quite important for politics in his thought.

As with reason, though, religion is prone to pathologies when it exists alone. One of the unfortunate mutations of the Christian heritage, in Benedict's view, was the rise of voluntarism and fideism— religion decoupled from reason—that took place in medieval nominalism and the Protestant Reformation. Unless religion is "purified and structured" by the "controlling organ" of reason, as Ratzinger put it in his dialogue with Habermas, it is liable to collapse into sectarianism and violence.[18] Benedict writes mindfully of the rise of religious terrorism around the world in the past couple of decades, manifested most vividly in the attacks of September 11, 2001.[19] He advocates, then, that religion be tethered to the mooring of reason just as he cautions against reason floating free from religion.

Altogether, Benedict believes that faith and reason each make a vital and distinctive contribution to politics, that each must complement the other, and that when twinned as they are in Christianity, faith and reason are crucial for sustaining just political orders. It is on the basis of these convictions that he worries about the marginalization of Christianity in the West. Unsurprisingly, the mutual necessity of faith and reason is also the central message in Benedict's dialogue with other religions, especially Islam.[20] In both Islam and in the West, an absence of the synthesis of faith and reason creates the danger of a descent into the mass injustices so many of which Benedict witnessed in his own lifetime.

RECONCILIATION: COMPLEMENTING AND ENACTING THE BENEDICTINE SYNTHESIS

Christian advocacy of reconciliation finds its setting in a global wave of political efforts to address massive past injustices of the kind that have influenced the life and thought of Benedict. In the past generation, over ninety countries have sought to leave behind dictatorships and make a transition toward democracy; since the end of the cold war, a historically dense spate of settlements of civil war and genocide has taken place; over the past decade, Western powers like the United States have struggled to leave behind stability and a modicum of democracy in the aftermath of interventions in Iraq and Afghanistan and elsewhere. Efforts to deal with such past injustices include over forty truth commissions; two international tribunals and now an International Criminal Court; national trials; community-level justice forums; reparations schemes; an outbreak of apologies such as U.S. President Bill Clinton's for not intervening in Rwanda; dramatic instances of forgiveness; memorials, museums, commemorations, and ceremonies; and scores of forums, seminars, and initiatives conducted by nongovernmental organizations (NGOs) and other civil society organizations.

But what notions of justice govern these efforts? The thinking that enjoys the greatest prestige among the institutions and networks involved—the United Nations, Western governments, human rights organizations, international lawyers, and other activists devoted to "transitional justice"—is what can be termed "the liberal peace."[21] The sociologist Jonathan Van Antwerpen has called the liberal peace the global orthodoxy for dealing with past injustices in the political realm.[22] Rooted in Enlightenment thought, some of whose ideas about law and institutions Benedict affirms, the liberal peace advances human rights, the rule of law, free markets, and judicial punishment, justified either on retributive or utilitarian grounds. Judicial punishment ranks as the queen of the virtues among international lawyers and human rights activists; the International Criminal Court is their signature accomplishment. The greatest mortal sin in their catechism is blanket amnesty. *¡Nunca mas!* they cry.

Yet both leaders and ordinary citizens inhabiting sites of catastrophe have articulated and performed other efforts of repair that do not fit easily into the liberal peace: citizens acknowledge the suffering of victims through truth commissions and related forums; perpetrators confess and offer acts of reparation within community justice forums; political leaders apologize; victims forgive; the state builds public memorials; religious leaders seek to overcome hatred and enmity among citizens. Such activities often go under the name "reconciliation." Defined most concisely and traditionally as "restoration of right relationship," reconciliation has emerged recently and vigorously in numerous settings of past (and sometimes ongoing) war and dictatorship. *Reconciliation* was eponymous for truth commissions in Chile, South Africa, Peru, Sierra Leone, Timor Leste, and elsewhere.

Disproportionately, but not exclusively, it is the religious who advocate reconciliation. Religious leaders espousing reconciliation have exercised leadership in political proceedings regarding past injustices in South Africa, Sierra Leone, Timor Leste, Peru, Uganda, Chile,

Guatemala, and postunification Germany. Churches and religious NGOs have conducted reconciliation efforts within civil society in locales across the globe. Theologians have reflected on reconciliation in recent years as well.

If the liberal peace is the global orthodoxy, Van Antwerpen argues, reconciliation has become the global "heterodoxy." In other words, it has achieved the status of a paradigm that poses an alternative to the orthodoxy but is less embedded in powerful global institutions and networks than the orthodoxy.

Like the global wave of efforts to deal with past injustices, reconciliation has entered the stage of global politics relatively late in history. It has little place in the Western tradition of political thought and practice. In Christian history reconciliation was long confined to the confessional, the church community, families, and other immediate relationships. It was in the late nineteenth and early twentieth century that theologians began to articulate reconciliation as a political ethic, the theologian John de Gruchy documents. Protestant theologians like Albrecht Ritschl, Scotland's P. T. Forsyth, and Switzerland's Karl Barth, who otherwise differed greatly in their orientation, commonly argued that Christian doctrines of justification, atonement, and reconciliation carried relevance for politics. De Gruchy follows reconciliation forward through the German theologian Dietrich Bonhoeffer and the Czech scholar Jan Milic Lochman, whose theology influenced the anti-apartheid movement in South Africa.[23] South Africa has indeed served as a prime site for reconciliation's entry into global politics, an entry that dates to the 1960s and that laid the intellectual groundwork for Archbishop Desmond Tutu to make reconciliation the primary theme of South Africa's famous truth commission of the 1990s.[24] Contemporary Protestant theologians of reconciliation include Miroslav Volf, Christopher Marshall, Donald Shriver, de Gruchy himself, and other scholars.[25]

In the Catholic tradition, it is Pope John Paul II who is most responsible for introducing reconciliation as a political ethic. His all too overlooked encyclical of 1980, *Dives in Misericordia* (Rich in Mercy), was revolutionary for commending the virtue of mercy to social and political orders, to be practiced through forgiveness and reconciliation. Seldom found in statecraft, political forgiveness had been rare in Church teaching as well. Its only previous appearance had been Pope Benedict XV's urging of forgiveness on European states at the end of World War I. John Paul II would resound his teaching of reconciliation and forgiveness for political orders several times again, including in his call for an examination of conscience in the Church in the years running up to the Jubilee Year, 2000; his Message for the World Day of Peace in 1997; and, most famously, his Message for the World Day of Peace in 2002, when, months after the attacks of September 11, 2001, he appended to Pope Paul VI's famous dictum "no peace without justice" the corollary "no justice without forgiveness."[26]

Benedict has commended reconciliation for politics as well. In 2004 he gave two addresses, one of them at the German cemetery near Caen, France, on the sixtieth anniversary of the Normandy invasion, where he spoke of reconciliation between Germany and its allies after World War II. He grounded reconciliation in the atoning sacrifice of Christ and argued that it was a Christian notion of reconciliation that drove European statesmen like Konrad Adenauer, Robert Schumann, Alcide de Gasperi, and Charles de Gaulle—all Catholics, in fact—to promote European unity after World War II.[27]

After Benedict became pope, he took the opportunity of his first general audience in Saint Peter's Square to explain how he chose his name. In part he meant to evoke Saint Benedict of Nursia of the sixth century, but he also wanted to honor Pope Benedict XV, who, he said, "was a prophet of peace who struggled strenuously and bravely, first to avoid the drama of war and then to limit its terrible consequences." "In his footsteps," Benedict continued, "I place my ministry, in the service of reconciliation and harmony between peoples, profoundly convinced that the great good of peace is above all a gift from God.[28]

Reconciliation defined Benedict's ministry from the outset. Over the course of his pontificate Benedict has invoked reconciliation frequently in political contexts. In the war in Lebanon in summer 2006, for example, he made reconciliation a central theme of his diplomacy for peace. Pardon and reconciliation were central, too, in his 2007 letter to the Catholic Church in China, where he sought to heal divisions within the Chinese Church and between the Chinese Church and the Chinese government.[29] Then, in his Message for the World Day of Peace of 2011, he framed his central theme of religious freedom—a cause close to his heart that he associates closely with the synthesis of faith and reason—as a message of peace and reconciliation. Remarkably, he counseled Christian communities suffering persecution to practice forgiveness as a witness to the gospel, even as he called the global Church to show solidarity with these victims.[30] Benedict also established reconciliation as the governing idea for the Church's political and social engagement in Africa in his exhortation to the Church in Africa of 2011, following the synod of African bishops.[31] These do not exhaust the occasions when Benedict turned to reconciliation to frame problems of a political nature.

Benedict, then, has joined his powerful voice to that of other religious leaders who proclaim reconciliation in an era when so many societies are addressing dolorous pasts of massive injustice. His message of reconciliation, I believe, complements his preaching of the synthesis of faith and reason as a response to the political evils of the past century. As I argued above, not only does overcoming past evils require that a society recover sound shared beliefs about the foundations of justice, ones reflecting the synthesis of faith and reason, but it also requires that it address the wounds that past evils have left behind. As I am about to argue, political reconciliation also embodies and illustrates the very synthesis that Benedict calls for, incorporating and conjoining the distinctive logics of faith and reason.

I wish to promote this complementarity and embodiment by developing further some of the core ideas of an ethic of political reconciliation. If both John Paul II and Benedict XVI have introduced and ensconced reconciliation firmly in Catholic social teaching, many questions remain about the application of reconciliation to politics. How do its core theological ideas translate into the political order? How does an ethic of reconciliation confront ethical questions such as, What sort of punishment do human rights violators merit? Are amnesties justifiable? May trials be foregone in order to achieve a peace agreement? May leaders apologize on behalf of nations? Can states practice forgiveness? Does forgiveness imply compromising a struggle against an unjust regime or the waging of a just war? While

I cannot begin to answer all such questions here, I propose the broad outlines of an ethic.[32]

AN ETHIC OF POLITICAL RECONCILIATION: CORE THEOLOGICAL CONCEPTS

In Benedict's exhortation to the Church in Africa he declares that reconciliation is a "pre-political reality" and then goes on to establish its relevance to political orders. In Christianity reconciliation means above all God's reconciliation of the world to himself through the death and resurrection of Jesus Christ. This "vertical" reconciliation, as it might be called, also makes possible a "horizontal" reconciliation between humans. Crucially for the argument at hand, Benedict makes the point that reconciliation is a matter of actual restoration of persons and relationships.

That reconciliation is restorative in character is evident in the New Testament, where the word *reconciliation* (or *reconcile*) appears fifteen times, twelve of these in the letters of Saint Paul.[33] English versions of the New Testament translate *reconciliation* and *reconcile* from the Greek *katallage* and *katallosso*, which can mean either an exchange of goods or money or the transformation of enmity and hostile separation into a state of peace or friendship.[34] Both of these scriptural senses come together in the atoning action of God in Christ, who exchanges places with humanity, bears the burden of humanity's sin, and defeats sin and death, thereby setting humans free and enabling their right relationship with God and one another. Biblical reconciliation can be understood both as a process of restoring relationship and as a resulting state of right relationship.

A surprising upshot of the biblical notion of reconciliation is its resemblance to the biblical meaning of justice. Surprising, because to modern Westerners justice means a particular version of "due" that revolves around rights and desert: human rights, civil rights, rights to a distribution of economic goods, rights that arise from contracts, and the punishment that a criminal deserves. The resemblance to justice will be surprising as well to many advocates of reconciliation and even

more to many of its critics, both of whom understand reconciliation
as something other than justice—something that stands in tension
with or supplements justice but is not itself justice. From the Bible,
though, arises the idea that reconciliation is a concept of justice.

In English versions of the Bible, the words that translate into justice also commonly translate into righteousness. Righteousness, in
turn, means living by the duties that govern relationships in every
sphere of life as specified by God's covenants. In Old Testament Hebrew it is the terms *sedeq* and *mishpat* that translators render as both
"justice" and "righteousness." These terms often occur together, one
denoting justice and the other righteousness. For example, Psalm 97:2
reads "Cloud and darkness surround the Lord; justice *(mishpat)* and
right *(sedeq)* are the foundations of his throne." When the terms are
thus paired they carry social and political implications, conveying a
justice that kings and other officials are called to promote.[35] The New
Testament Greek follows the same pattern, presenting a family of
words that begin with the *dik-* stem *(dikaiosunē, dikaioō, dikaiōma,
dikaiōs, dikaiōsis, dikaiokrisia, dikaios)* that translate into English words
that are rooted in "right" (righteous, righteousness, rectify, require-
ment, uprightly) as well as English words that are rooted in "just"
(justice, to justify, justly, righteous judgment, and acquittal, which relates to justice).[36]

In the entire Bible justice words denote not only a condition of
righteousness or right relationship but also a process of restoring a
relationship after it has been severed. This restoration is holistic and
variegated. The Old Testament speaks of justice as involving liberating people from poverty, debt, and slavery; alleviating the condition of
the poor and the dispossessed; providing bread to the hungry; canceling debt; and judging and punishing oppressors.[37] It is in Second Isaiah (chapters 40 through 60 or so) that the restorative nature of justice
is clearest. *Sedeq* here describes God's comprehensive restoration of
the people of Israel, who have strayed from his covenant, and augurs
a messianic suffering servant as the ultimate fulfillment of this restoration. Characteristic of this portion of Scripture is the term *saving
justice,* describing a renewal that is active and transforming. It is Second Isaiah that Jesus then quotes in the Gospel of Matthew, where he

explicitly identifies himself with this messianic servant, one who brings "justice to victory." In like spirit, Saint Paul, in his letters, closely links justice with the idea of justification, by which he means the action through which God, acting through Jesus Christ, frees humanity from the bondage of sin but also, equally importantly—as the Council of Trent took pains to emphasize—restores the sinner to a state of righteousness, or right relationship.

If biblical justice means comprehensive righteousness or right relationship, understood both as a process of restoration and as a state of being restored, and if biblical reconciliation means a process of restoring relationship or a state of right relationship, then, in a biblical interpretation, we may say that reconciliation is a concept of justice.

How does this justice compare with the justice of rendering another what is his due? Again, the modern West has come to understand justice as due in terms of rights and desert. In my view reconciliation encompasses rights and desert but is also wider and more comprehensive than rights and desert. Rights, after all, and desert, too, themselves describe crucial dimensions of right relationship, involving complex duties and claims between persons. It is also my view that rights can be found in the Bible, especially the Old Testament.[38] They appear later in the Christian tradition as well, including medieval canon law and the thought of sixteenth-century Spanish scholastics, and have been affirmed strongly by the post–Vatican II magisterium, not least by Benedict.[39]

But in three ways the right relationship of the Bible exceeds the duties and claims that rights describe. First, there are duties of such sufficient width that they involve no corresponding right. Philosophers describe a wide duty as one whose discharge on the part of its performer is open-ended. The action is obligatory but unspecified as to when, where, how, and exactly toward whom it is to be performed. The biblical obligation to serve the poor, for instance, fits this description. To be sure, the poor have specific rights. But the obligation of those who are not poor to serve the poor is not limited by what these rights describe and is unspecified in the realm in which it exceeds these rights. Second, the Bible's account of the justice of restoration—God's saving justice, for instance—is also wider

than rights and desert. As recounted throughout Scripture, most saliently in God's atoning act in Christ, and as affirmed consistently in
Christian tradition, this restoration takes the form of a gift—that is,
something to which recipients do not have a right or a claim. If this
restoration is indeed justice, then it is a justice that involves no corresponding right. The third respect in which the justice of reconciliation
is wider than rights again involves justice as a process of restoration. It
is that even when justice fulfills a right it also restores wounds to right
relationship that are not strictly entailed in the right. For instance,
international law has developed rights to reparation and to knowledge
of the truth on behalf of victims. The practices that fulfill these rights,
however, involve more than just fulfilling rights. Acknowledgment, as
it takes place at a truth commission, for instance, not only satisfies a
right to know the truth but also involves the recognition of the victim by fellow citizens, thus redressing the wound of social isolation
and ignorance. Such a restoration, whose value exceeds what rights
describe, is also a part of justice when we are talking about the justice
of reconciliation.

The justice of reconciliation, then, encompasses but exceeds
rights. This account of justice might seem to diverge from Benedict's
account in *Charity in Truth*. There he defines justice as what is due
and holds that love includes but also exceeds this justice. It would
seem, then, that he defines love in the way that I define the justice of
reconciliation. It turns out, however, that in separate discourses Benedict also affirms a justice that exceeds rights and that expresses the
saving action of God. In his Lenten Message of 2010, for instance,
he describes justice in terms of the restorative action of God. The
meaning of *sedeqah* (using the feminine form of *sedeq*), he says, is
linked to the God who "lifts the needy from the ash heap" (quoting
Psalm 113:7) and to the command to give to the poor in restorative
fashion. Discussing Paul's concept of justification, he translates Romans 3:21–22 as "the justice of God . . . manifested through faith in
Jesus Christ." In a General Audience delivered in 2008, he makes
clear that for Paul justification is a process whereby we *become* just and
thus restored to righteousness (again as Trent would have it and in
contrast to Luther and Calvin's notion of justification merely *declaring*

us just).[40] In the Lenten Address, he goes on to say that the justice of God comes from grace and is the loving act of a God who restores. He even says that this is a justice of gift, of "the fullness of charity," of salvation, enlivened by love, a justice that is in fact contrary to what everyone is due. Such divine justice is "profoundly different from its human counterpart," he observes, drawing an explicit contrast with justice as due. Yet this divine justice is not detached from or foreign to human affairs. Strengthened by it, Benedict exhorts, "the Christian is moved to contribute to creating just societies . . . enlivened by love." In these addresses, then, Benedict articulates a justice that goes beyond due or rights, that does not negate these rights, that converges with love, that is rooted in the biblical texts, that restores right relationship, and that converges substantially with what I have described as the justice of reconciliation.[41]

The justice of reconciliation takes on even more fullness through its connection with two other concepts derived from the Bible: peace and mercy. Peace, the first of these notions, converges with the aspect of reconciliation that is a state of affairs—a state of being reconciled, a state of right relationship, a state of justice. The word for "peace" found in the Old Testament, the Hebrew *shalom,* describes the proper life of the Jewish community and means health and prosperity, economic and political justice, and honesty and moral integrity in relations between persons—a condition much like comprehensive righteousness.[42] Certain Old Testament Scriptures explicitly spell out this intimate link between peace and the justice of right relationship.[43] *Eirene,* the Greek New Testament word for "peace," is a direct translation of *shalom* via the Septuagint, the Greek translation of the Jewish Scriptures, and here again involves the several dimensions of right order in a community.[44] The concept of peace informed by justice—what is often called "positive peace" and distinguished from a "negative peace" that is a mere absence of overt violence—has recurred in the Catholic tradition of thought, arguably present in Augustine's writings, for instance, and is resounded time and again in modern encyclicals. Benedict's exhortation to the Church in Africa is typical in arguing that "reconciliation and justice are the two essential premises of peace . . . and . . . to a certain extent, they also define its nature."[45]

If peace converges with reconciliation as a state or condition of justice, the concept that converges with reconciliation as a process of restoration of justice is mercy. A notion of mercy that involves holistic restoration is, here again, one that will ring strange in modern Western ears, to which mercy is much narrower and more conditional—a departure from deserved punishment, as when a judge lets a defendant "off the hook."[46] Mercy in the Bible, though—expressed by the Hebrew *hesed* and *rahamin* and the Greek *eleos* in the New Testament—means something far broader and more transformational. Pope John Paul II explained this biblical concept of mercy in his 1980 encyclical, *Dives in Misericordia*, writing that mercy is "manifested in its true and proper aspect when it restores to value, promotes and draws good from all the forms of evil existing in the world and in man." Thus understood, mercy is quite close in meaning to the justice that restores relationship, the justice that is reconciliation.

From the Bible, then, we can argue that reconciliation is a concept of justice that involves a restoration of relationship, animated by mercy, and a resulting state of right relationship, equivalent to peace. To import these core concepts into politics is to manifest a vision resonant with what Benedict proposed in *Charity in Truth*. Reconciliation proposes a politics that is not confined to the justice of rights and due but is infused with virtues and practices that are grounded in God's saving justice—or, as Benedict renders it in *Charity in Truth*, God's gratuitous love. Reconciliation, then, involves a robust role for faith in politics that far exceeds performing as a corrective to reason. As we shall see, though, reconciliation also involves a robust role for reason, especially insofar as it involves human rights, which, as Benedict persuasively argues, find their strongest grounding in natural law.

ENACTING RECONCILIATION IN POLITICS

How is this biblical notion of reconciliation to be realized in modern politics? Modern Catholic social thought has followed Thomas Aquinas in considering political authority indispensable for achieving important human goods in common. An ethic of political reconciliation might interpret this idea as follows: political authority secures vital dimensions of right relationship. In the modern world governments rightly concern themselves with that dimension of relationship that involves people's roles as subjects of public law—the rights, duties, and virtues that go with being citizens of political orders or that are rightfully owed to or claimed by foreigners. Restoring such right relationship between citizens is indeed the primary goal of political reconciliation in societies that have suffered war, genocide, and dictatorship. Today the main site of political reconciliation is the state, though it might also take place between states that have warred or between an intervener state and its target state, the United States and Iraq, for instance. But if it is legitimate for states to pursue reconciliation, the political sphere also has its proper boundaries. The common good promoted by the state is only a subset of the comprehensive biblical justice of right relationship within a community and between its members and God, which also pertains to friendships, families, economic dealings, conduct in the religious community, and so on. It exceeds the authority, and usually the competence, of the state to promote reconciliation between people in these other respects. The state, then, may foster reconciliation—political reconciliation—and remain a limited state, much as modern liberal democracy envisions the state.

Reciprocally, post–Vatican II magisterial thought teaches that the Church ought to refrain from performing the state's governing tasks but rightfully contributes to the political order—including, arguably, by promoting political reconciliation.[47] In recent decades the Church and Catholic organizations like Catholic Relief Services have respected these roles as they have worked to bring repair to persons and relationships who have suffered great wounds in conflicts in Rwanda, Colombia, Burundi, Guatemala, and elsewhere; in publicly urging governments to address past injustices in Timor Leste, South Africa, Chile, El Salvador, and many other places; in offering its prelates as truth commissioners or even organizers of truth commissions; and in setting forth norms of justice for the state's activities.[48]

Carried out by the state and by the Church in interaction with the state, political reconciliation seeks to restore justice in political communities. Right relationship in political communities is broken by political injustices, which may be defined as unjust actions or structures that people perform or build in the name of political agendas and ideals. Perpetrators of political injustices include both agents of the state and soldiers in opposition forces. Most of the political injustices of concern here are systemic ones, taking place on a large scale and affecting not only combatants but also wide swaths of civilians. But then the question becomes, Which acts and laws are unjust? Here we turn to human rights. The actual institutions that have carried out practices of political reconciliation—truth commissions, courts, implementers of lustration policies, negotiators of reparations settlements, and practitioners of political apologies—have appealed repeatedly to the international conventions that define human rights and the laws of war to define political injustices as war crimes, crimes against humanity, genocide, torture, more recently, rape, and sometimes violations of other political, civil, social, and economic rights. Human rights, of course, also enjoy a strong place in Catholic social thought, especially in the encyclicals of the Second Vatican Council and afterward, which root human rights in natural law and in the dignity of the person created in the image of God.

But if human rights define political injustices, the respects in which these injustices wound persons and relationships are far wider than rights alone describe. Correspondingly, the practices that make up an ethic of political reconciliation aim not only to restore human rights but also to redress this wide range of wounds, as well as the emotions of hatred, fear, revenge, and alienation from the political order to which these wounds give rise. These restorative practices are legitimate for the political order because the wounds were inflicted within the political order and because redressing them helps to secure the strength and health of the political order. The reasoning runs strongly parallel to the logic through which Benedict argues in *Charity in Truth* that the sustaining of justice (the justice of rights and due) itself depends on love.

It is wounds and practices that give specific and practical definition to political reconciliation. The wounds take on at least six forms. The first one approximates the very definition of political injustice: the violation of the victim's basic human rights or prerogatives under the laws of war. Human rights not only define political injustice, but their violation is one of the wounds of political injustice. Again, though, the wounds run far wider than violated human rights. A second form of wound encompasses the wide range of injuries that political injustices inflict on victims, including death, the death of family and friends, permanent bodily injury from torture or assault, trauma, humiliation, sexual violation, the loss of wealth and livelihood, and many other harms. A third wound, common in both war and dictatorship, is victims' ignorance of the source and circumstances of the political injustices that were inflicted on them. Commonly giving voice to this ignorance are the relatives of the missing and the dead. A fourth wound deepens the harm of political injustices even more: it is the lack of acknowledgment of victims' suffering, out of either ignorance or indifference, on the part of members of the surrounding community. The failure of public acknowledgment is "actually . . . a redoubling of the basic violation," writes the South African political philosopher André du Toit.[49] Such refusal, in a Christian theology of reconciliation, is a failure of the solidarity with the suffering that imitates Christ's identification with the poor and the afflicted. The fifth and sixth wounds focus primarily on the perpetrator. The fifth is what may be called the "standing victory" of the perpetrator's political injustice.[50] One of the harms that an injustice leaves behind is the undefeated "moral fact" of the perpetrator's disregard for the dignity of the victim. This moral fact is the standing victory of injustice. When human rights activists speak of the injustice of impunity, what they have in mind is something much like this standing victory. Finally, the sixth wound is the harm that the perpetrator inflicts on his own soul when he commits an act of injustice. In the Christian tradition sin does not merely result in a mark in a "debit column," but has real and debilitating consequences for the sinner; in cases of violence these frequently include severe psychological damage. "The wages of sin is death," as Saint Paul wrote in his Letter to the Romans (6:23).

Reflecting harms that political injustices impose directly, all these wounds may be called "primary wounds." In episodes of systemic injustice—civil war, dictatorship, and genocide—thousands, sometimes millions, of people, suffer them. But primary wounds also cause harm in a secondary and indirect sense, namely, by contributing to judgments through which citizens and collectives proceed to commit further injustices such as massacres, genocide, torture, and other war crimes and international aggression, or else to withhold allegiance from fledgling constitutional orders and peace agreements. Such further injustices may be called "secondary wounds," for they arise from emotions of fear, hatred, resentment, and revenge that emanate from the original injustices.[51] To understand secondary wounds and grasp how they can undermine political orders and relations between states, sometimes for generations, one need think no further than Rwanda, Northern Ireland, Bosnia, Kosovo, the Basque Country, Iraq, Israel and Palestine, Kashmir, the Rape of Nanking, Hiroshima, and Dresden.

Six practices, then, aim to transform wounded persons and relationships into a condition of greater human flourishing. Each practice addresses one or more wound in a different way; each reflects the restorative logic of an ethic of political reconciliation. The practices are interdependent and often complementary and together make up a holistic ethic of political reconciliation.

1. *Building regimes based on human rights and building relations between states based on respect for international law.* Again, human rights and respect for law between states are a crucial dimension of right relationship in modern political orders. Ensconcing human rights in the rule of law brings repair with respect to the wound of the violation of human rights. It is here that the ethic of political reconciliation most converges with the liberal peace, in which rights occupy center stage. This practice is indispensable if reconciliation is not to be cheap, taking the form of an amnesty, an agreement between enemies, or an otherwise "negative peace" that does not involve justice for all.

2. *Acknowledgment* of the suffering of victims on the part of other citizens in the political community. Acknowledgment is recognition, which addresses social ignorance of victims' suffering on the part of the community. Conferring such recognition are truth

commissions, as well as museums, monuments, commemorations, and rituals of remembrance. Theologically, acknowledgment reflects God's own remembrance and recognition of the poor, the victim, and the forgotten and his will for their restoration as recorded throughout the Bible and realized most fully in Jesus Christ.

3. *Reparations,* a material payment in the form of money, mental and physical health services, and the like, to victims of political injustices on the part of perpetrators, the state, or both. The purpose of reparations is in part to compensate victims materially insofar as that is possible. More deeply, the material payment expresses the community's recognition of the victim's suffering symbolically, much like acknowledgment does. The theological grounds for reparations are largely the same as those for acknowledgment, though they stress that God's restoration of victims involves a material dimension, as with the liberation of slaves and the granting of the just claims of the poor and the otherwise oppressed. Restitution, meaning something much like reparations, was in fact the central response to crime within the Jewish community, as the law of the Torah set forth. Reparations have also played an important role in the Christian tradition. In the sixteenth century, for instance, Bartolomé de Las Casas thought that reparations, or *restitutio,* were owed to indigenous peoples of the New World for a wide range of injuries done to them by European conquerors.

4. *Punishment,* today frequently pitted against reconciliation in debates about just responses to past evil around the world. Critics of reconciliation equate it with amnesty and thus reject it. An ethic of reconciliation, though, need not exclude punishment and can in fact justify it on a restorative rationale that promotes the restoration of relationships between perpetrators, victims, and members of the community. The *Compendium of the Social Doctrine of the Church* holds that "there is a twofold purpose [in judicial punishment]. On the one hand, *encouraging the reinsertion of the condemned person into society;* on the other, *fostering a justice that reconciles,* a justice capable of restoring harmony in social relationships disrupted by the criminal act committed."[52] Imprisonment,

even long-term imprisonment, need not be foreign to restorative punishment and is appropriate for masterminds of large-scale human rights violations. Restorative punishment is realized most fully, though, in community forums where victims, perpetrators, and community members gather in a common place and recite their stories and their claims and where community elders deliver a penance that takes the form of restitution or reintegrative community service.

5. *Apology*, growing increasingly common in global politics. A succession of German leaders, for instance, have voiced repentance for the Nazis' perpetration of the Holocaust, most dramatically in the case of Chancellor Willy Brandt kneeling at the monument to the victims of the Warsaw Ghetto Uprising in 1970 and in the case of President Richard von Weizsäcker's speech to the German Bundestag of 1985. In practicing apology, a perpetrator nullifies the standing victory of his injustice, commits himself to the restoration of his soul, and confers recognition on victims. When a leader of a nation or other collective performs an apology, he speaks on behalf of the political community in whose name the injustice was committed, though the leader may not himself have been involved in the injustice. In Christian theology, repentance, confession, and apology are essential for the moral and spiritual restoration of a perpetrator and his appropriation of forgiveness.

6. *Forgiveness*, the rarest of the six practices to take place in political orders but also the most distinctively Christian and, I would argue, the most potentially transforming. The liberal peace has little place for it; its proponents often criticize it. South Africa's Nelson Mandela is one of the few heads of state to have practiced it, though accounts of the aftermath of violence in countries like South Africa, Rwanda, Sierra Leone, and Uganda reveal that victims have practiced it more widely. In a robust Christian theological framework, forgiveness involves not only the victim's renunciation of resentment but also his or her construction of right relationship. "It is by granting and receiving forgiveness that the traumatized memories of individuals and communities have

found healing and families formerly divided have rediscovered harmony," Benedict writes in *Africae Munus*. Jesus frequently commands forgiveness in the New Testament, even calling for it to be practiced seventy-seven times (or seventy times seven times in one version of the command). Forgiveness also can be viewed more deeply not just as a following of Christ's teachings but also as a victim's participation in the act of forgiveness that God performed through the death and resurrection of Jesus Christ. For societies recovering from past injustices, forgiveness helps to defeat the standing victory of injustice, contributes to the restoration of victims, and helps to work against cycles of revenge and counter-revenge. Most vividly of the six practices, forgiveness expresses the mercy and the justice that wills to restore relationship, and it helps to restore just peace in political orders. Pope John Paul II indeed argued in his Message for the World Day of Peace of 2002 that social peace is possible only through forgiveness and reconciliation.[53]

To speak of reconciliation, peace, and forgiveness in sites of massive past political injustice admittedly sounds utopian. It is worth stressing that all six practices, wherever they take place, will remain partially accomplished, compromised by power, hindered by differing concepts of justice among victims, perpetrators, and other citizens, laden with sheer complexity, and hampered by political institutions that often have been wrecked and then repaired only partially if at all. Pertinent to an ethic of political reconciliation is original sin, which reminds us that the work of restoration will be accomplished in partial and fragmentary ways this side of heaven. To conceive of justice and peace holistically is not to insist that peace and justice will be achieved holistically in the political realm. In part, the function of an ethic of political reconciliation is to provide standards according to which we can assess the justice of efforts at restoration. Still, the ethic of political reconciliation is not an ethic of mere ideals. In the real world, all these practices do occur, even if roughly. In these occurrences we can find a mixture of breakdown and breakthrough, of terrible failures as well as instances when "hope and history rhyme," in the words of the poet Seamus Heaney. The resulting predicament is that restorative practices take place but are suffused with blemish. It is just this predicament that begs an ethic. Were the practices ineffectual, the ethic would be futile; if the practices did not involve partiality, compromise, and excruciating dilemmas, the ethic would be pointless.

CONCLUSION

Much more can be said about the content of an ethic of political reconciliation. What I want to stress is how it reflects and complements Benedict's synthesis of faith and reason. The ethic builds on and encompasses human rights, which define the political injustices that political reconciliation addresses as well as the basis of the regime or relationship between states that political reconciliation seeks. Reconciliation without human rights would be cheap reconciliation or perhaps an oppressor's rationale: Drop your demands, and let us reconcile! Human rights, which Benedict believes to be grounded in natural law, serve to moor reconciliation much in the way that Benedict desires for reason to moor the influence of faith in the political realm.

Reconciliation also brings into politics a religious logic, one firmly grounded in God's reconciliation of the world to himself and in scriptural concepts of justice, peace, and mercy. Resounding *Charity in Truth*, such reconciliation encompasses but also exceeds the rights that are "due" and is informed by God's gratuitous and saving action. It is an ethic that the Church itself can advocate and perform out of its deepest purposes even while remaining differentiated from the state in its role and responsibility.

The ethic is situated in the aftermath of the kind of catastrophic evils that have informed Benedict's life and thought. It is worth noting that regimes or factions that explicitly rejected God or for whom religious faith had very little import perpetrated virtually all the great atrocities of the twentieth century. Even those violations of human rights committed by professedly Christian regimes—Pinochet's Chile, Videla's Argentina—were carried out in direct contravention of the Church's ethical teachings. The prevalence of secular statist violence makes all the more urgent Benedict's call for reincorporating faith, moored by reason, into politics.

It is also practices grounded in faith that have the capacity to bring repair to the wounded persons, relationships, and societies that these massive injustices have left behind. The balm of reconciliation redresses wounds that are wider than those that human rights can describe, involves measures wider than restoring human rights, and indeed effects the kinds of restoration that greatly strengthen a regime based on human rights. Justice rooted in reason depends greatly on the mercy, love, grace—and yes, distinctive justice—found in faith.

NOTES

1. Joseph Ratzinger, *Values in a Time of Upheaval*, trans. Brian McNeil (San Francisco: Ignatius Press, 2006). On the theme of crisis in Benedict's thought, see also Samuel Gregg, *The Modern Papacy* (New York: Continuum, 2009); Tracey Rowland, *Ratzinger's Faith: The Theology of Pope Benedict* (Oxford: Oxford University Press, 2009). In this essay I use the name Benedict when referring to him either in the inclusive sense, meaning throughout his career, or else specifically during the time when he has been Pope Benedict XVI, whereas I use the name Joseph Ratzinger only to refer to him prior to his papacy.

2. Joseph Cardinal Ratzinger, *Homily, Mass Pro Eligendo Romano Pontifice,* April 18, 2005. Available at www.vatican.va/gpII/documents/homily -pro-eligendo-pontifice_20050418_en.html.

3. Benedict XVI, *Faith, Reason, and the University: Memories and Reflections,* September 12, 2006. Available at www.vatican.va/holy_father/ benedict_xvi/speeches/2006/september/documents/hf_ben-xvi _spe_20060912_university-regensburg_en.html. On the ensuing debate, see Miroslav Volf, Ghazi bin Muhammad, and Melissa Yarrington, eds., *A Common Word: Muslims and Christians on Loving God and Neighbor* (Grand Rapids, MI: Eerdmans, 2010).

4. Jürgen Habermas and Joseph Ratzinger, *The Dialectics of Secularization: On Reason and Religion,* ed. Florian Schuller, trans. Brian McNeil (San Francisco: Ignatius Press, 2006).

5. Joseph Ratzinger, "The Subiaco Address," reprinted in Rowland, *Ratzinger's Faith*, 158–59, 163.

6. Benedict XVI, "The Listening Heart: Reflections on the Foundations of Law," September 22, 2011. Available at www.vatican.va/holy_father/benedict_xvi/speeches/2011/september/documents/hf_ben-xvi_spe_20110922_reichstag-berlin_en.html.

7. Habermas and Ratzinger, *Dialectics of Secularization*, 78.

8. Benedict XVI, "Address at Westminster Hall," September 17, 2010. Available at www.vatican.va/holy_father/benedict_xvi/speeches/2010/september/documents/hf_ben-xvi_spe_20100917_societa-civile_en.html.

9. Benedict XVI, "The Listening Heart."

10. Habermas and Ratzinger, *Dialectics of Secularization*, 67–72.

11. Benedict XVI, "Address at Westminster Hall."

12. Alvin Plantinga, "On Christian Scholarship." www.calvin.edu/academic/philosophy/virtual_library/plantinga_alvin.htm.

13. See, for example, Benedict XVI, "Christmas Address December 22, 2006," at www.vatican.va/holy_father/benedict_xvi/speeches/2006/december/documents/hf_ben_xvi_spe_20061222_curia-romana_en.html; Ratzinger, "The Subiaco Address," 164; Benedict XVI, "The Listening Heart."

14. Habermas and Ratzinger, *Dialectics of Secularization*, 76.

15. Ratzinger, "The Subiaco Address," 156–65, quote on 161.

16. Joseph Cardinal Ratzinger, *Truth and Tolerance: Christian Belief and World Religions*, trans. Henry Taylor (San Francisco: Ignatius Press, 2004), 247, 256.

17. Benedict XVI, *Caritas in Veritate*, June 29, 2009. Available at www.vatican.va/holy_father/benedict_xvi/encyclicals/documents/hf_ben-xvi_enc_20090629_caritas-in-veritate_en.html.

18. Habermas and Ratzinger, *Dialectics of Secularization*, 77; Ratzinger, *Values*, 108–9.

19. On the tendency of religion to descend into violence when it is left alone, see also Benedict XVI, "Address at Westminster Hall," September 17, 2010; Benedict XVI, *Faith, Reason, and the University*, September 12, 2006.

20. Habermas and Ratzinger, *Dialectics of Secularization*, 73–76.

21. In her "conceptual history of transitional justice," Paige Arthur describes the field of transitional justice as "an international web of individuals and institutions whose internal coherence is held together by common concepts, practical aims, and distinctive claims for legitimacy" that formed in common response to practical dilemmas. "The field of transitional justice, so

defined, came directly out of a set of interactions among human rights activists, lawyers and legal scholars, policymakers, journalists, donors, and comparative politics experts concerned with human rights and the dynamics of 'transitions to democracy,' beginning in the late 1980s." She also discusses debates that occurred within this web despite their broad agreement on certain values—over the desirable extent and justification for judicial punishment, for instance. See Paige Arthur, "How 'Transitions' Reshaped Human Rights: A Conceptual History of Transitional Justice," *Human Rights Quarterly* 31 (2009): 324, 353, 354, 358. For other helpful surveys and assessments of transitional justice, see Bronwyn Leebaw, "The Irreconcilable Goals of Transitional Justice," *Human Rights Quarterly* 30, no. 1 (2008): 95–118; Ruti G. Teitel, "Transitional Justice Genealogy," *Harvard Human Rights Journal* 16 (2003): 69–94.

22. Jonathan Van Antwerpen, "Reconciliation as Heterodoxy" (2010), unpublished manuscript. Van Antwerpen was discussing reconciliation in the context of transitional justice, a domain somewhat narrower than peacemaking or peace building, but his point applies rather well here nevertheless.

23. John W. De Gruchy, *Reconciliation: Restoring Justice* (Minneapolis, MN: Fortress Press, 2002), 67–76.

24. Erik Doxtader, *With Faith in the Work of Words: The Beginnings of Reconciliation in South Africa, 1985–1995* (East Lansing: Michigan State University Press, 2008), 35–73.

25. De Gruchy, *Reconciliation;* Miroslav Volf, *Exclusion and Embrace: A Theological Exploration of Identity, Otherness, and Reconciliation* (Nashville, TN: Abingdon Press, 1996); Christopher D. Marshall, *Beyond Retribution: A New Testament Vision for Justice, Crime and Punishment* (Grand Rapids, MI: Eerdmans, 2001); Donald W. Shriver, *An Ethic for Enemies: Forgiveness in Politics* (New York: Oxford University Press, 1995). Most of the theologians— as well as practical examples—offered here are from Protestant and Catholic sources. What about the Orthodox Church? To be sure, it has always harbored a deep theology of reconciliation, one that reaches back to the early Church fathers and that is profoundly restorative, as in its concept of divinization. Orthodox theologians, though, at least to my knowledge, have not developed a theology of reconciliation for the political realm to the extent that Protestant and Catholic theologians did during the twentieth century.

26. The post–September 11 address was his "No Peace without Justice. No Justice without Forgiveness. Message for the Celebration of the World Day of Peace," January 1, 2002. Available at www.vatican.va/holy_father/ john_paul_ii/messages/peace/documents/hf_jp-ii_mes_20011211_xxxv -world-day-for-peace_en.html.

27. Ratzinger, *Values,* 119–26, for the portions discussed here.

28. See "Pope tells why he chose the name of 'Benedict XVI,'" www
.catholicnewsagency.com/resource.php?n=493.

29. See "Letter of the Holy Father Pope Benedict XVI to the Bishops,
Priests, Consecrated Persons and Lay Faithful of the Catholic Church in the
People's Republic of China," www.vatican.va/holy_father/benedict_xvi/
letters/2007/documents/hf_ben-xvi_let_20070527_china_en.html.

30. Benedict XVI, "Religious Freedom, the Path to Peace: Message of
His Holiness Pope Benedict XVI for the Celebration of the World Day of
Peace," January 1, 2011. Available at www.vatican.va/holy_father/benedict
_xvi/messages/peace/documents/hf_ben-xvi_mes_20101208_xliv-world
-day-peace_en.html.

31. Benedict XVI, "*Africae Munus*: Post-Synodal Apostolic Exhortation
of His Holiness Pope Benedict XVI to the Bishops, Clergy, Consecrated
Persons and the Lay Faithful on the Church in Africa in Service to Reconciliation, Justice, and Peace," November 19, 2011. Available at www.vatican.va/
holy_father/benedict_xvi/apost_exhortations/documents/hf_ben-xvi
_exh_20111119_africae-munus_en.html.

32. My arguments herein draw from Daniel Philpott, *Just and Unjust
Peace: An Ethic of Political Reconciliation* (Oxford: Oxford University Press,
2012). For a shorter statement of the book's argument in a Catholic context,
see Daniel Philpott, "Reconciliation: A Catholic Ethic for Peacebuilding in
the Political Order," in *Peacebuilding: Catholic Theology, Ethics, and Praxis,* ed.
Robert Schreiter, R. Scott Appleby, and Gerard F. Powers (Maryknoll, NY:
Orbis Books, 2010), 92–124.

33. De Gruchy, *Reconciliation,* 46, 51.

34. Ibid., 51.

35. Moshe Weinfeld, *Social Justice in Ancient Israel* (Minneapolis, MN:
Augsburg Fortress, 1995), 25–33.

36. Marshall, *Beyond Retribution,* 38.

37. Ibid.

38. See Nicholas Wolterstorff, *Justice: Rights and Wrongs* (Princeton, NJ:
Princeton University Press, 2008); Christopher D. Marshall, *Crowned with
Glory and Honor: Human Rights in the Biblical Tradition* (Telford, PA: Pan-
dora Press, 2001); David Novak, *Covenantal Rights: A Study in Jewish Political
Theory* (Princeton, NJ: Princeton University Press, 2000).

39. Brian Tierney, *The Idea of Natural Rights: Studies on Natural Rights,
Natural Law, and Church Law, 1150–1625* (Atlanta, GA: Scholars Press,
1997).

40. Benedict XVI, "General Audience," St. Peter's Square, Wednesday,
November 19, 2008.

41. Benedict XVI, "The Justice of God Has Been Manifested through Faith in Jesus Christ," Pope's Lenten Message for 2010. Available at www .vatican.va/holy_father/benedict_xvi/messages/lent/documents/hf_ben-xvi _mes_20091030_lent_2010_en.html.

42. Perry Yoder, *Shalom: The Bible's Word for Salvation, Justice, and Peace* (Newton, KS: Faith and Life Press, 1987), 10–23; Howard Zehr, *Changing Lenses* (Scottdale, PA: Herald Press, 1990), 130–32.

43. Ps 85:10 and Is 32:16–17.

44. Ulrich Mauser, *The Gospel of Peace: A Scriptural Message for Today's World* (Louisville, KY: Westminster/John Knox, 1992), 33.

45. Benedict XVI, *"Africae Munus"*; perhaps the most important modern encyclical that defines peace is Pope John XXIII, *Pacem in Terris*, in *Catholic Social Thought: The Documentary Heritage*, ed. David J. O'Brien and Thomas A. Shannon (Maryknoll, NY: Orbis Books, 1992), 129–62.

46. See Claudia Card, "Mercy," *Philosophical Review* 81, no. 2 (1972): 182–207; Jeffrie G. Murphy and Jean Hampton, *Forgiveness and Mercy* (New York: Cambridge University Press, 1988). In Murphy and Hampton, see especially the essays by Murphy.

47. Pontifical Council for Justice and Peace, *Compendium of the Social Doctrine of the Church* (Dublin: Veritas, 2005), #181–83.

48. On the role of churches in political efforts to address past injustices, see Daniel Philpott, "When Faith Meets History: The Influence of Religion on Transitional Justice," in *The Religious in Response to Mass Atrocity: Interdisciplinary Perspectives*, ed. Thomas Brudholm and Thomas Cushman (Cambridge: Cambridge University Press, 2009), 174–212.

49. André du Toit, "The Moral Foundations of the South African TRC: Truth as Acknowledgment and Justice as Recognition," in *Truth v. Justice: The Morality of Truth Commissions*, ed. Robert I. Rotberg and Dennis Thompson (Princeton, NJ: Princeton University Press, 2000), 133.

50. Murphy and Hampton, *Forgiveness and Mercy*, 124–38.

51. On the role of emotions in ethnic conflict, see Roger D. Peterson, *Understanding Ethnic Violence: Fear, Hatred, and Resentment in Twentieth-Century Eastern Europe* (Cambridge: Cambridge University Press, 2002).

52. *Compendium*, #173–74. Emphasis in original.

53. See *Compendium*, #224–25; John Paul II, "No Peace without Justice. No Justice without Forgiveness," no. 9; John Paul II, *An Ever Timely Commitment: Teaching Peace. Message for the Celebration of the World Day of Peace*, January 1, 2004, no. 10, at www.vatican.va/holy_father/john_paul_ii/ messages/peace/documents/hf_jp-ii_mes_20031216_xxxvii-world-day-for -peace_en.html.

chapter seven

DEVELOPMENT DRIVEN BY HOPE AND GRATUITOUSNESS

The Innovative Economics of Benedict XVI

SIMONA BERETTA

Hope and gratuitousness characterize Pope Benedict XVI's social teaching and give a thicker meaning to that "inquiry into nature and the causes of the wealth of nations" which should be the core of economics. Development, driven by human work and social creativity, captures the essence of economic inquiry; and development prominently appears in the full title of *Caritas in Veritate (CV)*, Benedict XVI's encyclical letter on "integral human development in charity and truth."[1]

At first glance hope and gratuitousness seem to be extraneous to both economic language and economic logic; quite the opposite, they are central especially today, as we face the "powerful new forces" of globalization: "Charity and truth confront us with an altogether new and creative challenge, one that is certainly vast and complex. It is about *broadening the scope of reason and making it capable of knowing and directing these powerful new forces,* animating them within the perspective of that 'civilization of love' whose seed God has planted in every people, in every culture" (*CV* 33).[2]

This challenge of charity and truth calls economics to search for a deeper and more realistic understanding of the economic dimension of human experience, as persons and members of one human family. Today *"the social question has become radically an anthropological question"* (*CV* 75), not simply because of advances in biotechnology allowing manipulations of life, but, more radically, because a "conscience that can no longer distinguish what is human" (*CV* 75) tends to prevail in social as well as economic analysis. The whole breadth of reason is called for, overcoming dualisms[3] and fragmentation that disempower the scope of human reason and frustrate economic theory and practice. Fragmentation and dualisms also risk sterilizing the seeds of the "civilization of love," making it harder to initiate and sustain dialogue among different cultures and traditions.

Caritas in Veritate spurred a reappraisal and a revaluation of many practices of love in the economy, such as economy of communion, reciprocal gift economies, social responsibility, and hybrid profit-nonprofit forms of commercial entities; it also revived important lines of research on the "civil" economy and on pre-Smithian traditions in economic thought.[4] This encyclical also attracted much interest among non-Catholics, "bridging" Catholic social teaching—as presented in Pope Benedict's encyclicals—with other contemporary lines of sociopolitical inquiry.[5]

The witnessing of deeds of charity and the practice of virtues—also within the economic dimensions of life—are a language that speaks clearly to those who want to listen, opening new questions: Why do these practices happen at all? What can we learn from them? If these questions are not asked, the witness of deeds becomes reduced to "best practice"—possibly with a technocratic flavor. When the inner drivers of a good practice go unmentioned, the most intriguing part of the witness of deeds—that is, how human reason and love shape that practice—remains invisible, and the common mentality remains unchallenged. But exploring why deeds of charity and practices of virtue occur, how they can be sustained even through hard times, allows one to better appreciate how innovative Pope Benedict's social teaching is.

The basic structure of Pope Benedict's "development economics" is fully fleshed out in the introduction to *Caritas in Veritate* and summarized in the very first lines of the encyclical:

> Charity in truth, to which Jesus Christ bore witness by his earthly life and especially by his death and resurrection, is the principal driving force behind the authentic development of every person and of all humanity. Love—*caritas*—is an extraordinary force which leads people to opt for courageous and generous engagement in the field of justice and peace. It is a force that has its origin in God, Eternal Love and Absolute Truth. (*CV* 1)

All persons are called to live their daily lives in charity and in truth; in fact, *Caritas in Veritate* originally defines Catholic social teaching (CST) as "caritas in veritate in re sociali." Christians are protagonists in shaping the economy, society, and polity in which they live as they "remain" in Jesus, incarnated Love and Truth, freely entering the inner dynamism—the creative tension—between love and truth.

ECONOMIC REALITY AND THE WHOLE BREADTH OF REASON

In his addresses, Benedict XVI invites us to "open the window" of our reason in facing reality, realistically acknowledging that we live in a world we did not make. For example:

> In its self-proclaimed exclusivity, the positivist reason which recognizes nothing beyond mere functionality resembles a concrete bunker with no windows, in which we ourselves provide lighting and atmospheric conditions, being no longer willing to obtain either from God's wide world. And yet we cannot hide from ourselves the fact that even in this artificial world, we are still covertly drawing upon God's raw materials, which we refashion into our

own products. The windows must be flung open again, we must see the wide world, the sky and the earth once more. (Address to the Bundestag, Reichstag Building, Berlin, September 22, 2011)

Reality is a fascinating sign: it brings with it the dynamic experience of the mysterious; it urges those who look at it with an open mind to search ever deeper. Reality is genially complex: the closer the grip of dominion—technocratic and/or disciplinary—over reality, the less we end up understanding. Benedict explains in his Aparecida Address of May 13, 2007:

> What is real? Are only material goods, social, economic and po-litical problems "reality"? This was precisely the great error of the dominant tendencies of the last century, a most destructive error. . . . Anyone who excludes God from his horizons falsifies the notion of "reality" and, in consequence, can only end up in blind alleys or with recipes for destruction. . . . Yet here a further question immediately arises: who knows God? . . . only his Son, . . . true God, knows him. . . . If we do not know God in and with Christ, all of reality is transformed into an indecipherable enigma.

There are good reasons for seriously considering the possibility that economic reality is an "indecipherable enigma"; as to development, economists and social scientists have succeeded in providing good ex-planations of development scenarios in a given past and in a given region, but they seem to lack similarly good explanations of what to do in order to generate development and justice, as no socioeconomic mechanism seems to work even for what should be the easiest aspect of development—namely, increasing material production.

Acknowledging ignorance can be a healthy start for rethinking development, engaging reality with the full breadth of reason. Reality, in its truth, "is first of all *given* to us. In every cognitive process, truth is not something that we produce, it is always found, or better, re-ceived. Truth, like love, 'is neither planned nor willed, but somehow imposes itself upon human beings'" (*CV* 34, quoting *Deus Caritas Est*). In the adventure of knowledge—in searching for and finding truth—we need to love reality: "charity is not an added extra, like an appendix to work already concluded in each of the various disciplines: it engages them in dialogue from the very beginning" (*CV* 30).

The *Compendium of the Social Doctrine of the Church* describes CST as "knowledge illuminated by faith" (*CSDC* 72), in "friendly dialogue with all branches of knowledge" (76). Each branch of knowledge—including economics—is a precious ally in dialogue, and friendly interdisciplinary dialogue requires only that participants love the truth of reality. There is in fact a "specific responsibility of reason, which is not absorbed by faith" (Address to La Sapienza, January 17, 2008).

The whole breadth of reason includes valorizing each branch of knowledge for what it can contribute to a deeper understanding of reality. This "inclusive" perspective, which appreciates all efforts of *recta ratio*, appears in many important addresses by Benedict XVI.[6] *Caritas in Veritate* in particular speaks highly of "economic logic."[7] A similar inclusive perspective could usefully be applied also in economics, appreciating its branches for what each can contribute:[8] any "true" detail can fit into the wide horizon of a reason that is ready to "host" reality.[9]

SOUND ECONOMICS REQUIRES SOUND ANTHROPOLOGY

CST announces that Jesus Christ fully reveals man to man and that the integral development of every person and of humanity is inscribed in the fact of his Incarnation, death, and Resurrection. This announcement unifies the entire human experience: there is no gospel for the soul which is not also for the body, and for the raw fabric of the material world; reality as a whole is redeemed. Benedict XVI uses a beautiful image: participating in the Incarnation, death, and Resurrection of Christ through baptism allows for a real "evolutionary leap" in the history of humankind:

If we may borrow the language of the theory of evolution, it is the greatest "mutation," absolutely the most crucial leap into a totally new dimension that there has ever been in the long history of life and its development: a leap into a completely new order which does concern us, and concerns the whole of history. (Easter Vigil, Homily of His Holiness Benedict XVI, Vatican Basilica, Holy Saturday, April 15, 2006)

There are four features of Christian anthropology, fully revealed in Christ, that belong to the tradition of CST and are emphasized in Pope Benedict XVI's teachings. These features make it very interesting for economics to enter the friendly interdisciplinary dialogue surrounding CST, so as to contribute to integral human development. In short, this Christian anthropology is relational, dynamic, realistic, and "whole."

Relational Anthropology

Thinking about development "so that integration can signify solidarity rather than marginalization ... requires a deeper critical evaluation of the category of relation. This is a task that cannot be undertaken by the social sciences alone" (*CV* 53). That is, rethinking development requires a metaphysical interpretation of the *humanum* in which relationality is a constitutive element (*CV* 55), as we are the image of God. It also requires that "*God has a place in the public realm*, specifically in regard to its cultural, social, economic, and particularly its political dimensions" (*CV* 56): the relation with God fosters the true encounter between persons. We are thus challenged to explore the analytical, not simply the ethical, relevance of constitutive relations: both horizontal relations (be they *do ut des* or "reciprocal" relations) and relations with the transcendent, since God is "indispensable" (*CV* 31).

Relations inherently define both individual persons and society. Benedict XVI suggests a definition of the common good which is also intrinsically relational: "There is a good that is linked to living in society: the common good. It is the good of 'all of us,' made up of individuals, families and intermediate groups who together constitute society" (*CV* 7). The common good includes, but does not coincide with, the setting of material and institutional conditions that allow the flourishing of society; the most prominent good we have in common is the fact of our living together.[10]

As relations are the deep fabric of all human actions, adding "relational goods" to the traditional categories of economic goods, and maintaining that these goods add to economic welfare and to constructing a "civil" society, represents a necessary but insufficient step. Rethinking economic development within a relational anthropology entails much more. CST as *caritas in veritate in re sociali* shapes the relational perspective on development around "love" and "truth," two essentially relational words that are indispensable also in economic analysis.

Dynamic Anthropology

CST uses the word *vocation* to characterize both human labor and development, as generative processes that occur in the concreteness of time and space. The word *vocation* recurs throughout *Caritas in Veritate*; essentially, vocation means that labor and development themselves are constitutively a relation, in real time and real space: there is someone calling and someone giving a response, freely deciding whether and how to answer the call: "*Integral human development presupposes the responsible freedom* of the individual and of peoples: no structure can guarantee this development over and above human responsibility" (*CV* 17). The dynamism of freedom present in this calling and answering actually moves history, which can never be reduced to "necessity." No antecedent automatically produces development, as human freedom is the ultimate driver of work and development.

Realistic Anthropology

One traditional feature of realism in CST—dating to Saint Paul—recalls our wounded nature: "Ignoring the fact that man has a wounded nature inclined to evil gives rise to serious errors in the areas of education, politics, social action and morals. In the list of areas where the pernicious effects of sin are evident, the economy has been included for some time now" (*CV* 34, quoting *Catechism of the Catholic Church, #407, Centesimus Annus* 25).

Christian realism is truly poignant in Benedict XVI, yet truly disarming. His realism does not mean pessimism; in fact, Benedict XVI recalls original sin in *CV* 34, devoted to the joyful experience of receiving gifts (*joy* is one of the most frequently words in Benedict XVI's speeches, especially impromptu ones).[11] Even ignorance—a clear matter of realism!—seems to be no reason for pessimism in Benedict XVI's social teachings. Broadening the scope of our search, acknowledging our ignorance, is the opposite of a gloomy experience; rather, it is the condition for receiving the overwhelming gift of truth.[12] Correspondingly, Benedict XVI is very outspoken against technocratic ideology (*CV* 14, 70), in which one's limitations and one's ignorance are actually ignored.

"Whole" Anthropology

Pope Benedict said, "We are the image of a Trinitarian God, Logos and Agape, fullness of perfection. In God's love and truth, we are invited to participate in God's life, living our unified, dynamic and open existence in time and space, overcoming fragmentation, and schizophrenic dualisms. . . . [H]uman beings are in need of the infinite. . . . This is why God's presence and approachability are so important. . . . God's goodness present, his truth present, the true infinity for which we thirst."[13] In baptism, we are introduced to living a "whole" experience of development, with a unity of sense and direction because we "know the Way."[14] Hence, "*Development needs Christians with their arms raised towards God* in prayer, Christians moved by the knowledge that truth-filled love, *caritas in veritate,* from which authentic development proceeds, is not produced by us, but given to us" (*CV* 79).

In this new life, reason and affection are not distinct and potentially clashing dimensions, as reason is connected primarily with power over reality—including calculating and technical rationality—

while affection is driven by subjective and fluctuating emotions. Bene-dict points out that we need a new humanistic synthesis: "The dif-ferent aspects of the crisis, its solutions, and any new development that the future may bring, are increasingly interconnected, they imply one another, they require new efforts of holistic understanding and a *new humanistic synthesis*" (*CV* 21). This synthesis would allow recon-sideration of virtue in nonmoralistic terms: "being good" and "well being" need not be enemies; the objective ethics of duty need not clash with the subjective ethics of emotions. This unity, this wholeness of human experience, is very attractive. Within this wholeness, virtue can be learned by sympathy, by admiration, by imitation. Nothing short of virtue can address the complex challenges of our times.

TRACES OF A FRUITFUL DIALOGUE BETWEEN ECONOMICS AND CST

The anthropology of CST valorizes many advances in economic re-search. Good economic theory teaches that building personalized relationships is often essential for trade and for pursuing one's more general objectives; this is especially the case when it is costly or virtu-ally impossible to gather all relevant information, when information is asymmetrically distributed, when economies of scale and market power are relevant, or when we face uncertainty. In many cases, it is also important that personalized relationships be durable; hence, the substantive quality of the relationship matters.

Referring to basic economic experience, economists recognize that perceptions, expectations, motivations, and hopes are the driving forces of material economic decisions and actions; in other words, no material condition can be described without reference to its immate-rial dimension.[15] At the micro level any manager (including a house-wife) can confirm that human motivations make the difference in work performance; in fact, managing human resources typically en-tails a concerted effort to sustain workers' motivation. At the macro level nations flourish and decay for reasons that seem only loosely connected to material wealth and largely related to the substantive set of expectations, beliefs, and motivations of the "all of us" that constitute the nation.[16]

Human work and development may indeed be organized from a technocratic perspective, as if material and objective dimensions were all that mattered; but when this perspective prevails the organization of life in societies, firms, or institutions remains helpless in facing change. Human labor and development, on the contrary, consists in facing the unexpected and driving change, in sharing with other people problems that would find no solution when faced alone. Each step of the development path requires distinguishing good from evil, life from death, bettering of the human condition from worsening. The same applies to societies: development is an intrinsically dynamic process wherein static categories such as *means* and *ends* are totally inappropriate; it is a process we can recognize and measure only by its actual *crescendo*, from less to more "good" things. In a globalized and plural world, we need shared criteria that fit with elementary human experience across a wide spectrum of cultures: Love and truth, beauty, justice, happiness essentially capture the truly "basic needs" for development of each and all persons and societies. Indeed, sound economics needs to address the issues of love and truth.

GRATUITOUSNESS, GIFT, AND ECONOMIC ACTION

Pope Benedict XVI invites us to consider that the economy actually thrives on gifts, even if we do not often stop to think about it.

> Gratuitousness is present in our lives in many different forms, which often go unrecognized because of a purely consumerist and utilitarian view of life. The human being is made for gift, which expresses and makes present his transcendent dimension. Sometimes modern man is wrongly convinced that he is the sole author of himself, his life and society. This is a presumption that follows from being selfishly closed in upon himself. (*CV* 34)

The unreasonable presumption of human omnipotence is unfortunately quite common; the knowledge, physical capital, and infrastructures we actually thrive on are simply the legacy of previous generations to the current generation.[17] The relational logic of gifts is clearly exemplified in transmitting knowledge: it requires an élan for freedom in both the teacher teaching and the pupil paying attention. Human traditions can also be thought of as gifts: what previous generations found valuable to transmit to the next one had to be willingly received. Even material goods actually received from past generations keep challenging human freedom, as they bring with them a symbolic dimension that can be either treasured or disregarded.

There is no need to be romantic about gifts: we know from experience that receiving and giving are ambivalent realities. Gifts do not simply transfer something from one person to another; they convey a meaning: they can be meant to offer true friendship but also to buy injustice, to manipulate others, and to bind them into submission. Gifts, in life as in fairy tales, may be "poisonous";[18] still, the logic of gifts seems omnipresent in nurturing relationships such as market contacts, diplomatic initiatives, and business transactions. Curiously enough—at least from a materialist's point of view—these gifts must be perceived as spontaneous and sincere, or "gratuitous," in order to win a friend or even a client.

The ambivalence of gifts is one aspect of the ambivalence of relations: there is nothing intrinsically good about personal and durable relationships: they may be necessary for reaching one's objectives, no matter how "good" those objectives *(mafias)* are. Ambivalence can be found in the notion of reciprocity as well; reciprocity is one of the most elementary, commonly observed forms of interpersonal and social relationships: *do ut des* in markets and politics, *tit for tat* in repeated games, even *eye for eye, tooth for tooth*. Hence, reciprocity might sustain the pursuit of a good life in common when a true "good" received is reciprocated, but it might equally lead to the disintegration of society, through retaliation.

In addition to recalling that we all thrive on gifts, Pope Benedict XVI affirms that "in *commercial relationships* the *principle of gratuitousness* and the logic of gift as an expression of fraternity can and must *find their place within normal economic activity.* This is a human demand at the present time, but it is also demanded by economic logic" (*CV* 36).

What can we make of this statement? What kind of gratuitousness is required by economic logic? The adjective *gratuitous* has various meanings: it may indicate receiving a useful good without paying money (positive use value, zero exchange value); it may be synonymous with unmotivated, unjustified, and possibly irrational behavior. The kind of gratuitousness *Caritas in Veritate* refers to is connected to the logical priority of receiving; that is, the *gracious* aspect of gratuitousness is demanded by economic logic. Gratuitousness leads us to risk a benevolent action, and this decision flows from having treasured with gratitude the "superabundant" experience of *receiving* (especially receiving the gifts of truth and love, which mean so much for human and social development): "The human being is made for gift, which expresses and makes present his transcendent dimension. . . . [E]conomic, social and political development, if it is to be authentically human, needs to make room for the *principle of gratuitousness* as an expression of fraternity" (*CV* 34).

Gratuitousness relates to fraternal reciprocity (*CV* 38); and fraternity can only be received. We are brothers as we receive paternity; we feel like brothers in recognizing such paternity—that is, in sharing the common belonging which is the source of our freedom.[19] The only perfect Giver (from whom all gifts, all gratuitousness come) is God, Creator Redeemer and Giver of Life. Hence, recognizing that all persons are the image of God founds society: "[C]harity in truth is a force that builds community, it brings all people together without imposing barriers or limits. The human community that we build by ourselves can never, purely by its own strength, be a fully fraternal community" (*CV* 34).

Human gratuitousness, so to speak, can only tend to being "purified" gift: an act of freedom aimed at pursuing what is beautiful, just, true, admirable; what is worthwhile in itself—no matter what (i.e., whether or not this act will be visible, appreciated, reciprocated). In a sense, there is no such thing as "my" gratuitousness, because what is truly beautiful and perfect precedes me and transcends me, and draws me into more deeply desiring it. A truly gratuitous gift is always exceeding the expression of "our own" gratuitousness, as the presence of God's Love is there.

In his address given at the Collège des Bernardins on September 12, 2008, Benedict XVI powerfully exemplified how gratuitousness drives human and social development, referring to the monastic tradition and its tangible and lasting impact on European culture, technology, and economic development. The impressive material development we still benefit from was the unexpected, truly "gratuitous" consequence of the basic content of the monks' daily life: *quaerere Deum* in prayer and imitating God in work *(ora et labora):*

> Their goal was: *quaerere Deum.* Amid the confusion of the times, in which nothing seemed permanent, they wanted to do the essential—to make an effort to find what was perennially valid and lasting, life itself. . . . They wanted to go from the inessential to the essential, to the only truly important and reliable thing there is. . . . [T]hey were seeking the definitive behind the provisional. . . . Monasticism involves . . . a culture of work, without which the emergence of Europe, its *ethos* and its influence on the world would be unthinkable. Naturally, this *ethos* had to include the idea that human work and shaping of history is understood as sharing in the work of the Creator, and must be evaluated in those terms. Where such evaluation is lacking, where man arrogates to himself the status of god-like creator, his shaping of the world can quickly turn into destruction of the world.

The crisis we are experiencing today puts us in a position to see both the creative and the destructive part of human work, and to realistically assess our wounded nature. When God is expelled from our understanding of reality, we experience destruction—yet solutions remain indecipherable. At least as a cry for help, we sense that gratuitousness in charity and truth is needed for society to exist and to develop, that economic activity does require gratuitousness, and that there is no justice without gratuitousness (*CV* 36, 38, 39). But is gratuitousness in charity and truth just a pious aspiration? Can we actually detect and measure it?

These serious questions engage the full breadth of reason, including acknowledging ignorance: reality exists even before we discover it; and not knowing how to measure it does not imply it does not exist. Surely, gratuitousness belongs to the immaterial dimension of human actions, and measurable acts (e.g., volunteer work in a community, not-for-profit initiatives in a population) would work at best as rough approximations: so much gratuitousness goes unnoticed, and the appearance of gratuitousness may be just that. Acts of gratuitousness in charity and truth are different from cheap voluntarism, as they involve the entire person, mind and deeds; they are acts of full-fledged reason, judging what is just and what is unjust, and acts of will, choosing what is just. We may find it hard to isolate gratuitousness in charity and truth; but we can easily detect the *lack* of it, both in micro and macro situations. As Pope Benedict tells us, "Without truth, without trust and love for what is true, there is no social conscience and responsibility, and social action ends up serving private interests and the logic of power, resulting in social fragmentation, especially in a globalized society at difficult times like the present" (*CV* 5).

In the economy, we detect lack of gratuitousness whenever we observe the all-consuming desire for profit and the thirst for power, which are wealth accumulating and wealth appropriating—but definitely not wealth creating. We can also detect lack of gratuitousness in terms of insufficient development-generating actions, such as investment and innovation. Any investment decision is in fact a sort of leap into the void: following one's intuition that it is possible to realize something beautiful, good, and just, in the reasonable hope of improving the human condition, at the cost of risking today some material goods that one could selfishly keep and treasure.

Gratuitousness and hope back all investment: in physical capital (starting a new enterprise), in human capital (from the most obvious, giving birth to a child, to taking care of people, transmitting knowledge, teaching apprentices), in social capital (which also requires investment); in being solicitous to "just" institutions, as opposed to exploiting existing institutions and even depleting their contribution to the common good. So it is only fair to maintain that gratuitousness drives development.

THE ECONOMICS OF HOPE AND CHRISTIAN HOPE

Benedict XVI's teachings on hope include a powerful social dimension, with special reference to development. Development is a path, driven by human gratuitous action in pursuit of what is beautiful, good, and just; it is a risky path, requiring at times a leap of faith that must be sustained by a reasonable, trustworthy hope.

> We see as a distinguishing mark of Christians the fact that they have a future: it is not that they know the details of what awaits them, but they know in general terms that their life will not end in emptiness. Only when the future is certain as a positive reality does it become possible to live the present as well. So now we can say: Christianity was not only "good news"—the communication of a hitherto unknown content. In our language we would say: the Christian message was not only "informative" but "performative." That means: the Gospel is not merely a communication of things that can be known—it is one that makes things happen and is life-changing. The dark door of time, of the future, has been thrown open. The one who has hope lives differently; the one who hopes has been granted the gift of a new life. (*Spe Salvi* 2)

It surely makes sense in economics that "only when the future is certain as a positive reality does it become possible to live the present as well": we need a trustworthy hope to activate our freedom and be economically and socially generative. Any action for development occurs in the present, but it stretches from the past (we thrive on gifts we gratefully received) into the future (a trustworthy hope motivates investment).

Human development is embedded in gratitude—the memory of a received gift, experiencing the gratuitousness of God, Creator and Redeemer—and is driven by hope. Hope and gratuitousness are indeed closely related: "Hope encourages reason and gives it the strength to direct the will. It is already present in faith, indeed it is called forth by faith. Charity in truth feeds on hope and, at the same time, manifests it. As the absolutely gratuitous gift of God, hope bursts into our lives as something not due to us, something that transcends every law of justice. Gift by its nature goes beyond merit, its rule is that of superabundance" (*CV* 34).

In its essence, any reasonable hope is based on recognizing the ultimate goodness of creation. The world is good, "indeed very good": the more we discover about the universe, the more we are surprised by the incredible number of favorable coincidences that made human life on earth possible.

The anthropology of CST in general, and Pope Benedict's teaching on hope in particular, resonates with some contributions at the frontier of economic research on reasonable human decisions in conditions of uncertainty. There is a well-developed body of economic research concerning decisions in risky situations, most of which can be summarized along the lines of expected utility based on prior probabilities. Yet recent thoughtful research[20] helps push forward our understanding of human action in uncertain environments—especially in "strong" uncertainty.[21] In many circumstances, ignorance is simply a fact: it is rational to recognize that one does not have sufficient information to form probability priors and behave accordingly. Deciding on the basis of expected utility would be quite unreasonable! In these cases some sort of compromise is needed: one can refer to a "default" choice that has been developed and accepted within a community (as in health professions) or incorporate "caution" in decisions (we could say, exercise the virtue of prudence). As a minimum condition, a reasonable choice under uncertainty requires that one not hold beliefs contrary to objective available data and to logical reasoning. An even higher standard of rationality demands subscribing only to beliefs that can be persuasively justified to others (a narrative can be provided to those who ask for the reasons of our decisions).

That is, sound economic analysis maintains that community belonging, virtue, and dialogue matter for qualifying decisions under uncertainty as rational.[22] This broader view of what is rational in uncertain situations resonates very much with a relational, dynamic, realistic, and "whole" anthropology. Default practices are inherently developed and dynamically adapted within a community; caution is a way of expressing the virtue of prudence; realistically acknowledging ignorance and giving justification for one's beliefs is a way of saying that we are in relation to (material and immaterial) reality and others. Indeed, we are not "lost atom[s] in a random universe" (*CV* 29).

Strong uncertainty is enhanced in periods of systemic change, as today. Which decision would be most reasonable (effective and efficient) under structural change? Which attitude is more conducive to providing an effective answer to human needs, which are unfinished by nature? If any answer can be given to this question, it must include the word *hope*. The founders of monasteries, the great travelers of the past, the many saints that created huge enterprises (often aimed at reducing the negative effects of uncertainty in the lives of the poor and the needy), and even artisans and entrepreneurs have been protagonists of changes that went beyond their calculated intentions. Their work was the answer to a calling they perceived in reality, challenging their freedom; they discerned the possibility to transform problems into opportunities. They took the risk of action, as hope moved them—a reasonable, trustworthy hope. They held beliefs they could share with others; they were able to persuade others to get involved in their human adventure, providing reasonable justifications for their intentions and deeds. They could give good reasons for their hope. Hope is completely different from illusion, utopia, and dreams. Deciding on the basis of hope implies being aware of one's ignorance, one's limits, and even one's "wounded nature"—just the opposite with respect to the presumption of omnipotence.

HOPE AND JUST INSTITUTIONS

Strong uncertainty is deeply ambivalent. Many social institutions we are accustomed to would have no reason to exist in a world of "certainty": pacts and alliances among human beings; reliance on third-party authority to resolve controversies; money itself, which is a peculiar form of language—these would have no role in a "certain" world. These institutions indicate that human beings can cope with strong uncertainty, not simply because it is unavoidable, but because it is viewed as an opportunity for sharing more than just a temporary convergence of interests. Strong uncertainty requires strong relations, including social organizations devoted to assisting the unlucky who will end up suffering the most from current uncertainty.

In today's globalized world, which "makes us neighbours but does not make us brothers" (*CV* 19), integration with solidarity (*CV* 53) requires institutions of justice. While injustice can occur between individuals and within small communities, it cannot be denied that injustice can also stem from the actions of local, national, and international institutions and organizations, both governmental and nongovernmental.

How can our generation contribute to building just institutions? This crucial topic was interestingly addressed by Benedict XVI during his opening speech at Aparecida before the Latin American Bishops' Conference, in a tight question-and-answer format that is so typical of him.

> In truth, just structures are a condition without which a just order in society is not possible. But how do they arise? How do they function? Both capitalism and Marxism promised to point out the path for the creation of just structures, and they declared that these, once established, would function by themselves. . . . [T]his ideological promise has been proved false. The facts have clearly demonstrated it. . . . Just structures . . . neither arise nor function without a moral consensus in society on fundamental values, and on the need to live these values with the necessary sacrifices, even if this goes against personal interest. . . . [J]ust structures must be sought and elaborated . . . with the full engagement of political, economic and social reasoning. They are a question of *recta ratio.* . . . Just structures will never be complete in a definitive way. As history continues to evolve, they must be constantly re-

newed and updated. (Address of Benedict XVI to the Inaugural Session of the Fifth General CELAM Conference, Aparecida, May 13, 2007, par. 4, *Social and Political Problems*)

Spe Salvi connects building institutions for social justice and social progress with hope. Hope, in fact, drives the élan of freedom that constantly renews and updates those institutions.

> Let us ask once again: what may we hope? And what may we not hope? First of all, we must acknowledge that incremental progress is possible only in the material sphere. Here, . . . we clearly see continuous progress towards an ever greater mastery of nature. Yet in the field of ethical awareness and moral decision-making, there is no similar possibility of accumulation for the simple reason that man's freedom is always new and he must always make his decisions anew. . . . This, however, means that . . . [t]he right state of human affairs . . . can never be guaranteed simply through structures alone, however good they are. Such structures are not only important, but necessary; yet they cannot and must not marginalize human freedom. Even the best structures function only when the community is animated by convictions capable of motivating people to assent freely to the social order. . . . If there were structures which could irrevocably guarantee a determined— good—state of the world, man's freedom would be denied, and hence they would not be good structures. (*Spe Salvi* 24)

The term *moral consensus* that we find in the Aparecida Address is reformulated in *Spe Salvi* as "convictions capable of motivating people to assent freely to the social order." These expressions are especially interesting to social scientists, as they innovate with respect to the notion of both overlapping consensus (minimum common ground) and democratic consensus (majority rule). Moral consensus is a relational procedure, requiring argumentative dialogue on core values that all persons share, as they can be learned from elemental human experience.[23]

Love and truth are indeed the shortest list of such values. Hence, action for justice comes from true love and expresses true love. Benedict XVI repeatedly elaborates on justice and charity, claiming that "love—*caritas*—will always prove necessary, even in the most just society" (*Deus Caritas Est* 28).

> *Ubi societas, ibi ius:* every society draws up its own system of justice. *Charity goes beyond justice,* because to love is to give, to offer what is "mine" to the other; but it never lacks justice, which prompts us to give the other what is "his." . . . [J]ustice is inseparable from charity, and intrinsic to it. Justice is the primary way of charity. . . . On the one hand, charity demands justice: recognition and respect for the legitimate rights of individuals and peoples. It strives to build the *earthly city* according to law and justice. On the other hand, charity transcends justice and completes it in the logic of giving and forgiving. The *earthly city* is promoted not merely by relationships of rights and duties, but to an even greater and more fundamental extent by relationships of gratuitousness, mercy and communion. (*CV* 6)

Justice in charity, we read, is offering what is "mine" to the other. But: can we say something is truly "our own"? What is really "mine"? The answer is: my freedom, myself in action, driven by the Infinity for which I thirst. This tension with the infinite truth and love keeps us working for justice and not surrendering to the logic of power and interest. For Christians, being workers of true justice is rooted in "gratuitously" being made just:

> As Christians, we must constantly be reminded that the call of justice is not something which can be reduced to the categories of this world. . . . [O]nly when we Christians grasp our vocation, as having been created in the image of God . . . can we address the urgent social problems of our time from a truly Christian perspective. To be workers of this true justice, we must be workers who are being made just by contact with Him who is justice itself: Jesus of Nazareth. The place of this encounter is the Church,

nowhere more powerfully present than in her sacraments and liturgy. (Cardinal J. Ratzinger, Homily, St. Peter's Basilica, March 18, 2005, Conference "Call to Justice" on the fortieth anniversary of *Gaudium et Spes*)

WHAT ELSE COULD DRIVE DEVELOPMENT?

The alternative to gratuitousness and hope could be programs, projects, techniques, policies. These alternatives seem rather obvious to our generation, since we live in a world characterized by the preeminence of the sphere of production of goods and services and by a technocratic ideology (cf. *CV* 14, 70) in which "too much attention is given to the 'how' questions, and not enough to the many 'why' questions underlying human activity" (*CV* 70). For example, if you care about reaching a predefined, internationally agreed on set of development indicators, you will rationally look for the best technical solutions to be efficiently implemented. The more seriously you care about material outcome, the more you will be inclined to technocratic solutions; as a consequence, all the more you will focus on material conditions, and not human freedom, as the crucial driver of growth. You will control resources, and allocate them; and maybe appropriate them, or simply waste them.

Bread may become stones, as in this passage from Benedict XVI's *Jesus of Nazareth*:

The German Jesuit Alfred Delp, who was executed by the Nazis, once wrote: "Bread is important, freedom is more important, but most important of all is unbroken fidelity and faithful adoration."

When this ordering of goods is no longer respected, but turned on its head, the result is not justice or concern for human suffering. The result is rather ruin and destruction even of material goods themselves. When God is regarded as a secondary matter that can be set aside temporarily or permanently on account of more important things, it is precisely these supposedly more important things that come to nothing. It is not just the negative outcome of the Marxist experiment that proves this.

The aid offered by the West to developing countries has been purely technically and materially based, and not only has left God out of the picture, but has driven men away from God. And this aid, proudly claiming to "know better," is itself what first turned the "third world" into what we mean today by that term. It has thrust aside indigenous religious, ethical, and social structures and filled the resulting vacuum with its technocratic mind-set. The idea was that we could turn stones into bread; instead, our "aid" has only given stones in place of bread. The issue is the primacy of God. The issue is acknowledging that he is a reality, that he is the reality without which nothing else can be good.[24]

Caritas in Veritate is very effective and sharp in denouncing how technocratic perspectives in development easily end up serving the interests of those in power—both state and nonstate actors—and yield no benefit to the poor. Resistance to technocratic perspectives entails giving God the right place in the world; hence, it is a matter of truth: "Development, social well-being, . . . all need this truth. . . . Without truth, without trust and love for what is true, there is no social conscience and responsibility, and social action ends up serving private interests and the logic of power, resulting in social fragmentation, especially in a globalized society at difficult times like the present" (*CV* 5).[25]

In our plural world, pursuing development—integration with solidarity—by trying to reach abstract universal agreements is either impossible (because culturally specific values and priorities may never fit together in any meaningful, operational way) or sterile (agreements can be formally reached only on "cloudy" notions that do not encounter strenuous opposition, and for the same reason cannot really make the difference). Trying to strike deals, to reach a compromise, is a necessary but by no means sufficient action. Global development stems from human freedom "in action," rooted in gratuitousness and driven by hope, steadily pursuing the humble path of a dialogue where truth is loved per se and loving aspires to *true* love. So development is a humble and fascinating path along which plurality can be recognized and valorized, within the basic grammar of human dialogue: "All people feel the interior impulse to love authentically: love and truth never abandon them completely, because these are the vocation planted by God in the heart and mind of every human person" (*CV* 1).

NOTES

1. The full title of the letter is "Encyclical Letter *Caritas in Veritate* of the Supreme Pontiff Benedict XVI to the Bishops, Priests, and Deacons, Men and Women Religious, the Lay Faithful, and All People of Good Will on Integral Human Development in Charity and Truth."

2. Quotations from encyclicals are taken from the English version of the official Vatican website, www.vatican.va. Italics are reproduced as in the original texts. For *Caritas in Veritate,* see http://www.vatican.va/holy_father/benedict_xvi/encyclicals/documents/hf_bene-xvi_enc_20090629_caritas-in-veritate_en.html.

3. *CV* repeatedly challenges dualisms: moral evaluation and progress (14), life ethics and social ethics (15), culture and nature (26), ethics and scientific research (31), economic science and ethics (32), economic action and political action (36). In economics *CV* denounces the juxtaposition of economics to politics, state to market, and market to society; the separation of "private" and "public" and "profit" and "nonprofit" organizations (36, 39, 41, 46); the "real" and "financial" economy (45), efficiency and ethics (50).

4. As to Italy, we can mention studies on the civil economy (L. Bruni and S. Zamagni, *Dizionario di Economia Civile* [Rome: Città Nuova Editrice, 2009]) and on business oganizations pursuing social ends (L. Bruni and A. Smerilli, *La leggerezza del ferro* [Milan: Vita e Pensiero, 2011]).

5. For example, in Anglican milieus, the point is raised that the economics of Benedict XVI, dealing with the civil economy, is tracing a much needed "third way" between the excesses of markets and the state, thus providing what seems to be a plausible way out of the global economic crisis—a way likely to attract consensus both within the Christian world and in other milieus. A. Pabst, ed., *The Crisis of Global Capitalism: Pope Benedict XVI's Social Encyclical and the Future of Political Economy* (Eugene, OR: Cascade Books, 2011).

6. For example, in his address given at Westminster Hall on September 17, 2010, Benedict XVI made the point that objective norms which

govern righteous actions are accessible to reason; reason helps purify religion, and religion purifies reason. In his address to the UN Assembly on April 18, 2006, he called for a rediscovery of the authentic image of creation, where the rational use of technology and science never requires choosing between science and ethics.

7. Limiting excessive disparities in wealth distribution and prioritizing the goal of access to steady employment for everyone are required by "economic logic" (*CV* 32); economic logic also demands that the principle of gratuitousness and the logic of gift as an expression of fraternity can and must find their place in normal economic activity (*CV* 36).

8. Innovating economic thinking is often spelled out in terms of abandoning the "mainstream" for an exploration of "alternative" economic models and perspectives, but this is neither necessary nor sufficient. Cheap economic reasoning that reduces economics to optimizing techniques is wrongly taking a detail for the whole; yet sound and sharp mainstream economics can be very useful, both in exploring economic decisions and their consequences and in showing under which (usually very strict) conditions those explorations can be taken to hold.

9. A. Scola, *Ospitare il reale: Per una "idea" di università* (Rome: Pontificia Università Lateranense-Mursia, 1999).

10. This innovative definition of the common good allows exploring the social order in today's plural world in a way that can overcome the limitations of narrow contractualist or communitarian perspectives. See A. Scola, *Buone ragioni per la vita in comune: Religione, politica, economia* (Milan: Mondadori, 2010).

11. As an Ambrosian Catholic, I cannot help thinking about Saint Ambrose's *felix culpa.*

12. Each researcher, each discipline, discovers this "superabundance" (*CV* 34) in specific ways, and we can experience superabundance precisely because we do not *produce* reality.

13. Interview with the Holy Father Benedict XVI during the flight to Mexico, Friday, March 23, 2012, www.vatican.va/holy_father/benedict_xvi/speeches/2012/march/documents/hf_ben-xvi_spe_20120323_incontro-giornalisti_en.html.

14. See Benedict XVI, Aparecida Address, May 13, 2007, on the way and the Way to justice and development.

15. Extremely poor people actually describe their experience of being poor using words such as humiliation, fear, shame, despair. See N. Deepa, R. Patel, K. Schafft, A. Rademacher, and S. Koch-Schulte, *Voices of the Poor: Can Anyone Hear Us?* (New York: Oxford University Press for the World Bank, 2000).

16. This is suggested by a variety of authors, from A. de Tocqueville, *Democracy in America*, 1835–40, to M. Olson, *The Rise and Decline of Nations: Economic Growth, Stagflation, and Social Rigidities* (New Haven: Yale University Press, 1982).

17. The logic of gift in human work and development is clearly spelled out also in Pope John Paul II's encyclicals, especially *Laborem Exercens*. See S. Beretta, "Wealth Creation in the Global Economy: Human Labor and Development," in *Rediscovering Abundance: Interdisciplinary Essays on Wealth, Income and Their Distribution in the Catholic Social Tradition*, ed. H. Alford, C. Clark, S. A. Cortright, and M. Naughton (Notre Dame: University of Notre Dame Press, 2005), 175–201.

18. J. T. Godbout, *Ce qui circule entre nous: Donner, recevoir, render* (Paris: Editions du Seuil, 2007). Benedict XVI refers to some forms of international aid as potentially "poisonous" gifts (*CV* 22, 28, 47, 58).

19. In Latin, the same word expresses being free and being a son.

20. I. Gilboa, A. Postlewaite, and D. Schmiedler, "Is It Always Rational to Satisfy Savage's Axioms?" *Economics and Philosophy* 25 (2009): 285–96, and related literature.

21. "Strong" uncertainty refers to many circumstances in which we simply cannot list all possible outcomes of a choice. This is the case when initiating scientific research, introducing innovation in processes and products, experimenting with new treatments for terrible illnesses, bombing a potential enemy, and so on. In all these situations, which are among the most critical for economic, social, and personal lives, we do choose—either to act or to withdraw action; so understanding how we choose is essential for understanding development.

22. Schmeidler and his coauthors appropriately notice that this compromise is similar to compromises made in moral dilemmas, and that we must be prepared to face conflicts between different demands of rationality: sometimes we may need to relax internal consistency, sometimes to lower our standards of justification for choice.

23. L. Giussani, *The Religious Sense*, trans. John Zucchi (Montreal: McGill-Queen's University Press, 1997).

24. Benedict XVI, *Jesus of Nazareth: From the Baptism in the Jordan to the Transfiguration*, trans. Adrian J. Walker (New York: Doubleday, 2007), 33–34.

25. See also Benedict XVI, address prepared for the visit at the Università La Sapienza, Rome, January 17, 2008.

God Is Love

chapter eight

PAPAL ECCLESIOLOGY

FRANCESCA ARAN MURPHY

AN ECUMENICAL ECCLESIOLOGY

To many Catholics, Ratzinger's "universalist" ecclesiology represents a top-down idea of the Church, that is, a conception of the Church as a Platonic Idea that generates its local variants. If I had had any interest in ecclesiology before I went to Aberdeen in 1995, those Catholics could have included me, alongside Cardinal Kasper. Fourteen years later I entertained my friend and teacher, the biblical scholar Richard Bauckham, at dinner in my home. He began to tease me, saying that all German theologians are Lutheran theologians, and, therefore, Joseph Ratzinger is a Lutheran theologian. I had to take this teasing with good humor, because it made sense of teaching Ratzinger's theology to Protestants in Aberdeen. To these Presbyterians, Ratzinger was not starting from an abstract Platonic Idea but from the biblical God whose actions are concrete works of salvation. They were not put out by Ratzinger's claim that "for Paul the Church is constituted as a subject by her head"; that is, "she continues to be a unified entity only by grace."[1] Ratzinger is in tune with their belief in the priority of God and of grace. The Protestants liked Ratzinger's biblical-mindedness.

We taught the first-year theology students using two textbooks, Karl Barth's *Credo* and Ratzinger's *Introduction to Christianity*. This early book exemplifies Ratzinger's continuous practice of keeping Protestant interlocutors within earshot. He draws on Barth's claim that in the *name* Jesus Christ "existence and mission are identical": Christ's *sending* is his very being. Ratzinger can use the formula ecumenically, because it unites the Catholic and Orthodox focus on the *being* of Christ with the Protestant focus on his salvific action and deed. Christ's being, Ratzinger says, "is *actualitas*, . . . going out from self, . . . the act of being sent," and his "'doing'" "reaches down into the depths of being and coincides with it."[2] This intuition has stayed with Ratzinger: he claims in his second book, about Jesus of Nazareth, that "Being with him includes the missionary dynamic by its very nature, since Jesus' whole being is mission."[3] Just as Christ is "the Apostle of the Father," the one sent by the Father, "so . . . those whom he sends as apostles represent what he is in himself."[4] "Being a Christian," Ratzinger claims, "means changing over from being for oneself to being for another."[5] Apostolicity is the "being" and the doing of the Church, its expression of love.

In 2005 I ran a conference at Aberdeen, on *Ut Unum Sint*. The 1995 encyclical asks Orthodox and Protestant Christians to say how papal primacy can be configured so as to be a mark of unity rather than division. Either *Ut Unum Sint* made a mark on Ratzinger or he set his mark on it. Many of his signature themes are in the encyclical, from the power of prayer to the healing of memory by apology and forgiveness and love. Because Ratzinger's understanding of love is *dispossessive*, he is open to organic development of Petrine jurisdiction. That includes, of course, not only the first but also the second millennium of Christian life.

Ratzinger is a fundamentally pastoral theologian. So he often buttonholes Lutherans about where they go wrong. But he also assimilates what he thinks is valuable in the "other" that is Protestantism. So here we have a theologian conversant with Lutheranism to whom it has been said, "Thou art Peter, and I give you the keys of the kingdom." Simultaneously, we find one who is qualified to appreciate the theological meaning of these words. This essay is a reflection on a "papal ecclesiology" conducted in an irenic and ecumenical spirit. Ratzinger is profoundly out of tune with what he sees as the absence of love in Luther's theology.[6] The essay thus concludes by mentioning the place of love in the developing relations between Catholic and Orthodox Christians.

THREE PATHS, THE KEY, AND THE DOOR IT UNLOCKS

The three paths on which Ratzinger's theology circles are tradition, Scripture, and the Church. He sees tradition not as a companion to Scripture but as the source of Scripture. He treats tradition as an anthropological datum. Ratzinger is one of those German thinkers, like Adam Möhler and Josef Pieper, who are fascinated by the idea of a "primordial" tradition, a divine revelation to the first human beings. He doesn't imagine that, at the dawn of civilization, human beings were given a divine revelation. Rather, featherless bipeds were *humanized* by their reception and transmission of revelation. Human "nature" is not a static essence but a historically original ability to hear the divine word. Ratzinger says, "Primordial revelation . . . mean[s] that there occurred . . . the formation of subjects who would be bearers of tradition. . . . [I]t . . . mean[s] also the possibility of fall, of infidelity, of pride. . . . [O]riginal sin, then, . . . mean[s] this: the *humanum* is rooted in tradition, to the beginnings of which there belongs, above all, the ability to hear the Other (whom we call God)."[7] So human nature and its sinfulness are alike rooted in the capacity to hear and transmit the Word of God, the capacity for tradition.

In his 1967 commentary on *Dei Verbum* Ratzinger praises the Vatican II constitution for avoiding "ecclesio-monism" and instead focusing on "listening, an attitude in which the Church transcends itself, for it is not there for its own sake, but only to lead to . . . God the Lord." Ratzinger observes that revelation comes to its end in Christ, because "in him God has . . . said himself. In him the dialogue of God has attained its goal; it has become a union."[8] All "subsequent history" is the effort to "catch up . . . gradually" with what has been said in Christ, meaning "to catch up all humanity" in "the one and only Adam." That is the slow, historical "osmosis" of Christ's divine word into the members of his body the Church, making all into hearers of the Word. Fifteen years later, in *Principles of Catholic Theology*, Ratzinger asks how theologians can really *listen* to God speaking through Scripture instead of testing and measuring it by their own "philosophical" ideas. He notes two suggestions from Gregory of Nyssa. One is that there is in us a "longing to break out" of self-absorption, which is a "pointer toward unending love." This "longing" is the spot in which the human being "is a mirror" and "reflection" of God. So, although we human beings cannot "transcend" ourselves, "God can enter" that space of resemblance, which is longing. This brings a second insight, that "this entering of God into man took a historical form in the Incarnation. . . . God wounds the soul—the Son is this wound, and we are thereby laid open. The new agent, the Adam who is becoming one in the Church, is in touch with the Son and, thus, with the threefold God himself, from within. Thomas Aquinas framed these two ideas in metaphysical terms in the principles of analogy and participation and thus made possible an open philosophy, which is able to accept the biblical phenomenon in all its radicalism."[9]

Nonetheless, Scripture was composed by human beings over many millennia, and the interpretation of it has changed over time. Hindsight shows that every epoch which imagined it had uncovered "the truth" of Scripture was merely reflecting itself back into Scripture. If human nature is historical and if Scripture and its interpretation are human phenomena, then it is not easy to see how to uncover a "true" interpretation of the revelation of God contained in the human word of Scripture. Just as historical consciousness raises the question of whether there is some one single truth about human nature, so too it creates the dilemma of whether Scripture is a single unified whole. Ratzinger comments that "we always find the Church in the tension between what is changeable and what is unchangeable."[10] The tension between the changeable and the unchangeable is at bottom the tension between the mortal and the eternal. It is the

Resurrection of Christ which pulls together all the strands of Scripture into a single, canonical whole. The Resurrection reframes the past, refiguring all the historic biblical images around itself. Reading Scripture ecclesially means reading it in the resurrected body of Christ: this is the key to the problem of hermeneutics.

It would be depressing if the key to ecclesial reading of Scripture opened a door into a more knowledgeable ecclesiology. In fact, the door opens on eternal life. The keys of the kingdom are keys to immortality. The keys of the kingdom are given to address human "longing" for God. Without the gift of the keys, the door to eternity remains locked. "Justification by works," Ratzinger says, means striving "to construct a little immortality" of our "own." He compares "the philosopher," like Plato, who tries to auto-immortalize, with "Peter on the lake, wishing to step beyond mortality . . . but not succeeding, indeed sinking beneath the waves. For all his capacity to speculate about immortality . . . he cannot stand. . . . Only the Lord's outstretched hand can save sinking Peter, that is, humankind. . . . Philosophical understanding . . . yields no solid ground. Only God incarnate can draw us out of the waters by his power and hold us firm." "Immortality points to a praxis of receiving": it is, Ratzinger claims, essentially relational. Self-sufficient human individuals are not hard-wired for immortality: rather, it is the "relatedness . . . constitutive of human nature" which orients it to eternity. Echoing Gabriel Marcel's contention that the lover's belief that his beloved will never die points to the reality of God, Ratzinger argues that "desire for immortality" springs "from the experience of love, . . . communion, . . . the Thou." God himself, he says, is relationship, meaning, is love. But relationship as an eternal essence does not make for immortality. Rather, our immortality flows from God's own deed: "The living and dying of Christ tells us that God himself descends into the pit of Sheol, that in the land of absolute loneliness he makes relationship possible, . . . giving life in the midst of death." Since the gift of immortality is the result of Christ's dispossession of self, "martyrdom with Christ" belongs to the defeat of death. It consists in "granting truth more importance than self." If "death" is the closing down of communication, then its opposite is "the movement of love itself."[11]

These opening remarks about the three paths, the key to which they lead, and the door it opens have implicitly depicted most of Ratzinger's ecclesiology. I began by noting a rather Lutheran-sounding defect in tradition: tradition conjointly bears human nature and human sinfulness. I conclude this section by noting Ratzinger's solution to that dilemma: it is that the life, death, and resurrection of Jesus Christ is a historical remaking of primordial tradition: "the Christian sees in Jesus a point of access to the center of tradition, . . . where tradition is . . . a breakthrough to what was in the beginning . . . reveal[ing] the ground on which it rests." Reading tradition in line with Jesus' relation to the Father shields the Christian against falsified tradition and against fleeing tradition for false reasons. The Christian "interprets tradition in conversation with God, the Father of Jesus Christ. . . . What Jesus reveals as a basic . . . tradition is . . . not a multiplicity of tenets, but the simple and ancient credo of Israel: God is. . . . Jesus is a radical Jew—it is a question of God's existence as God. . . . The Resurrection is but the most extreme concretization of this statement: God is. It shows that God is in-deed *[wirklich]*, for being is doing and God's being is the life that overcomes death. That God is in-deed means that there is a truth of man in which the goals of his intellectual inquiry find their limits and their measure."[12]

THE "INSTITUTIONAL CHURCH" VERSUS THE "LIVING CHURCH"

Ratzinger speaks autobiographically about having been stirred by Romano Guardini's phrase, "the Church is awakening in men's souls." To the young Ratzinger, this was a wonderful insight, for it presents the Church "not like some machinery that exists over against us but as something . . . alive within us[,] . . . the organism of the Holy Spirit, something alive that embraces us all from within." He says that before Guardini, "the question of papal primacy was so much foregrounded that the Church appeared . . . as a centrally directed institution . . . which [one] only encountered externally."[13]

In the same book, Ratzinger bluntly denigrates a document produced by the Anglican–Roman Catholic ecumenical committee, which speaks of "our two traditions" and claims that "Apostolic succession" could belong to one of these two, but not the other, without their unity being impaired. Is this an unjustifiable sideswipe? Not really. That ARCIC document is a prolongation of the same scholastic, institutional conception of the Church as a lego structure from which unwanted pieces can be detached by fiat of a clerical committee. It is as a "pneumatic" champion of the "living Church" against the institutional bureaucracy that Ratzinger complained that that ARCIC document had an external and mechanistic conception of Church unity and tradition.[14]

Ratzinger observes that Augustine teaches that the Holy Spirit "causes us to abide in God, and God in us. But love does this." Love "abides," builds a home. Hence, the "activity of the Spirit is 'the house,' the granting of the home. Unity. Because the Spirit is love." The activity of the Spirit is known by love, just as unholy spirits are discerned by the opposite. Hence, for Augustine, the Church is *most authentically* herself in her pneumatological aspect: "the Church herself— when she truly exists as Church—is a creation of the Spirit."[15] Cyril O'Regan has brilliantly shown in his essay in this volume the depth of Ratzinger's engagement with Augustine.

Nonetheless, Augustine's idea of the Church "truly" existing under certain conditions can be problematic. It can make one imagine that there are two churches, the authentically true and the false! The Reformers made much of Augustine's "dichotomy" between the personal and the impersonal aspects of the Church.[16] Ratzinger claims that Augustine was the source of a dualistic conception of the Church as enclosing a "true," interior, elect kernel, which extrudes an external, "apparent" husk. When instrumentalized in the late Middle Ages alongside the use of excommunication as a political weapon, this remnant of "Augustinian" ecclesiology fired the excommunicate Luther's bullish belief that *he* constituted the interior, elect group. The sense of the Church as communion had long been depreciated by the sale of episcopal sees: as Ratzinger tells the story, Luther only made that loss apparent. Luther ratified his break with the Church's communion by eliminating from the eucharistic celebration the element which unifies the participants. Ratzinger invented his "communio ecclesiology" to avoid "Augustinian" dualism. The divine action which welds the practice of interior spirituality and the external Church into a single subject is the Eucharist.[17] When Ratzinger says that Christ is "contemporaneous with us" and we with him, because the "Church is the presence of Christ," he means "presence" literally.[18]

COMMUNIO ECCLESIOLOGY

Ratzinger's communio ecclesiology has three aspects: the Church as "subject," as "communion," and as "eucharistic."

The Church as "Subject"

In his simple and effective book about Ratzinger, Laurence Hemming notes that the theologian took from Bonaventure the principle that "Divine Revelation is God's approach *toward* man. God's divine self-disclosure—. . . his *disclosing* of himself . . . is *God's*, not *our*, initiative. Such an initiative . . . is always *for*, and so *given to*, some*one*."[19] To call the Church a "subject" means that she is the *recipient* of divine self-disclosure. To say she is the *subject* of revelation means God speaks about himself *to* her.

The Church as subject also *sees* the divine form of Christ. Describing how in Luke's Gospel, a scene in which Jesus prays precedes the scene of Peter's confession, Ratzinger says that "the disciples" are allowed "to see" Jesus "the one who . . . speaks face-to-face with the Father. . . . They are privileged to see him in his utterly unique filial being. . . . This seeing is the wellspring of their faith, their confession; it provides the foundation of the Church."[20]

Seeing and really assenting to the revelation gives the Church a stock of life-forming images. There is a pattern in human life and human history whereby we forget and dimly recall and remember our basic images. The Church as subject *remembers* the revelation, pondering God's words and actions. The "memory of the Church" is thus the "seat of faith," that place in the heart of the subject-recipient where the revelation comes back to haunt us. The Church remembers, and is formed by the one whom she remembers. It's this remembering which makes her an integral subject. As *subject* of God's initiative, the Church is Communio, because the Triune God is communio, an "ecstatic" and entire "going out from himself." The divine dialogue partner shapes his Thou as Communio.[21]

The Church as "Communion"

The notion of the Church as "communion" flows from conceiving the dialogue between God and humanity as not just verbal but sacramental. Following *Lumen Gentium,* the Church as communion is conceived as *the sacrament* of God. Communion is less virtual than dialogue and more physically intimate. In communion persons come together around a table. The Church is *sacrament* because, Ratzinger says, "she is God's communing with men and hence the communion of men with each other."[22] In this sense the ecclesiology of communion is a development of "mystical body ecclesiology," which imagines the Church as a human "participation" in "that communion between man and God which is the Incarnation." There are one or two lovely Greek myths in which a pair of gods, posing as elderly travelers, dine with a pair of poor and ignorant but hospitable humans. I read those stories as a child and thought it would be marvelous to eat with Zeus and Athena but rather a comedown to be turned into a tree as a reward. Plato was the heir to such primordial traditions, and, according to Ratzinger, he imagined sacrifice and the cult as aiming at "reciprocal communion between the gods and men ('η περι θεους κοινωνια)," a communion that gives rise to human community. When such communion is achieved, it is not as the result "of a new synthesis of *thought,* but [as] the fruit of a new *reality* which was previously nonexistent." In Christ, the triune love of God dines with human beings, "unveil[ing] his innermost life" as "a dialogue of eternal love." The Church as communion is the Church as transforming participation in that love. Paul's word for "participation" is the same as

Plato's: "the cup of blessing" and the "bread which we break" are each
κοινωνια in the body of Christ. As a "relationship created by the love
of Christ" the Church "founds a new relationship between men. We
can echo those beautiful words of Plato and say that the Eucharist is
in fact the 'healing of our love.'"[23]

The Church as "Eucharistic"

The third element of communio ecclesiology is thus the Church as
"eucharistic." It originated in Henri de Lubac's reminder of the patristic and early medieval habit of referring equally to the Eucharist and
the Church as "the body of Christ." The Eucharist as body was perceived to create the Church, its embodiment. "There now arose," Ratzinger recalls, "a eucharistic ecclesiology which people also liked to term
an ecclesiology of communion."[24] Communio ecclesiology started life
as a eucharistic image of the Church. For Ratzinger, the point of it was
to mediate between external conceptions of the Church, such as ultrapapalism, and internalist or charismatic ecclesiologies. As Aidan
Nichols puts it, Ratzinger is, "along with Henri de Lubac, one of the
first Catholic thinkers to adopt a . . . 'Eucharistic ecclesiology'. In the
sacrament of the true sacrifice of Christians, lies the inner *Leib-
Christi-Sein* of the holy, their existence as the body of Christ. . . .
[M]ost inwardly of all . . . lies the *caritas* which *is* the Spirit of Christ."[25]
"The biblical and patristic word κοινονια unites in itself the two
meanings 'Eucharist' and 'community' (fellowship)," says Ratzinger the
scriptural and patristic scholar.[26] "The word κοινονια unites two realities[,] . . . communion as sacrament and communion as a social and
institutional reality."[27] Fellowship entails the ability to see Christ in
our fellows, especially the poor. We can only see Christ in the poor if
we know what he looks like, only if we know his face: that face is up
close and personal in the Eucharist.[28] The Church as subject, as communio, and as Eucharist is created by receiving the Word of the Lord:
to "say that the last supper is the origin of the Church . . . means . . .
that the eucharist links men and women . . . with Christ and . . . in this
way . . . turns people into the Church." Hence the Church both as institution and as charismatic "lives in eucharistic communities."[29]

THE BISHOPS: APOSTOLIC SUCCESSION

Luther defines the Church as truly existing where the gospel is proclaimed and the sacraments rightly performed. At the very beginning of his *Church Dogmatics* Barth explains that theology is "a function of the Church." He says that what the Church does is to "confess God" by speaking about God: the Church "does so first by its existence in the action of each individual believer. And it does so secondly by its specific action as a fellowship, in proclamation by preaching and the administration of the sacraments, in worship, in its internal and external mission including works of love amongst the sick." Barth defines the Church as an event of *witnessing* to God's revelation:

> When the Canon, the staff which commands and sets moving and points the way, is moved by a living stretched-out hand, . . . then it bears witness, and by this act of witness it establishes the relation of the Church to revelation, and therewith establishes the Church itself as the true Church. . . . By its witness! Witnessing means pointing in a specific direction beyond the self and on to another. Witnessing is thus service to this other in which the witness vouches for the truth of the other, the service which consists in referring to this other. This service is constitutive for the concept of the prophet and also for that of the apostle. . . . Standing in this service, the biblical witnesses point beyond themselves. If we understand them as witnesses . . . then their self must be . . . understood by us from the standpoint of its form as a reference away from themselves. . . . [W]hat makes man a witness is solely and exclusively that other, the thing attested, which constrains and limits the perfect or imperfect human organ from without.

Thus, for Barth, the Bible as a text is God's revelation as a "deposit," but ecclesial proclamation and witness to the revelation is the *living* Word, the revelation as brought to life in the event of pointing to God. It is "apostolic succession" which holds together the Bible as text and the Bible as proclaimed word:

The apostolic succession of the Church must mean that it is guided by the Canon, that is, by the prophetic and apostolic word as the necessary rule of every word that is valid in the Church. It must mean that the Church enters into the succession of the prophets and apostles in their office of proclamation, and does so in such a way that their proclamation freely and independently precedes, while that of the Church is related to it, is ventured in obedience on the basis of it, is measured by it, and replaces it only as and to the extent that it conforms to it.[30]

Barth defines apostolic succession in terms of proclamation and witness.

Ratzinger embraces these conceptions of apostolic succession and of the Church and takes them to a Catholic conclusion. Thus when he explains apostolic succession he considers the practice of the early Church and cites Paul's Letter to the Romans: "But how are men to call upon him in whom they have believed? And how are they to believe in him of whom they have never heard? And how are they to hear without a preacher? And how can men preach unless they are sent?" (Rom 10:14–15). As Ratzinger conceives it, the New Testament envisages "the word" of God, as "the word that is *heard* and, as such, preached, not a word that is read." Hence, "when the true *successio apostolica* is found in the word, it cannot just be found in a book. . . . [A]s *successio verbi*, it must be *successio praedicantium,* and this . . . cannot be without a 'sending', a 'mission'—that is, without a personal continuity deriving from the apostles. It is . . . for the sake of the word—which in the New Covenant is not supposed to be a dead letter, but *viva vox*—that a *viva successio* is demanded."[31] Ratzinger states that by "apostolic succession" he does not mean "the formal ritual of an unbroken laying-on of hands, but the problem of personal responsibility for the witness that has been given."[32] Being a successor to the apostles means being "taken into the service" of God's word, to witness to it and proclaim it. Following the Protestant patristic scholar Campenhausen, Ratzinger contrasts the early Church's assertion that it had an unbroken *succession* with the contemporary gnostic claim to possess an unwritten tradition. When the Christian church

insisted it had "living διαδοχη," a live "transmission," it was not arguing that it had the *real* "oral tradition" stemming from Christ, which
beside its Scripture countered the Gnostic, counterfeit traditions.
Rather, it was *contrasting* the living διαδοχη, the succession, with the
Gnostic *paradosis agraphos,* or unwritten tradition. The early Church
contended that no unwritten traditions existed: all that existed was
the living διαδοχη, the apostolic succession. Against Campenhausen,
Ratzinger argues that this living, apostolic succession preceded the
New Testament. This anteriority is due to the early Church understanding "Scripture" to mean the *Old Testament* while conceiving its
New Testament as the lens through which the Old Covenant is understood and proclaimed.

Turning to the East, as he encourages us to do in the sacred liturgy, Ratzinger observes that Orthodox and Catholic do not disagree
about apostolic succession: both maintain that "the pneumatological
rite of the imposition of hands and prayer points . . . to the unbroken
content of ecclesial tradition as the *situs* of the Spirit."[33] But he criti-
cizes the Eastern notion of the five patriarchates, calling it state-
imposed diminution of the primitive theological concept of apostolic
sees.[34] He also disparages the Western medieval development by
which episcopal consecration came to mean "juridical power" separate
from pastoral care and sacramental power. *Lumen Gentium* recovered
the genuine meaning of episcopacy in its statement, "That divine mission, which was committed by Christ to the apostles, is destined to
last until the end of the world (cf. Mt 28.20), since the gospel which
they were charged to hand on is, for the Church, the principle of all
her life for all time."[35]

PETER IN THE COMMUNIO

Ratzinger defines *Roman Catholic* thus: "The 'Roman' guarantees true
catholicity; the actual catholicity witnesses to the rights of Rome." He
adds: "The formula expresses the twin breach that runs through the
Church: first, the breach between 'catholicism' and Christianity of the
mere word of Scripture and, then, the breach between Christianity

related to the Roman office of Peter, and Christianity that has separated itself from this." Ratzinger's observations about formal, institutional ecclesial structure are based in Scripture and early Christian history, both considered as having enduring theological significance. Ratzinger presents the original ecclesial structure as layered like an "onion." All the bishops of the early Church are entrusted with standing by the Word of God, and so every one of them is the tradition in person. Insofar as each of them is "the personal form of the tradition (παραδοσις)" the original episcopate in its entirety represents apostolic succession or is "in the 'succession' (διαδοχη) of the apostles." The next layer consists of those early bishops who held an actual apostolic see: the episcopate as *sedes apostolicae* represents the wider episcopacy, and binds it to the more direct and literal lineage of the "succession." At the core of the *sedes apostolicae* is the *sedes Romana*, binding and representing the entire episcopate. It is this representative function, creating the catholicity of the whole onion, that makes the pope "the ecumenical bishop" and gives his ex cathedra decrees infallibility and irreformability. The character of his "infallibility" as a sign of *catholicity* entails that the pope depends on the correlative witnessing to him of the whole episcopate.[36]

Ratzinger told a German magazine in summer 2004, the summer before he was elected to the papacy, that papal conclaves could not, in his opinion, be guided by the Holy Spirit: there have been too many bad popes, he asserted, for the papal election results to be the work of the Spirit. By contrast, he reminds us that Vatican I teaches that the bishops are "appointed by the Holy Spirit." Ratzinger means that, legally and formally, the bishops are not papal appointees but hold their sees "by divine law." Vatican I also teaches that the pope has "ordinary jurisdiction" over the Church as a whole: he has direct episcopal authority over the entire onion. Vatican I terms the pope *apostolicus primatus,* the first apostle. All apostolic succession is ultimately linked with his. This principle does not stand alone, with reference to the see of Rome. For only a few early Church sees were taken to be apostolic: all the others were so tangentially, by reference to the major sees of the early Church, such as Corinth and Ephesus. Rome was always taken to have primacy among these *sedes apostolicae.*[37]

Episcopacy comes down to personal responsibility for the Word. The God of the Old Testament names himself, and gives names to those whom he calls and commissions. The New Testament intensifies and real-izes this divine action: baptism is the naming of each new Christian, and the "eucharistic prayer" invokes the sacred names of the early saints of the Church. Paul writes in his own name, telling his congregations that his life is the existential witness to his teaching: "corresponding to *the* witness of Jesus Christ," Ratzinger says, "are *the* witnesses, who because they are witnesses, vouch for him by name."[38] This is why ecclesial "leadership . . . has never been anonymous."[39] Simon is named as Peter because he witnesses to the divinity of Christ, that is, Ratzinger thinks, to the Trinity. "Thou art Peter" hangs on "You are the Christ." Simon is Peter because he confesses the Trinity, and his confession cannot be separated from the subject and the person which he is made to be by God. No neutrally "objective" content of faith exists in separation from the named, existent subject who teaches it.

Ratzinger's compression of the ideas of "naming" and "witnessing," the thesis that to be commissioned by God to witness is to be "named" by God with a personality that fits this role inevitably calls to mind the other twentieth-century Catholic theologian who wrote in German and conversed with Karl Barth, in Switzerland. As Hans Urs von Balthasar has it,

> The Apostles are witnesses of the Resurrection and of the whole life of Jesus that underlies it: the form of their objectivity coincides with the form of their witness. They are not uninvolved . . . reporters. . . . Scripture . . . testifies to their giving of testimony. The two coincide when Paul writes a letter and, in it, testifies with his whole life to the truth of revelation, putting God's action at the centre but including himself. . . . [H]e is speaking dramatically: he shows how the drama comes from God, via Christ, to him, and how he hands it on to the community, which is already involved in the action and must bring it into reality. What Paul and the other writers do in the Letters, the evangelists do in their own way: they do not recount stories in which they are not

involved; in fact, they know that their only chance of being objective is by being profoundly involved in the event they are describing. They exercise objectivity by giving their witness before the Church and the world, handing on the drama of Jesus' life, the life of the incarnate Word of God, a catechesis designed to incorporate the lives of the young Christians into the mystery of Christ's life.[40]

A singular name from God is the cross that Peter bears: carrying a singular name from God achieves its fullest existential reality in that moment of Christian witness which is martyrdom. Ratzinger claims that "martyrdom as response to the cross of Christ is . . . the final confirmation of this principle of named personal responsibility."[41]

CARDINAL REGINALD POLE

No one would claim that Ratzinger is Anglican-oriented. If one had to number Ratzinger's theological allergies, state-run churches would head the list. In England, the queen who sought to revoke the supremacy of the crown over the Church goes by the name "bloody Mary." Eamon Duffy has argued that the Church rebuilding undertaken by Mary Tudor and her right-hand man, Reginald Pole, anticipates the Catholic reformation initiated at Trent. The blueprint for Mary's reform was Reginald Pole's work of ecclesiology, originally addressed to Henry VIII, in 1536, and titled *Pro Ecclesiasticae Unitatis Defensione.* Pole's defense of the unity of the Church is based in a typically English historical argument, a narrative about God's providential love for England. Pole presents the martyrdoms of Saint John Fisher and Thomas More as the most recent evidence of God's "special love" for England: "These two men . . . were special legates from God to England." Pole affirmed that Fisher and More "'have accomplished their embassy; they have reported; they have brought back the most certain opinion of Christ.' 'God has sent us books against your deceitful wisdom. . . . [W]e have these writings from the finger of God, the very holy martyrs of God[,] . . . a certain book written not with ink but with blood.'"[42] The last phrase calls to mind Benedict's description of the Turin Shroud as an "icon written in blood." He has for decades been familiar with Pole's defense of the unity of the Church. As a contributor to the Council of Trent, Pole represents a starting point for reflection on the primacy which is organically rooted in the Church's tradition.

Ratzinger noted that in Pole's "theology of martyrdom the primacy represents the guarantee of the opposition of the Church in its catholic unity to all particular secular power." He likes Pole's idea of papal primacy because it is Christological. He refers to Pole's exposition of Isaiah 9:6–7, "for to us a child is born": Pole states, "When you hear that Christ is born for us as a child and sent to us, with regard to his vicar relate this to his election. It is . . . his birth. . . . [H]e has not been elected for himself, but . . . for the entire flock. In the office of shepherd he must regard himself and behave as the least." Pole read Isaiah's "strong hero" within the biblical meaning of *strength:* not power but "love as strong as death." Ratzinger comments that the "strength in which the vicar of Christ must become like his Lord is the strength of the love that is ready for martyrdom." Above all, Ratzinger appreciates the fact that, for Pole, "the cross is the real *locus* of the vicar of Christ."[43] Ratzinger treats that martyrdom as *the* sacrament of truth. He does not take martyrdom as a sign of subjective authenticity but as an expression of the power of God at work in the death and resurrection of Christ, exhibiting "the beauty of love that goes 'to the very end' and thus proves to be mightier than falsehood and violence."[44]

"THE VICTORY OF LOVE"

However much one appreciates Ratzinger's reaching back to the fathers of Trent for a dispossessive image of the papacy, no English Catholic can feel entirely at ease reading Ratzinger on Reginald Pole and recalling that the reform which Cardinal Pole masterminded killed very many Protestants. The Protestant and the Catholic Reformations wounded Christ's body. So too did the schism of 1054, between Catholic and Orthodox. Let me turn in conclusion to Ratzinger's reflection on the early days of the "healing" of that memory. Orthodox observers were invited twice to the Second Vatican Council and twice declined the invitation. In September 1963 Paul VI wrote a third time, to Patriarch Athenagoras, recalling Philippians 3:13 and proposing that the past be forgotten. Athenagoras now replied in kind, citing 1 Corinthians 13:7, "we can give one another no better gift than the gift of love": Paul affirms that love excuses, trusts, hopes, and endures. Paul VI now went to the Holy Land and met the patriarch on the Mount of Olives. Following that, in September 1964, the Synod of Patriarchs decided to accept the invitation to send observers to the Council. The great turning point came in December 1965, when, in St. Peter's in Rome and the Cathedral of Phanar in Constantinople, Catholics and Orthodox renounced their mutual bans of excommunication. Paul VI stated, "Just as harmony once served us well, so it later served us ill that on both sides . . . charity grew cold." The moment has come to "be bound together by love. . . . Therefore we want to follow the path of fraternal love on which we may be led to full union." In a letter a few weeks after the historic lifting of the bans of anathema, Pope Paul spoke of the longing "to leave the past in God's hands so that we may direct our energies to preparing a better future." As Ratzinger interprets it, the "negative" forgetting of the past is the necessary first step toward the "positive" step of restoring love. Rearranging and changing our stock of images of the past is the prerequisite condition for healing the wounded body of the Church: "Love is made possible," he says, "by a changed memory." An altered interpretation of the past changes what the past is for us by "forgetting" and "forgiving": "The character of the events of 1054 in the history of the Church has been changed." The old has gone, and the new has come, and the Church sees the beginning of "resurrection" when the "old memory" is "replaced by a new one—a memory of love."[45] The foundation of Ratzinger's ecclesiological insight is Christological. Reflecting on the fact that Christ on the cross prays "as his body," including "all of our struggles, our voices, our anguish, and our hope . . . in his praying," Ratzinger says that "at the same time, Jesus' suffering is a Messianic Passion. It is suffering in fellowship with us, in a solidarity—born of love—that already includes redemption, the victory of love."[46]

NOTES

1. Joseph Ratzinger, *Principles of Catholic Theology: Building Stones for a Fundamental Theology*, trans. Sister Mary Frances McCarthy, S.N.D. (San Francisco: Ignatius Press, 1987), 132, 199. One must confess that the "she" did cause them to blanch, when I spelled it out in terms of the doctrine of the Immaculate Conception.

2. Joseph Ratzinger, *Introduction to Christianity*, trans. J. R. Foster (San Francisco: Ignatius Press, 1990, 2004), 229–30.

3. Benedict XVI, *Jesus of Nazareth: Part Two: Holy Week: From the Entrance into Jerusalem to the Resurrection*, trans. Vatican Secretariat of State (San Francisco: Ignatius Press, 2011), 172.

4. Ratzinger, *Principles*, 273.

5. Ratzinger, *Introduction*, 252.

6. Joseph Ratzinger, *Church, Ecumenism, and Politics: New Essays in Ecclesiology*, trans. Robert Nowell and Fridesiwide Sandeman, O.S.B. (New York: Crossroad, 1988), 11–12.

7. Ratzinger, *Principles*, 89.

8. Joseph Ratzinger, "Dogmatic Constitution on Revelation: Origin and Background," trans. William Glen-Doepel, in *Commentary on the Documents of Vatican II*, 5 vols., ed. Herbert Vorgrimler (London/New York: Burns & Oates/Herder & Herder, 1969), 3:175.

9. Ratzinger, *Principles*, 118.

10. Ibid., 131.

11. Joseph Ratzinger, *Eschatology, Death and Eternal Life*, trans. Michael Waldstein (Washington, DC: Catholic University of America Press, 1988), 94, 98, 99, 151, 157–58.

12. Ratzinger, *Principles*, 99.

13. Ratzinger, *Church, Ecumenism, and Politics*, 3–4.

14. Ibid., 74–80.

15. Joseph Ratzinger, "The Holy Spirit as *Communio*: Concerning the Relationship of Pneumatology and Spirituality in Augustine," *Communio* 25, no. 2 (Summer 1998): 325.

16. Ratzinger, *Church, Ecumenism, and Politics,* 35–36. See also Ratzinger, *Principles,* 196–97.

17. Aidan Nichols, O.P., *The Thought of Benedict XVI: An Introduction to the Theology of Joseph Ratzinger* (London: Burns & Oates, 2005), 37–38.

18. Ratzinger, *Church, Ecumenism, and Politics,* 5. Here Ratzinger is drawing on Möhler's statement that the erroneous idea of the Church is that "Christ in the beginning established the hierarchy and by doing so did enough to look after the Church until the end of time." Ratzinger thinks Möhler's insight is expressed magnificently by the opening lines of *Lumen Gentium*: "'because Christ is the light of the nations' there exists the mirror of his glory, the Church, that reflects his radiance."

19. Laurence Paul Hemming, *Benedict XVI: Fellow Worker for the Truth: An Introduction to His Life and Thought* (London: Continuum, 2005), 145.

20. Benedict XVI, *Jesus of Nazareth,* II, 291.

21. Ratzinger, *Principles,* 23–25, 132.

22. Ibid., 53.

23. Joseph Ratzinger, *Behold the Pierced One: An Approach to a Spiritual Christology,* trans. Graham Harrison (San Francisco: Ignatius Press, 1986), 86–90.

24. Ratzinger, *Church, Ecumenism, and Politics,* 7.

25. Nichols, *Thought,* 47–48, 135–36.

26. Ratzinger, *Behold,* 99.

27. Ibid., 75.

28. Joseph Ratzinger, *On the Way to Jesus Christ,* trans. Michael J. Miller (San Francisco: Ignatius Press, 2005), 29.

29. Ratzinger, *Church, Ecumenism, and Politics,* 8.

30. Karl Barth, *Church Dogmatics I.i: The Doctrine of the Word of God,* trans. G. W. Bromley (Edinburgh: T & T Clark, 1975), 3, 103–4, 111–12.

31. Joseph Ratzinger, *God's Word: Scripture, Tradition, Office,* trans. Henry Taylor (San Francisco: Ignatius Press, 2008), 29.

32. Ratzinger, *Principles,* 9.

33. Ibid., 245.

34. Ratzinger, *God's Word,* 34–35.

35. Ratzinger, *Principles,* 243, citing *Lumen Gentium* 3.20.

36. Ratzinger, *God's Word,* 39, 35–36, 38.

37. Ibid., 15–16, 31–33.

38. Ratzinger, *Church, Ecumenism, and Politics,* 34.

39. Ibid.

40. Hans Urs von Balthasar, *Theo-Drama: Theological Dramatic Theory. II. The Dramatis Personae: Man in God,* trans. Graham Harrison (San Francisco: Ignatius Press, 1990), 57–58.

41. Ratzinger, *Behold,* 34–36.

42. Eamon Duffy, *Fires of Faith: Catholic England under Mary Tudor* (New Haven: Yale University Press, 2009), 9, 34, 36.

43. Ratzinger, *Church, Ecumenism, and Politics,* 38, 41–42.

44. Ratzinger, *On the Way,* 39.

45. Ratzinger, *Principles,* 202–12.

46. Ratzinger, *Jesus of Nazareth,* II, 215–16.

chapter nine

THE BAPTISM OF JESUS

On Jesus' Solidarity with Israel and
Foreknowledge of the Passion

GARY A. ANDERSON

In this essay I would like to consider the problem of Jesus' participation in the baptism of John, an event that appears near the beginning of all three synoptic Gospels. It is one of those rare moments in
the history of Jesus research concerning which all scholars are in
agreement—that the event itself is part of the historical record and
cannot be an invention of the early Church.[1] But observe my wording:
though the event itself is regarded as historical, the particular depic-
tions that our gospel writers provide have been subject to dramatically
different interpretations. Before turning to those problems, let us re-
familiarize ourselves with the story itself. I have chosen the version
from the Gospel of Mark, the earliest witness to the event.

> John the baptizer appeared in the wilderness, proclaiming a bap-
> tism of repentance for the forgiveness of sins. And people from

the whole Judean countryside and all the people of Jerusalem were going out to him, and were baptized by him in the river Jordan, confessing their sins. . . . In those days Jesus came from Nazareth of Galilee and was baptized by John in the Jordan. And just as he was coming up out of the water, he saw the heavens torn apart and the Spirit descending like a dove on him. And a voice came from heaven, "You are my Son, the Beloved; with you I am well pleased." (Mk 1:4–5, 9–11)[2]

Benedict XVI has succinctly summarized the challenge the gospel text provides the Christian reader:

The real novelty [in our text] is that he—Jesus—wants to be baptized, that he blends into the gray mass of sinners waiting on the banks of the Jordan. We have just heard that the confession of sins is a component of Baptism. . . . Is that something Jesus could do? How could he confess sins? How could he separate himself from his previous life in order to start a new one? This is a question that [the earliest] Christians could not avoid asking. The dispute between the Baptist and Jesus that Matthew recounts for us was also an expression of the early Christians' own question to Jesus: "I need to be baptized by you, and do you come to me?" (Mt. 3.14). Matthew goes on to report for us that "Jesus answered him, 'Let it be so now; for thus it is fitting for us to fulfill all righteousness.' Then he consented" (Mt. 3.15).[3]

Benedict is aware of how Jesus' participation in John's baptism has been used to launch a frontal attack on one of the most treasured teachings of the Church—the declaration that Jesus was sinless. Paul Hollenbach is an excellent representative of this school, and in his oft-cited article on the subject found in the prestigious series Der Aufstieg und Niedergang der römischen Welt, he declares that the rise of departments of religious studies in secular universities is allowing scholars to ask questions of the Jesus traditions that have been off-limits for centuries. He writes:

In this connection it is particularly important to focus on the traditional Christian belief in Jesus' sinlessness. This belief has colored most historical study of Jesus up to the present. Now it may be in some sense abstracted from history that Jesus never sinned, but historically speaking that issue cannot be determined one way or another. More important, the question whether or not Jesus was sinless in some sense abstracted from history is beside the point since it is clearly a theologically developed belief. *Historically the fact that Jesus came to John for baptism shows demonstrably that Jesus thought he was a sinner who needed repentance.* Indeed, if he had thought he was "without sin," that very thought clearly would have been a "sin of ignorance." For if he came to be baptized believing that he did not need it, but did it for some theologically appropriate reason, then he was in fact a deceiver, which was again reason enough indeed for him to need John's baptism of repentance even if Jesus himself was unaware of it. Hence, the only reasonable conclusion is that Jesus came to be baptized because he believed he was a sinner who needed the repentance John preached. Likewise, he must have believed the rest of John's message as it has been outlined above. Thus, from an historical point of view, the fact of Jesus' baptism and its meaning for Jesus are really not agonizing theological issues at all. They are and have been problematic only for Christians from the earliest days (Mt. 3:14–15) to the present.[4]

Hollenbach's logic appears to be unassailable: A. John the Baptist proclaims a baptism for the remission of sins; B. Jesus willingly submits to this baptism; ergo C. Jesus must have considered himself a sinner.

John Meier, however, has found a deep flaw in this syllogism. He writes, "In theory, a historian might inquire as to whether Jesus *considered* himself a sinner just as a historian might inquire as to whether Jesus' adversaries considered him a sinner (according to the Gospels, some did)." But by posing the issue this way, Meier goes on to say, "we are once again in danger of reverting to the psychologizing [tendencies] of the 'liberal lives' [of Jesus]." And as everyone will concede, the first monumental works of the nineteenth century—most famously

David Strauss's *Das Leben Jesu, kritisch arbeitet*—found in the so-called historical Jesus nothing other than an image of themselves. Meier raises the most pertinent issue when he asks: "What data allow us to enter into the depths of the individual conscience of the historical Jesus to find out whether he thought himself a sinner?"[5]

The way Hollenbach has framed the question, Meier continues, is more in accord with twentieth-century worries about *individual* as opposed to *collective* sin. This is really the rub of the question, so let's try to let this distinction settle into our consciousness. Meier correctly observes:

> Confession of sin in ancient Israel did not mean an unraveling of a lengthy laundry list of personal peccadilloes, with the result that worship of God was turned into a narcissistic reflection on self. . . . Confession of sin often meant recalling God's gracious deeds for an ungrateful Israel, a humble admission that one was a member of this sinful people, a recounting of the infidelities and apostasies of Israel from early on down to one's own day, and a final resolve to change and be different from one's ancestors. Even apart from the question of one's particular personal sins, one was part of this history of sin simply because one was part of this sinful people.[6]

But one need not take Meier's word as authoritative; the texts themselves bear this out. Consider the prayer of Ezra, for example, paying particular attention to the use of the first-person plural ("we"):

> O my God, I am too ashamed and embarrassed to lift my face to you, my God, for our iniquities have risen higher than our heads, and our guilt has mounted up to the heavens. From the days of our ancestors to this day we have been deep in guilt, and for our iniquities we, our kings, and our priests, have been handed over to the kings of the lands, to the sword, to captivity, to plundering, and to utter shame, as is now the case. . . . And now, our God, what shall we say after this? For we have forsaken your commandments, which you commanded by your servants the prophets, saying, "The land that you are entering to possess is a land unclean

with the pollutions of the peoples of the lands, with their abomi-
nations. They have filled it from end to end with their unclean-
ness.". . . Here we are before you in our guilt, though no one can
face you because of this. (Ezr 9:6–7, 10–11, 15b)

What Meier has said about early Judaism in general is even more
true for grand restoration movements like that of John the Baptist: it
was *collective* sin that was of primary importance. And any number of
penitential texts from this period put the emphasis squarely on the
nation's sin as opposed to the sins of individual persons.[7] An excellent
example of this very point can be found in the Book of Tobit. And to
that book let me turn.

As George Nickelsberg has noted, this book has two foci: the
plight of Tobit and the nation Israel.[8] It is impossible to read the book
correctly without attending to how the one is related to the other. In
this sense, Tobit shares some striking similarities to the figure of Jesus
whose life was also about himself and the people of Israel.

Tobit is a righteous Israelite who suffers miserably for his exemplary behavior. The nation Israel, on the other hand, is suffering the
consequences of its apostasy by enduring the harsh consequences of
the exile. Chief among those sins was the nation's violation of the pre-
scription to worship the Lord solely in Jerusalem.

I, Tobit, walked in the ways of truth and righteousness all the days
of my life. I performed many acts of charity for my kindred and
my people who had gone with me in exile to Nineveh in the land
of the Assyrians. When I was in my own country, in the land of
Israel, while I was still a young man, the whole tribe of my ances-
tor Naphtali deserted the house of David and Jerusalem. This city
had been chosen from among all the tribes of Israel, where all the
tribes of Israel should offer sacrifice and where the temple, the
dwelling of God, had been consecrated and established for all
generations forever. All my kindred and our ancestral house of
Naphtali sacrificed to the calf that King Jeroboam of Israel had
erected in Dan and on all the mountains of Galilee. But I alone
went often to Jerusalem for the festivals, as it is prescribed for all

Israel by an everlasting decree. I would hurry off to Jerusalem with the first fruits of the crops and the firstlings of the flock, the tithes of the cattle, and the first shearings of the sheep. I would give these to the priests, the sons of Aaron, at the altar; likewise the tenth of the grain, wine, olive oil, pomegranates, figs, and the rest of the fruits to the sons of Levi who ministered at Jerusalem. Also for six years I would save up a second tenth in money and go and distribute it in Jerusalem. A third tenth I would give to the orphans and widows and to the converts who had attached themselves to Israel. I would bring it and give it to them in the third year, and we would eat it according to the ordinance decreed concerning it in the law of Moses and according to the instructions of Deborah, the mother of my father Tobiel, for my father had died and left me an orphan. When I became a man I married a woman, a member of our own family, and by her I became the father of a son whom I named Tobias. (Tb 1:3–9)

Tobit, who came from the far northern province of Naphtali, made the trek to Jerusalem on a regular basis to fulfill the mandates of the Mosaic law. Yet in spite of this heroic obedience, he suffered the same fate as his disobedient fellow citizens and ended up being carted away to Assyria. There he continued his courageous obedience to the law in the face of similar apostasy among his fellow Israelites.

Later in the tale, after he goes out to retrieve a corpse for burial, he will have to put up with mockery for his religious dedication: "When the sun had set, I went and dug a grave and buried him. And my neighbors laughed and said, 'Is he still not afraid? He has already been hunted down to be put to death for doing this, and he ran away; yet here he is again burying the dead!'" (Tb 2:8). To make matters worse, his exemplary devotion to this commandment will lead to his becoming blind. Mocked by his fellow countrymen and subject to a humiliating test by his God, Tobit prays to be released from his misery and allowed to die.

But just prior to what he believes is his imminent death, he sends his only son on what seems to be a perilous journey in search of funds he had left on deposit in Media. God superintends the trip through his angel Raphael; Tobias finds a wife of the right pedigree and of considerable means and brings home a remedy for Tobit's blindness. So great is the transformation that Tobit declares that he has been raised from the dead. His life of almsgiving has brought him the reward that was his due.

Raphael exhorts Tobit and his son not to keep the news of his deliverance to himself but to trumpet it far and wide.

> Then Raphael called the two of them privately and said to them, "Bless God and acknowledge him in the presence of all the living for the good things he has done for you. Bless and sing praise to his name. With fitting honor declare to all people the deeds of God. Do not be slow to acknowledge him. It is good to conceal the secret of a king, but to acknowledge and reveal the works of God, and with fitting honor to acknowledge him. Do good and evil will not overtake you." (Tb 12:6–7)

And just moments later, in his song of thanksgiving, Tobit thanks God for raising him from the dead.

> Then Tobit said: "Blessed be God who lives forever, because his kingdom lasts throughout all ages. *For he afflicts, and he shows mercy;* he leads down to Hades in the lowest regions of the earth, and he brings up from the great abyss, and there is nothing that can escape his hand." (Tb 13:1–2; emphasis added)

And then Tobit goes on to pray that God will do the same for Israel, since it was common in biblical thought to see exile as a form of death.

> *He will afflict you for your iniquities, but he will again show mercy on all of you.* He will gather you from all the nations among whom you have been scattered. If you turn to him with all your heart and with all your soul, to do what is true before him, then he will turn to you and will no longer hide his face from you.
>
> So now see what he has done for you; acknowledge him at the top of your voice. Bless the Lord of righteousness, and exalt the

King of the ages. In the land of my exile I acknowledge him, and show his power and majesty to a nation of sinners: "Turn back, you sinners, and do what is right before him; perhaps he may look with favor upon you and show you mercy." (Tb 13:5–6; emphasis added)

The structure, then, of Tobit's life (vv. 1–2) and that of Israel (vv. 5 ff.) is strikingly parallel in form. From the description of verse 2, we could describe Tobit's life as follows:

A. A blind Tobit "descends" to Sheol.
B. In utter despair Tobit prays to God that he take his life.
C. God attends to his prayer and "raises" Tobit to new life.

And from verse 5, the life of Israel:

A. Israel is in exile (~Sheol) due to apostasy.
B. Tobit exhorts Israel to repent
C. In the hope that she too will soon be restored (raised from the dead).

In sum, the book of Tobit is both a personal and a national story. If there is a single message that it wishes to convey it would be this: the God who raised Tobit from the dead can do the same for Israel. Israel's hope for restoration is not in vain.

So let us now return to the problem of Jesus' confession of sins. As Hollenbach put the matter, the simplest historical interpretation of this act is that Jesus has come to the waters of the Jordan in despair over his personal plight as a sinner and seeks to restore his relationship with God. Meier countered this suggestion by reminding us that prayers of confession in the Second Temple period typically put an emphasis on communal and not personal sin.

The Book of Tobit is a good test case for this matter because it depicts its main character in a way very similar to that in which the writers of the Gospels depict Jesus: the book has been organized such that the concerns of the nation Israel are brought to the fore. In order to probe this more deeply, let us consider the prayer of contrition that

Tobit voices after he reaches the deepest point of his despair. If one knew only what had transpired in the first two chapters of the work and had to guess what type of prayer Tobit would utter at the beginning of chapter 3, there would really be only one possibility: a lament. All the classic markers of that genre would seem to be in place: innocence in the face of great suffering and the constant reproaches of his neighbors.

Psalm 26 is the prayer I would have chosen, had I been the author of the Book of Tobit!

> Vindicate me, O Lord,
> for I have walked in my integrity,
> and I have trusted in the Lord without wavering.
> Prove me, O Lord, and try me;
> test my heart and mind.
> For your steadfast love is before my eyes,
> and I walk in faithfulness to you.
> I do not sit with the worthless,
> nor do I consort with the hypocrites.
> I hate the company of evildoers,
> and will not sit with the wicked. . . .
> But as for me, I walk in my integrity;
> redeem me, and be gracious to me.
> My foot stands on level ground;
> in the great congregation I will bless the Lord.
> (Ps 26:1–5, 11–12)

I think this psalm constitutes a fitting prayer for the occasion of Tobit's lament, for in it the Psalmist protests his innocence ("Vindicate me, O Lord, for I have walked in my integrity, and I have trusted in the Lord without wavering") and contrasts his behavior to that of his neighbors ("I do not sit with the worthless, nor do I consort with the hypocrites. I hate the company of evildoers, and will not sit with the wicked"). Other laments like that of Psalm 3:7 go even further and demand of God that he silence the enemies of the just ("Rise up, O Lord! Deliver me, O my God! For you strike all my enemies on the cheek; you break the teeth of the wicked"), a plea that would also be fitting for Tobit.

Yet Tobit does not utter this sort of lamentation. The prayer of Tobit has more in common with the communal laments of the Second Temple period, such as Ezra 9. It begins with a declaration that the judgments of God are righteous and just (v. 2), which may refer not only to his own plight but also to the exile that has followed upon the apostasy of Israel. Yet, as the opening chapter makes quite clear, Tobit was heroically innocent. He suffers solely because of the sins of others. Yet he does not take this occasion to trumpet his innocence. Quite the opposite, he underscores his solidarity with his people.

> And now, O Lord, remember me
>   and look favorably upon me.
> Do no punish me for my sins
>   and for my unwitting offenses
>   and those that my ancestors committed before you.
> They have sinned against you,
>   And disobeyed your commandments.
>   So you gave us over to plunder, exile, and death,
>   to become the talk, the byword, and an object of reproach
>   among all the nations among whom you have dispersed us.
> And now your many judgments are true
>   in exacting penalty from me for my sins.
> For we have not kept your commandments
>   and have not walked in accordance with truth before you.
>   (Tb 3:3–5)

The prayer is remarkable for the way in which it expresses Tobit's identification with the plight of his people. Yet those very words seem to fly in the face of everything we have learned about Tobit in the first two chapters of the book. Unlike the people Israel, Tobit is innocent of any hint of apostasy. But the choice to put this communal confession ("And now your many judgments are true in exacting penalty from me for my sins") with that of the nation as a whole ("For we have not kept your commandments") fits well with the overall purpose of the book, that is, to make Tobit's life a parable for the larger nation. Tobit's moral and spiritual luster is not limited to a display of his own personal righteousness in the face of great apostasy but blossoms into an extraordinary expression of *solidarity* with his people that prevents him from disarticulating his fate from theirs.

In the person of the historical Jesus, I would like to suggest, we meet a similar person with a double-focused life. On the one hand, Jesus claims to be the Messiah, the very son of God who has come to do the bidding of his Father in Heaven. But at the same time he is a prophet anointed to preach about the coming Kingdom of God. And to facilitate that task he calls twelve disciples—not an accidental number by any means. This group constitutes an Israel in miniature. So the story of Jesus, similar to that of Tobit, centers on both a person and the nation he has come to redeem.

In summary, it is not just a distinct possibility that Jesus came to the Jordan to participate in a confession of *national* sin, but quite probable that this was the case. Benedict's claim that Jesus' consent to baptism was intended to express "solidarity with men who have incurred guilt but yearn for righteousness" is not some sort of apologetic veneer awkwardly pasted over the more sober and searing historical judgment proposed by Hollenbach; it is rather the likeliest historical reading of the event. And viewed this way, we also can see why the early Church found in the historical act of submitting to the baptism of John a window into the theological depth of Jesus' mission. By consenting to this baptism the innocent figure of Jesus was identifying with the people of Israel and recalling the message of the prophets about God's promise of restoration.

So much for the first question that Benedict treats in his chapter on the baptism. Alongside his consideration of Jesus' participation in the event, Benedict reminds his readers of the way in which the event was remembered in the Church. To illustrate his point, Benedict turns our attention to the way the baptism was presented in the iconographic tradition.[9] In this visual medium, the events of the baptism are juxtaposed to those of the crucifixion and resurrection. Descending into the Jordan was an anticipation of death, while rising from the waters foreshadowed the resurrection. For example, in one ancient reliquary from Tuscany (ca. ninth century), one can see how closely the two events were intertwined by noting the way in which the baptism and resurrection are depicted on opposite sides of a single cruciform object.[10]

But a personal favorite of mine is an icon with two registers from Saint Catherine's Monastery (tenth century).[11] In the top register we see the descent of Jesus into the Jordan; in the bottom register, Jesus' descent into the bowels of Hades to retrieve the figures of Adam and Eve. Yet, strikingly, the movement is depicted along a single vertical axis; it is as though Jesus falls through the Jordan into Sheol. Clearly, the imagery of Romans 6 has influenced the way in which the iconographers have depicted the historical event.

> Do you not know that all of us who have been baptized into Christ Jesus were baptized into his death? Therefore we have been buried with him by baptism into death, so that, just as Christ was raised from the dead by the glory of the Father, so we too might walk in newness of life. For if we have been united with him in a death like his, we will certainly be united with him in a resurrection like his. (Rom 6:3–5)

According to this text the entry into the baptismal waters becomes salvific for the newly minted Christian because it is identified with the descent of Christ into Hades. Going down to the water is symbolic of the individual's death, while rising out of the waters bespeaks a participation in the resurrection of Jesus.

The historical-critical reader, however, will have reason to worry. One question that naturally arises is how we can know whether the iconographic tradition has accurately captured what took place at the baptism itself.[12] Was Jesus conscious of the fact that his baptism was the first step in a journey that would lead to the cross? This appears to be the point the icons make when they depict the two events in such a similar fashion. But even here, I think, there are grounds for caution. When we look at an icon like the one from Saint Catherine's, we need not presume that the correlation of the two moments was already a conscious fact in Jesus' mind. It could be that the Church, functioning something like an omniscient narrator, has provided the viewer with a synthesis of two historical moments in Jesus' life that the actors in the story would not have seen.

But to view the matter this way is already to depart from the path laid out by premodern exegetes (and, indeed, by Saint John the Evangelist himself). For them, it was clear that Jesus was fully aware of what awaited him from the beginning of his earthly ministry. Recently, however, Fr. Thomas Weinandy has suggested that the imputation of such robust knowledge to the person of Jesus comes at the cost of affirming his full humanity. If he was a man like unto us, then he too must have experienced his life on earth like other *viatores*—that is, man "on the way," man trusting fully in God even as the full implications of that trust remain in the shadows. Weinandy argues that Jesus' experience of the Father

> did not reach its comprehensive and complete maturity until his resurrection. It is there that the Father raises him from the dead by the power of the Holy Spirit and makes him Son of God in power (see Romans 1:4). Only within his glorified and risen state does the Son of God obtain, through the full light of the Holy Spirit, the full human hypostatic vision of his Father and so the full human vision of who he is as the divine Son. This seems to be in accord with the Letter to the Hebrews' claim that he was "made perfect" through his death and resurrection (see Hebrews 2:10, 5:9, 7:28, 10:14). Only in the resurrection does Jesus become truly the *comprehensor*.[13]

Weinandy hastens to add, however, that certain forms of knowledge must be imputed to Jesus. These would include the fact that he was the Son of God and that his death would be on behalf of those whom he was sent to save. But presumably we would not have to declare that Jesus knew with utter confidence that his life was bound for the cross right at the beginning of his public ministry. This insight would have come only as Jesus witnessed the reactions to his ministry and prayerfully pondered them in light of his Scriptures. On this view, the icon from Saint Catherine's represents a back-to-front reading: only as Jesus matured did he come to see that the solidarity he had expressed for the people Israel would lead to his dying on their behalf.

However appealing this suggestion might appear, it should cause some worry for the theological reader of the New Testament. The appeal to post-Easter reconfigurations of the message of Jesus can easily slide into heretical judgments about the character of Israel's Messiah. Some New Testament scholars have used this distinction to claim that the Church imposed upon Jesus an identity that was completely different from what he had originally intended. Benedict provides numerous examples of this in his book. But just because this sort of approach to the person of Jesus has been misused does not mean it is wholly without value. In his laudatory review of Benedict's first volume, Raniero Cantalamessa, preacher to the pontifical household, permits himself "a small reservation" that is precisely on the question of the difference Easter makes in terms of assessing the full identity of Jesus of Nazareth. Cantalamessa cites with approval the statement of G. Theissen and A. Merz that "Christians, after Easter, spoke of Jesus more affirmatively (that is to say, they said greater and more important things) than the historical Jesus would have said about himself. This 'value plus' of post-Paschal Christology in respect of Jesus' pre-Paschal self-awareness, whether on the historical or on the objective level, is based on the actual event of Easter."[14]

Cantalamessa immediately points out that these two phases of self-awareness do not posit an unbridgeable gulf between the historical Jesus and the post-Easter Christ. Rather, the difference is akin to that of an implicit and explicit Christology. In other words, the event of Easter simply sets in sharper focus what could have been intuited from the earthly ministry of Jesus.

But we need not limit ourselves to the simple binary that a pre- and post-Easter perspective imposes. As Benedict himself notes, some significant scholars, including Rudolf Pesch, Gerhard Lohfink, and Ulrich Wilckens, have argued that Jesus began his public preaching by "offering the good news of God's kingdom and his unconditional forgiveness, but that he had to acknowledge the rejection of this offer and so came to identify his mission with that of the Suffering Servant." Though Benedict will eventually reject this proposal, he concedes quite readily its plausible nature. He writes, "This 'flexibility' on God's part is utterly characteristic of the paths that he treads with his people, as recounted for us in the Old Testament—he waits for man's free choice, and whenever the answer is 'no', he opens up a new path of love."[15] Easter is no longer the point of provocation but rather the growing knowledge about the kingdom that took place within Jesus' own lifetime. But we must also underscore the theological grounds for Benedict's concession that this position is plausible. Christ can grow in his knowledge of the Father's will in the way Pesch, Lohfink, and Wilckens propose because it accords with what we know about the character of God as revealed in the Old Testament. Rather than undercut the Church's claims about the divinity of Christ, it can be brought into harmony with it.

So where does this leave us in regard to Benedict's approach to the Bible? I think that Cantalamessa has captured the point well when he writes that the overall purpose of Benedict's two volumes on Jesus of Nazareth proceeds from the conviction "that the Christ of faith is also, rigorously, the Jesus of history." Many reviewers, especially in the English language, have misread the volumes when they fault the pope for not staying abreast of all the developments of modern criticism. "What was the pope supposed to have done," Cantalamessa asks, "write yet another historical reconstruction in which to confront and discuss all objections?" Rather, the pope's intention, it seems to me, was to present a portrait of Jesus that takes history seriously while at the same time not capitulating to the limits of purely historical inquiry. The result is a vibrant historical narrative that teems with theological insights.

In my own treatment I have provided additional evidence as to why the Christian reader need not be embarrassed by the fact that Jesus submitted to John's baptism, and why a robust Christological account need not presuppose that Jesus knew precisely where that baptism would take him. In the former undertaking I am at one with the pope; in the latter I have diverged slightly from the reading he has proposed.[16] But I hope my alternative reading will be seen as congruent with the overall aim of his project, that is, a portrait of Jesus that strengthens faith even as it takes the questions of historical reconstruction with utmost seriousness. For I do believe that that is the ultimate purpose of Benedict's two magnificent volumes: faith and reason are not at odds with one another, but each serves to enlarge the capacities of the other. Faith without reason is weak and prone to collapse; reason untempered by faith fails to come to terms with the questions most dear to the human heart.[17]

NOTES

1. John P. Meier, *A Marginal Jew: Rethinking the Historical Jesus*, vol. 2: *Mentor, Message, and Miracles* (New York: Doubleday, 1994).

2. All citations from Scripture are taken from the NRSV. In quoting Tobit 3:4, I have modified NSRV in light of the Morton recension of the Greek (Vatican).

3. Benedict XVI, *Jesus of Nazareth: From the Baptism in the Jordan to the Transfiguration*, trans. Adrian J. Walker (New York: Doubleday, 2007), 16–17.

4. "The Conversion of Jesus: From Jesus the Baptizer to Jesus the Healer," *Aufstieg und Niedergang der römischen Welt* II/25.1 (1982), 201–2. Emphasis added.

5. Meier, *Marginal Jew*, 113. Original emphasis.

6. Ibid., 113–14.

7. See Meier, *Marginal Jew*, 114–15, for a fuller listing of texts and an excellent discussion.

8. In his short commentary on the book (*The HarperCollins Bible Commentary*, ed. James Mays [San Francisco: HarperCollins, 2000], 791), Nickelsberg writes, "Parallel to the story of Tobit is the uncompleted story of Israel. Tobit's situation is paradigmatic for the exiled nation. As God has chastised Tobit, so Israel, suffering in exile, is being chastised. But God's mercy on Tobit and his family guarantees that this mercy will bring the Israelites back to their land. Since this event, described only in predictions, awaits fulfillment, one level of the double story is incomplete."

9. Benedict XVI, *Jesus of Nazareth*, I, 18–19.

10. See Anna D. Kartsonis, *Anastasis: The Making of an Image* (Princeton: Princeton University Press, 1986), figs. 26a and 26b (unpaginated).

11. Ibid., fig. 63.

12. In order to substantiate the Church's manner of reading the baptism, Benedict appeals to Joachim Jeremias's claim that John 1:29 ("Behold, the lamb of God, who takes away the sin of the world") represents a historical utterance of the Baptist himself (*Jesus of Nazareth*, I, 20–21). On these grounds, Benedict concludes, we can say that Jesus enters the Jordan knowing that his baptism has a redemptive purpose for the cosmos at large that will be configured through his Passion. Yet the claims of Jeremias have not been well received by New Testament scholars. See the excellent discussion by Fr. Raymond Brown, S.S., *The Gospel According to John I–XII* (Garden City, NY: Doubleday, 1966), 58–63, esp. 60. One should also note a curious aporia in the way in which Benedict lays out his argument. Having made the point that Jesus' assent to baptism was a way of expressing a "solidarity with men," Benedict goes on to say that "the [true] significance of the event could not fully emerge until it was seen in light of the Cross and Resurrection. Descending into the water, the candidates for Baptism confess their sin and seek to be rid of their burden of guilt. . . . Looking at the event in light of the Cross and Resurrection, the Christian people realized what happened: Jesus loaded the burden of all mankind's guilt upon his shoulders; he bore it down into the depths of the Jordan. He inaugurated his public activity by stepping into the place of sinners" (*Jesus of Nazareth*, I, 17–18). On this view, one could remain agnostic as to what the participants thought about the historical event of the baptism—it was the events of Easter that cast a light backward and illumined the true meaning of the occasion. In support of this position of reading the text "backward," see Fr. Raniero Cantalamessa's review of Benedict's volume (www.zenit.org/article-20129?l=english).

13. Thomas Weinandy, O.F.M. Cap., "Jesus' Filial Vision of the Father," *Pro Ecclesia* 13 (2004): 198. His proposal shares much in common with that of J. Galot, *La conscience de Jésus* (Gembloux: Ducolot-Lethielleux, 1971), and *Who Is Christ? A Theology of the Incarnation* (Chicago: Franciscan Herald Press, 1981), 319–43. The perspective of Weinandy and Galot has been subject to a strong critique by Thomas J. White in his "The Voluntary Action of the Earthly Christ and the Necessity of the Beatific Vision," *The Thomist* 69 (2005): 497–534, which Weinandy responded to in a subsequent issue: "The Beatific Vision and the Incarnate Son: Furthering the Discussion," *The Thomist* 70 (2006): 605–15. Finally, see the excellent discussion of all these articles in Edward Oakes, S.J., *Infinity Dwindled to Infancy: A Catholic and Evangelical Christology* (Grand Rapids, MI: Eerdmans, 2011), 210–21.

14. Cantalamessa's citation of Gerd Theissen and Annette Marz is from their *Der historische Jesus: ein Lehrbuch* (Göttingen: Vandenhoeck & Ruprecht, 1999), 624.

15. Benedict XVI, *Jesus of Nazareth: Part Two: Holy Week: From the Entrance into Jerusalem to the Resurrection*, trans. Vatican Secretariat of State (San Francisco: Ignatius Press, 2011), 120–21.

16. But even here it is significant to note that though I disagreed with Benedict's reading of John the Baptist's identification of Jesus as "the Lamb of God who takes away the sins of the world," it is striking that he uses historical-critical results to make his case for Jesus' knowledge as to what the telos of his baptism truly is. His approach is not simply to cite the words of the creed or the magisterium to make a historical case from the Gospels themselves. One has to wrestle with the evidence of the texts—but always in conversation with the claims the Church has made about the identity of Jesus as the Divine Son. It is that very goal that my own essay has attempted to embody.

17. On the epistemic value of faith, see the opening chapter of his *Introduction to Christianity*, trans. J. R. Foster (San Francisco: Ignatius Press, 2004), 39–81.

chapter ten

THE FEAST OF PEACE

*The Eucharist as a Sacrifice and a Meal in
Benedict XVI's Theology*

KIMBERLY HOPE BELCHER

Pope Benedict XVI's eucharistic theology is marked by a commitment to the traditional Roman Catholic doctrine, stated clearly in the Council of Trent, that the Mass is a sacrifice. His understanding of the sacrifice of the Mass, however, can overcome the dichotomy of meal and sacrifice as it has been portrayed all too often since the Reformation period. In order for the Mass to be a complete participation in the sacrificial love of Son and Father, it must also take on the dimension of a meal. The festal dimension of the Eucharist, recovered in the high levels of eucharistic reception in contemporary Roman Catholicism, is integral to its sacrificial dimension.[1]

MEAL AND SACRIFICE IN BENEDICT XVI

In his essays on eucharistic theology published before his election to the papacy, Benedict XVI expressed deep concerns about the use of meal imagery to describe the Eucharist. In the essay "Form and Content in the Eucharistic Celebration," for instance, Benedict argues that speaking of a meal structure in the Mass, or calling the contemporary Eucharist a "meal" or a "sacrificial meal," "is based on a misunderstanding of the Eucharist's origins and leads to a false view of the sacrament."[2] Theologically, "there is no opposition between 'meal' and 'sacrifice,'" [because] "they belong inseparably together in the new sacrifice of the Lord." Nevertheless, theologies centered on meal language "reduce the sacrificial character of the Mass in favor of a meal-oriented theory."[3]

The meal theory seemed to threaten the doctrine of sacrifice because if the Eucharist had the structure of an ordinary Jewish or Greco-Roman meal in the early Church, one might suppose that it was a continuation of Jesus' radical table fellowship, and thus would be offered even to sinners. Pope Benedict XVI saw in this, quite reasonably, a precursor to a call for greater openness to communion in the modern day. More fundamentally, though, the idea that the Eucharist could have the "structure" or "form" of a meal and the "content" or dogmatic meaning of a sacrifice seemed problematic to him. In the liturgy, he argues, "the structure is not merely a ceremonial form, but at its core an indispensable manifestation of its essential content[;] it makes no sense absolutely to separate the one from the other."[4] And in fact, the form of the Mass, as was made clear by the liturgical movement, was "the inner expression of the spiritual reality which takes place within the Mass."[5] The spiritual reality taking place within the Mass, though, is the sacrifice of the cross, not a community meal. This conviction is so strong that Pope Benedict XVI concludes that in the form of the Eucharist "there *can* be no direct continuity between Jesus and the Church"; rather, in reaching out to embrace the Gentiles, the early Church legitimately and inescapably undergoes structural development which cements the Christian form of the Eucharist.[6] "The Last Supper of Jesus is certainly the basis of all Christian liturgy, but in itself it is not yet Christian. . . . [I]t has not yet attained a form, a structure *[Gestalt]* of its own as Christian liturgy. . . . [T]he Last Supper is the foundation of the dogmatic content of the Christian Eucharist, not of its liturgical form."[7] Despite this element of discontinuity, "there is no hiatus between Jesus and the Church. The Lord's gift is not some rigid formula but a living reality. It was open to historical development."[8]

There is, thus, also a continuity between the institution of the Eucharist at the Last Supper and the Church's Eucharist. This continuity comes from the words of Christ over the cup and the bread, which form the heart, in the Roman Rite, of the eucharistic prayer. In fact, the central form or structure of the liturgy, for Pope Benedict, is the *eucharistia*, the eucharistic prayer. To make this prayer in the Church is to participate in the whole Paschal Mystery, supper and sacrifice both: "The eucharistic prayer is an entering-in to the prayer of Jesus Christ himself; hence it is the Church's entering-in to the Logos, the Father's Word, into the Logos' self-surrender to the Father, which, in the Cross, has also become the surrender of mankind to him."[9] Although the Eucharist did include a community meal in its origins, that dimension was finally subordinated to the structure of the *eucharistia*, the eucharistic or thanksgiving prayer. Thus the Catholic Eucharist should not be called a meal.

In *The Spirit of the Liturgy,* originally published in 2000 in German, Benedict reaffirms this view. Celebration *versus populum*, with the priest facing the people, he argues, "brings with it a new idea of the essence of the liturgy—the liturgy as a communal meal."[10] But this is a "misunderstanding" of the eucharistic celebration, because "the Eucharist that Christians celebrate really cannot adequately be described by the term 'meal'. True, the Lord established the new reality of Christian worship within the framework of a Jewish (Passover) meal, but it was precisely this new reality, not the meal as such, that he commanded us to repeat. Very soon the new reality was separated from its ancient context and found its proper and suitable form."[11] In this book, however, the argument against seeing the Eucharist as a meal is an incidental support for the eastward orientation of the Christian assembly and the priest in the eucharistic celebration: the Eucharist should not be considered a meal because that supports the practice of having the priest face the people. Indeed, Benedict XVI concedes that even if we consider the Last Supper as a direct model for contemporary eucharistic celebrations, Greco-Roman din-ing practices would argue that Jesus as host and his guests would all recline on one side of the table, and this would reinforce the argument for celebration *ad orientem*, toward the East.[12] The concern, in other words, primarily concerns eucharistic practice and is not based on a theological conflict of meal and sacrifice.

Moreover, the Christian Eucharist should not be fully divorced from the festivity of meal practice, for after the liturgy "the joy that it contains [may turn] into a 'secular' feast, which is expressed in a common meal and dancing but does not lose sight of the reason for the joy, of what gives it its purpose and measure. This connection between the liturgy and cheerful earthiness ('Church and inn') has always been regarded as typically Catholic, and so it is still."[13] Though still committed to the centrality of the doctrine of eucharistic sacrifice, Pope Benedict seems, in *The Spirit of the Liturgy*, to be moving away from the idea that meal imagery threatens Catholic eucharistic theology.

"The Theology of the Liturgy," a paper delivered to the Fontgombault Liturgical Conference in July 2001, has a very similar focus. Here Pope Benedict critiques Catholic liturgical theology for its reticence about sacrificial language, its "modernity": "One can no longer imagine that human offences can wound God, and even less that they could necessitate an expiation such as that which constitutes the cross of Christ.... Thus the crisis of the Liturgy has its basis in central ideas about [humanity]. In order to overcome it, it does not suffice to banalise the Liturgy and transform it into a simple gathering at a fraternal meal."[14] This is a more nuanced presentation: the problem with meal language is that, due to contemporary cultural assumptions, especially in the context of a highly secularized Europe, a "simple" and "fraternal meal" will support a modern tendency to discount both Christ's sacrifice and human responsibility. He is stronger, too, about the continuity between the Passover meal and the Christian eucharistic sacrifice, acknowledging that "even in the earliest period, when the Passover was still a family feast, the slaughtering of lambs already had a sacrificial character. Thus, precisely through the tradition of the Passover, the idea of sacrifice is carried right up to the words and gestures of the Last Supper."[15]

In *Sacramentum Caritatis,* however, Benedict XVI's postsynodal apostolic exhortation on the Eucharist in 2005, and in *Deus Caritas Est,* later the same year, he uses meal imagery for the Eucharist very positively while of course not abandoning sacrificial imagery. In his homily at the inauguration of the synod, he begins with a reflection on the edible things, the bread and wine in the readings, and the "feast" in which they become "images of the gift of love." In this homily, meal and sacrifice are fused in feast: the Church celebrates "the mystery of the Eucharist, where the Lord gives us the bread of life and the wine of His love, and invites us to the feast of eternal love. We celebrate the Eucharist in the awareness that its price was the death of the Son—the sacrifice of his life, which is present in it. Whenever we eat this bread and drink this cup, we proclaim the death of the Lord until He comes, says St Paul (Cf. 1 Cor 11:26)."[16] In *Sacramentum Caritatis* the first image of the Eucharist is "the food of truth": "In this sacrament, the Lord truly becomes food for us, to satisfy our hunger for truth and freedom."[17] The sacrifice of Christ is presented using the Lamb of God imagery that evokes the Passover meal, and this leads directly, in the following paragraph, to a reflection on the institution at the Last Supper, which "took place within a ritual meal commemorating the foundational event of the people of Israel: their delivery from slavery in Egypt."[18] Meal and sacrifice are no longer at odds but complementary aspects of the one feast, and the continuity between the Last Supper and the Christian Eucharist is emphasized.

In his 2011 *Jesus of Nazareth: Holy Week,* too, Benedict is stronger on the connection between the Passover and the early Church's Eucharist than in any of these earlier writings. Here he argues that the Johannine chronology is most historically reliable and thus that the Last Supper was not itself a Passover meal, but that it was recognized as a Passover theologically based on early Church experience with eucharistic celebration. That is, the early Church recognized that the Eucharist was a continuing fulfillment of the Passover celebration of Israel, and on this basis the evangelists of the synoptic Gospels, relying on their liturgical experience, set the Last Supper as a Passover meal.[19]

This transition no doubt reflects many contextual factors: for example, Pope Benedict has long been aware that not all the Catholic world is threatened in the same way by secularization as his native country and continent. In *Christ Our Hope* he even recognizes secularism in the United States as a positive force, considering its unique history: the United States was "secular precisely out of love for religion in its authenticity, which can only be lived freely."[20] The *Instrumentum Laboris* for the 2005 synod also reflects the diversity of Catholic cultures: "In those countries enjoying a general climate of peace and prosperity—primarily western countries—many perceive the Eucharistic mystery as simply the fulfilment of a Sunday obligation and a meal of fellowship. Instead, in those countries experiencing wars and other difficulties, many understand the Eucharistic mystery more fully, that is, including its sacrificial aspect."[21] In less affluent societies, where a mother might regularly find herself deciding whether to eat or to feed her children, the fact that every meal is a sacrifice is more readily seen. While pastoral care might require catechesis on the nature of sacrifice in prosperous contexts, other contexts highlight other pastoral needs, which might be answered by a relative emphasis on the Eucharist as the banquet of the poor, especially as these cultures more readily understand its sacrificial aspect. Perhaps, too, the resurgence of theologies of sacrifice in recent theological scholarship played a role.

While I do not doubt the influence of these contextual and pastoral issues on the greater integration between meal and sacrifice in these papal teachings, I would argue that the inner theological dynamic of Pope Benedict XVI's understanding of the eucharistic sacrifice already implies its completion in a community meal. The Eucharist is the paradigmatic example of human worship for the pope, which means it is, as he puts it in *Spirit of the Liturgy*, "Peace in the universe through peace with God, the union of above and below."[22] The horizontal or meal dimension of the Eucharist flows naturally out of and is necessary to complete the vertical or sacrificial dimension, as soon as we understand how Benedict understands the connection between the Eucharist and the cross and the Trinitarian dimension of sacrificial worship.

LOVE AND SACRIFICE

Pope Benedict argues against Martin Luther's distrust of sacrifice, but he also recognizes Luther was responding to a fatally flawed vision of sacrifice. When the sacrifice of the Eucharist is seen as a work of a priest (or of a human institution of the Church) that overshadows or adds to the work of Christ on the cross, it becomes a trap for human pride. When Christians believe the sacrifice is offered to God as the judge who seeks to condemn us rather than our loving Savior, it becomes a trap for despair. Benedict disparages, in no uncertain terms, these understandings of Christian sacrifice. They are fused in the idea of sacrifice as destruction: by destroying something human beings would like to use, they "do something" for God, earning favor in the place of punishment. Thus the angry God is appeased by a human work. This understanding of any Christian sacrifice, Benedict argues, is ruled out by the image of God even in the Hebrew Scriptures who does not need human food, or want human worship belied by human injustice. The God of the Hebrew Scriptures is the unending giver, and the law exists to bring humans to justice and mutual love. The message of Judaism and Christianity is that God is liberator, savior.

In *The Spirit of the Liturgy,* Pope Benedict addresses these misunderstandings very clearly. Sacrifice is not only the heart and object of Christian worship; it is "at the heart of worship" in all religions.[23] Sacrifice springs from a twofold awareness intrinsic to humanity but expressed differently in different cultures: human beings are aware of the divine and "reach out toward God," and human beings are aware of themselves as both ontologically and morally divided from God.[24] In other words, sacrifice is a universal of human religion, according to Benedict, because human beings are transcendent and dependent. Sacrifice does not solely come from the fall of humanity; it is a "belonging oneself" to God, a willing submission to and acceptance of one's ontological dependence, that would be necessary (but not painful) even for a human race that had never fallen: "Belonging to God has nothing to do with destruction or non-being: it is rather a way of being. It means emerging from the state of separation, of apparent autonomy, of existing only for oneself and in oneself. It means losing oneself as the only possible way of finding oneself."[25]

How does this positive self-offering come to be misinterpreted as a "destruction, [a] definitive removal," of something precious from human use?[26] When human beings sin, they become morally as well as ontologically divided from God. After this, sacrifice includes elements of suffering: "the healing of wounded freedom, atonement, purification, deliverance from estrangement."[27] Human beings still experience longing for God, but now they also recognize that because of their sins they are unable to return to God on their own. Human beings and the whole cosmic order need reconciliation with God.[28] This knot, the need for God's aid, extends to the cosmic dimension in addition to addressing the human relationship with God. Traditional sacrificial cult preserves the integration of the relationship of human beings to God and to creation as a whole, but it is also apt to try to manipulate God with human worship.[29] This misunderstanding of sacrifice endangers all worship; only historical contact with a God who needs nothing and offers all can cleanse human worship from it, allowing true liturgy to take place.

True liturgy does not arise from the human desire to reach God (though that desire, implanted in humanity from creation, always exists); rather, it stems from the human awareness that the attempt to reach God is always a failure. Thus, although "in all religions sacrifice is at the heart of worship," it is in the exile that Israel finally learns (and thus can reveal to the world) what sacrifice is: "In this crisis the conviction became ever clearer that Israel's sufferings, through God and for God, the cry of her broken heart, her persistent pleading before the silent God, had to count in his sight as 'fatted sacrifices' and whole burnt offerings. It was the very emptiness of Israel's hands, the heaviness of her heart, that was now to be worship, to serve as a spiritual equivalent of the missing Temple oblations."[30]

This awareness of our own empty-handedness converts human beings from the belief that by destroying or giving over a valued good, we accomplish the healing of the world ourselves. This would be a liturgical enactment of pride, so that even worship would be a practice of deceptive self-sufficiency. Rather, the biblical testimony, especially in the Hebrew prophets, makes it clear that God has no need of human goods.[31] The human sacrifice to God, then, "the only real gift," is oneself.[32] Ritual sacrifice facilitates this self-offering; so while a human being "living righteously . . . is the true worship of God . . . [c]ult exists in order to communicate this vision and to give life in such a way that glory is given to God."[33] Cult is therefore important, giving structure to human society,[34] but the emphasis must remain on the self-offering, since that is the essential soteriological aspect of sacrifice. The self-offering of true sacrifice has as its ultimate object the *reditus* of the world back into God, so that transculturally, "worship is the attempt . . . to overcome guilt and bring back the world and one's own life into right order."[35] That right order, enacted by self-offering, is human participation in "love-transformed [humanity], the divinization of creation and the surrender of all things to God: God all in all. . . . That is the purpose of the world. That is the essence of sacrifice and worship."[36] True sacrifice affirms the structure of creation, in which all things exist because God loves them, and therefore the self exists for God and all God's creatures.

The late medieval understandings of sacrifice that Martin Luther protested, which suggested that the sacrifice of the Mass either competed with or added to the sacrifice of the cross, Pope Benedict condemns as "mistaken ideas."[37] Rather, the eucharistic sacrifice is a witness to the fact that God does not save us without our participation but rather "accepts us and takes us up, so that we ourselves become active with his support and alongside him, participating in the mystery ourselves."[38] This is key to the essential tension in Pope Benedict's soteriology: on the one hand, God's salvation is radically gracious and all-encompassing, requiring nothing of human beings; on the other hand, God's salvation is radically respectful of human freedom, not only leaving room for refusal, but liberating human beings for full participation in God's work. The sacrificial dimension of the Eucharist must be interpreted in terms of its historical contact with the liberating God, through the words of institution, "This is my body. . . . This is my blood."

These words, "This is my body. . . . This is my blood," have a threefold significance for Pope Benedict, which he addresses very clearly in the eucharistic essays collected in *God Is Near Us*. These essays represent an earlier period in Pope Benedict's eucharistic theology since they date to 1978, but they provide the necessary background for understanding how the pope sees the relationship between the eucharistic prayer, the sacrifice of the Mass, and the sacrifice on the cross. For Benedict, it is the words of institution that connect these theological realities. First, these words transform the execution of the cross "into the spiritual act of affirmation, into the act of self-sharing love; into the act of adoration, which is offered to God."[39] Second, they assert "that love is stronger than death," a promise about the structure of the world, which God verifies in the Resurrection. The words thus tie the Paschal Mystery, feast, cross, and resurrection together.[40] And third, the words are a gift, the core of the eucharistic prayer, that allows us to participate in the perfect sacrifice ourselves. Because "Jesus Christ transformed his death into verbal form—into a prayer . . . we can share in this death, because we can participate in this transforming prayer, can join in praying it. This, then, is the new sacrifice he has given us, in which he includes us all."[41] This is the solution to the age-old problem of representative sacrifice: it is never sufficient, but it points toward the possibility of our participating in the one sufficient sacrifice of Jesus on the cross.

If free self-offering, and a participative share offered to all humanity, is the core of the sacrifice of the cross, it is accomplished on both the human and the divine level. Within the Godhead, the Word eternally accomplishes this losing himself or giving himself up in order to attain his identity. I will come back to this Trinitarian layer later. At the same time, the human self-offering of Christ on the cross, a self-offering that takes the form of "painful expiation" because of the Fall,[42] is also the fulfillment of the Jewish—and indeed transcultural—tradition of representative sacrifice. Since human beings are aware that they do not give themselves freely to God, they try to heal this brokenness through representative sacrifice. They are always dimly aware, Pope Benedict argues, that such sacrifice, even of the firstborn child, falls short of the absolute self-giving required by God's very essence. In the Hebrew Scriptures, then, representative sacrifice is canonically authorized by the story of Abraham and Isaac but limited by the prophets. The reminder that representative sacrifice is inadequate, according to Pope Benedict, points to the eventual fulfillment (and abolishing) of the system by Jesus on the cross.[43]

The sacrifice of Jesus on the cross, at the human level, is *the* paradigmatic example of the self-offering that recovers what humanity is supposed to be. The historical ties of the crucifixion to the tradition of representative sacrifice in Judaism and elsewhere in human culture, however, also opens this sacrifice to all Jews and all humanity, so that on the cross, Jesus "gathers up and into himself all worship of God, takes it from the types and shadows into the reality of . . . union with the living God."[44] Because of the reality of the hypostatic union, this complete human self-offering is not only united with the whole of humanity, but becomes one with the inner life of God, so that the partial, flawed ritual self-offerings of human beings throughout history are united to God's own life: "the Word who is made flesh . . . draws 'all flesh' into the glorification of God. . . . He takes up into himself our sufferings and hopes, all the yearning of creation, and bears it to God. . . . In Jesus' self-surrender on the Cross, the Word is united with the entire reality of human life and suffering."[45] In this high priesthood the Passover is fulfilled, according to Pope Benedict, and all human worship is enabled to participate in the perfect self-offering of the cross, which is not destruction but "an act of new creation": "All worship is now a participation in this 'Pasch' of Christ, in his 'passing over' from divine to human, from death to life, to the unity of God and man."[46]

The sacrifice of the Eucharist, then, is no more than a sacramental participation in the self-offering of the Son to the Father, an offering historically accomplished on the cross and made eternally accessible for human participation in the eucharistic prayer. To say it is no more than this is not to minimalize the importance or salvific consequence of the eucharistic sacrifice; to participate in this self-offering is the best human beings can do, and all that they can do, and the fulfillment of human nature! The sacrifice of the cross is made present and effective in the Eucharist. It is neither extrinsic to the structure of salvation history (not some "other thing" that priests can offer an angry God to appease him) nor opposed to the Incarnation:

rather, the sacrifice of the Eucharist is the presence of the unity of God and humanity which is definitively offered to humanity in the Incarnation and consummated in the Pasch. Any theology that divides the sacrifice of the Mass from the sacrifice of the cross is simply a mistake. The self-offering of Jesus, which has its root in the self-offering of the Word to the Father, validates and completes the ritual offering of the Mass.

In *God Is Love,* Benedict XVI refers explicitly to the experience of human participation in the divine self-offering of the Trinity. The treatment of the Eucharist in this document is central, providing the ultimate revelation of the true love defined in the first half of the letter and the foundation for the Church's charity discussed in the second half. In this letter Benedict reaffirms that the sacrifice of the Mass is a participation in the cross: "Jesus gave this act of oblation an enduring presence through his institution of the Eucharist at the Last Supper."[47] The act of Christ on the cross, though, does not merely take up into God's life the ritual sacrifice of humanity but also makes present in history the eternal love relationship of Father and Son. This gives the cross its unique significance for salvation history: it brings human and divine self-offering together. Human participation in divine love unifies what Benedict calls the erotic and agapic aspects of love, its "ascending" reaching out and its "descending" receptive love. Precisely for this reason, it also unites contemplation and action, grace and mutual charity, and sacrifice and meal.

Even the "merely" human experience of erotic love draws human beings out of themselves, out of self-satisfaction and into the self-offering of true sacrifice: when "a real discovery of the other" takes place, "love . . . becomes concern and care for the other. No longer is it self-seeking, a sinking in the intoxication of happiness; instead it seeks the good of the beloved: it becomes renunciation, and it is ready, and even willing, for sacrifice."[48] Even in human love there is an interpenetration of *eros* and *agape,* active and receptive love. At the same time, human beings are not created to live by *agape* alone, and the drive to give only, never to receive, is a sign of a spiritual malaise, pride, or despair. Rather, "*eros* and *agape*—ascending love and descending love—can never be completely separated. The more the two, in their different aspects, find a proper unity in the one reality of love, the more the true nature of love in general is realized."[49]

This unity, the transformative integration of erotic and agapic, active and passive love, stems from the grounding of creation in the intra-Trinitarian relations of Father, Son, and Holy Spirit. It is manifest in the scriptural narratives of God's love: "God's *eros* for man is also totally agape . . . [because] it is bestowed in a completely gratuitous manner . . . [and] it is love which forgives."[50] God's gratuitous salvation, God's preservation of human freedom, and God's self-abandoning acceptance of the results of that freedom unite an element of passivity with God's passionate love for humanity. In volume 5 of *Theo-Drama,* Pope Benedict's friend Hans Urs von Balthasar describes the active passion of the Trinitarian love: already in the immanent Trinity there is a cycle of "ultimate self-giving, self-emptying (in the Word of God) and self-reacquisition (in the Holy Spirit)."[51] In the revealed God we see that "absolute self-giving is beyond 'power' and 'powerlessness': its ability to 'let be' embraces both."[52] The mystery of the cross reveals an essential truth of God's being: God "wishes to be almighty not solely by creating," that is, actively; "by begetting and breathing forth, and allowing [him]self to be begotten and breathed forth, [he] hands over . . . power to the Other—whoever that Other may be—without ever seeking to take it back."[53] The whole of creation, particularly humans, who are made in the Trinitarian image, expresses the truth that "to give oneself is not to lose oneself; it is the essential realization of oneself."[54] In the Trinity, the Son's consent to be begotten and the Spirit's consent to proceed are equiprimordial with the Father's absolute self-giving that gives over the divine substance, holding nothing back. As such, in the Trinity, neither activity nor passivity, neither *eros* nor *agape,* has the priority; both are united in the absolute love that constitutes the Godhead. "'Substance' is there for the purpose of 'transubstantiation,' for 'communion.'"[55] God desires to offer this love to humanity as well, but it requires our active and receptive participation: "Where absolute love is concerned, conceiving and letting be are just as essential as giving. In fact, without this receptive letting be and all it involves—gratitude for the gift of oneself and a turning in love toward the Giver—the giving itself is impossible."[56] For Balthasar, this is true of the Word and of human beings, who are conformed to the image of the Incarnate Word by their grateful reception of God's love and active return to the Father.

The Paschal Mystery, then, is the paradigmatic moment in which the structures of creation are revealed in their real purpose. In the Hebrew prophets, Pope Benedict argues, we already see that "God's passionate love for his people—for humanity—is at the same time a forgiving love. It is so great that it turns God against himself, his love against his justice."[57] This entrance of the agapic acceptance into history is fulfilled on the cross, "the culmination of that turning of God against himself in which he gives himself in order to raise man up and save him. This is love in its most radical form."[58] In love, on the cross, Jesus unifies the power of God's justice and the powerlessness of human death: "so great is God's love for man that by becoming man he follows him even into death and so reconciles justice and love."[59] Of course, this turning of God against himself is at the same time the essential manifestation in history of the God we know and proclaim: the God for whom love and justice, mercy and judgment are not at odds but have been brought paradoxically into reconciliation on the cross.

By eucharistic worship human beings participate in the sacrifice of the cross; by it the Church continues its unification of justice and mercy, of ritual and ethics. "The Eucharist draws us into Jesus' act of self-oblation. More than just statically receiving the incarnate *Logos*, we enter into the very dynamic of his self-giving."[60] This means, for Pope Benedict, that the sacrifice of the Mass also obliges Christians to one another and in fact to the whole of humanity: "Union with Christ is also union with all those to whom he gives himself. . . . Love of God and love of neighbor are now truly united: God incarnate draws us all to himself."[61] In 1978 Pope Benedict reflected that the true sacrifice is "a contrite heart,"[62] but in *God Is Love* he has united that prophetic utterance to those insisting that sacrifice is the practice of justice. "Is not this the fast that I choose," Isaiah says, "to loose the bonds of injustice, to undo the thongs of the yoke, to let the oppressed go free, and to break every yoke? Is it not to share your bread with the hungry, and bring the homeless poor into your house; when you see the naked, to cover them, and not to hide yourself from your own kin?" (Is 58:6–7 NRSV). The true sacrifice of the Eucharist, Pope Benedict says in *God Is Love*, leads to *caritas*, "the service of charity," which is as essential to the Church as "the sacraments and the Word."[63] Because the Eucharist is ongoing participation in Christ's self-sacrifice, this service, the organized and concrete practice of loving the neighbor, is intrinsically connected to eucharistic worship: "'Worship' itself, Eucharistic communion, includes the reality both of being loved and of loving others in turn. A Eucharist which does not pass over into the concrete practice of love is intrinsically fragmented."[64] In other words, for Pope Benedict, the sacrifice of the Mass is a ritual realization of the Trinitarian love of Father and Son, into which all humanity is invited by the event of the cross. Precisely for this reason its *lex orandi*, structure of prayer, issues forth as *lex vivendi*, structure of life.

FEAST OF PEACE

This connection of liturgy and ethics, the unity of the agapic and erotic aspects of the eucharistic sacrifice, is also a unity of the sacrificial aspects of the Eucharist and its meal aspects. The meal aspect of the Eucharist in Benedict XVI's papal writings is not a mere addition to the sacrificial aspect; still less does it detract from the sacrificial reality of the Eucharist. As I argued above, the sacrifice of the Mass is participation in the sacrifice of the cross to the fullest possible degree. The meal aspect is united to this reality because the sacrifice of the cross flows outward and naturally completes itself in a community meal, as evident in Benedict's theology in three ways: through the historical completion of the cross in Christ's Resurrection; through the sacramental completion of Christ's body in the Body of the Church; and through the revelation of divine beauty in the icon of the Eucharist.

As discussed above, the sacrifice of the cross remains accessible to humanity in the Mass because of the eucharistic prayer in all its forms, because by the meal in the upper room "Jesus Christ transformed his death into verbal form—into a prayer—and in so doing, changed the world."[65] By speaking the words of life that made bread and wine into his own body and blood, Christ realized the sacrifice of his whole existence as human: "his self-giving sacrifice [in the Incarnation], the mystery of the Cross and the mystery of the paschal sacrament that derives from it."[66] These sacrifices, however, are not complete alone; Good Friday is completed in Easter. "The words of institution alone are not sufficient," Pope Benedict says; "the death alone is not sufficient; and even both together are still insufficient but have to be complemented by the Resurrection, in which God accepts this death and makes it the door into a new life."[67] In the immanent Trinity, the Son must consent to be begotten; more, the Unoriginate Origin must consent to become Father and receive the gift of self from the one he generates. On the cross, too, God must consent to become the receiver of the gift for the sacrifice to become complete. When God accepts the sacrifice of the cross, death is transformed into victory, not only for the Victor on the cross, but for all humanity.

What is more, the completion of the cross in the Resurrection, already in the scriptural evidence, is made known to the disciples through meals: the fish in the upper room, the breaking of the bread on the road to Emmaus, the bread and fish at the seashore. On the cross Christ thirsts, but in the Resurrection he eats with his people. These meals affirm the truth of the Resurrection (in the face of understandable doubt) by affirming the continuity between the Son of Man and the risen Lord.

The meals of the Resurrection are also meals that found the new community, the new Body of Christ. The Resurrection, for Pope Benedict, is the foundation of the new humanity, and that humanity is drawn into one another and into God through the Eucharist. In *Spirit of the Liturgy*, for example, he writes:

Deliverance from death is at the same time deliverance from the captivity of individualism, from the prison of self, from the incapacity to love and make a gift of oneself. Thus Easter becomes the great feast of Baptism, in which man, as it were, enacts the passage through the Red Sea, emerges from his own existence into communion with Christ and so into communion with all who belong to Christ. Resurrection builds communion. It creates the new People of God. The grain of wheat that dies all alone does not remain alone but brings much fruit with it.[68]

The Resurrection thus completes the passing over and fittingly fulfills the feast of Passover. "Israel's Passover is the recalling of an act of God that was liberation and thus the foundation of the community";[69] similarly, Christian outreach even in the contemporary context is founded in the Christian feast. "Precisely because Christ has become for us the food of truth, the Church turns to every man and woman, inviting them freely to accept God's gift."[70] It is the festal dimension of the Eucharist, the communal love expressed in communal eating, that gives witness to its sacrificial dimension, just as it was the Resurrection that manifested that the crucifixion was the salvific work of God in the world. "By this everyone will know that you are my disciples, if you have love for one another" (Jn 13:35 NRSV).

In other words, the vertical, sacrificial dimension, as the work of God in the world, has the priority. Nonetheless, it is often the horizontal, communal meal that is first recognized as God's work, and this, theologically speaking, is no surprise. In fact, there is another theological domain, significant in both Balthasar's and Benedict's work, in which the earthly becomes the first manifestation of transcendence, the domain of beauty or of theological aesthetics. Beauty makes its appearance in the creaturely, but it captivates us because it speaks of God's love. It challenges the dichotomy of the bodily and the spiritual, because it presents a "living, efficacious form—it is a body animated by the spirit, a body whose meaning and whose principle of unity are dictated and imposed by the spirit," as Balthasar puts it. For the human being who has "a spiritual eye," beauty can realign body and spirit to exist in the same profound unity, which allows the human person to reach out to God and respond to God's invitation.[71] As Benedict XVI says in *Spirit of the Liturgy*, beauty arouses the erotic desire for God, which then prepares us to receive God's agapic love: "Through the appearance of the beautiful we are wounded in our innermost being, and that wound grips us and takes us beyond ourselves; it stirs longing into flight and moves us toward the truly Beautiful, to the Good in itself."[72]

Beauty, in the context of sacred art, is thus not merely an aesthetic appeal; it is a covenant call, just as liturgical aesthetic exists to serve the call to covenant: "However inferior the first images of the Christian tradition may often be in their artistic qualities, an extraordinary spiritual process has taken place in them. . . . The Resurrection sheds a new light on history. It is seen as a path of hope, into which the images draw us."[73] Beauty's purpose, from creation, is to draw human beings into the Trinitarian love of God; it arouses our desire, captivates us, and pulls us toward God, but it also calls us to see beyond established dichotomies between body and spirit, between human and divine, so that God may be all in all. The exultation that results is naturally expressed in a feast, a sacrifice, and meal: "The Lord himself has given us the essentials of this new worship. The Church, his Bride, is called to celebrate the eucharistic banquet daily in his memory. She thus makes the redeeming sacrifice of her Bridegroom a part of human history and makes it sacramentally present in every culture."[74]

The icon is the paradigm of this sacred art for Benedict: it is born of the artist's prayer and evokes prayer for the viewer.[75] Moreover, the paradigmatic icon is the *acheiropoietos,* the miraculous image not made by human hands, which is "a participation in the reality concerned, the refulgence and thus the presence of the One who gives himself in the image."[76] This image most clearly reveals the character of beauty as the *self*-revelation of the self-giving God, because there is no temptation in it to exult in human ingenuity and pride. The Eucharist is the culmination of God's visibility to human beings in salvation history, and it also develops the spiritual eye needed for the experience of sacred beauty.[77] The Eucharist, then, is very much like an icon not made by human hands. Perhaps it is not surprising that, for Benedict, eucharistic adoration becomes a uniquely Catholic kind of veneration, one in which the Eucharist dissolves the apparent conflict between contemplation and action, between seeing and eating, between communion with God and communion with one's brothers and sisters. These are revealed as "a false dichotomy" through the prayer of the Church, because "eucharistic adoration is simply the natural consequence of the eucharistic celebration, which is itself the Church's supreme act of adoration."[78] By the act of adoration, which springs from the Mass and leads back to it, one develops the faculty of spiritual sight necessary not only to see God, but to see God in and serve one another in charity: "it is precisely this personal encounter with the Lord that then strengthens the social mission contained in the Eucharist, which seeks to break down not only the walls that separate the Lord and ourselves, but also and especially the walls that separate us from one another."[79]

In the end, then, in *Deus Caritas Est* and in *Sacramentum Caritatis,* the Eucharist has become the self-gift of the Trinity come to dwell at home with human beings. In it, the sacrifice of Christ on the cross has given itself over and become complete in the community meal, and in it the eschatological call to community with God is recognized also as the moral call to be one in Spirit with my brothers and sisters.[80] The Eucharist is the fulfillment of human worship, "peace in the universe through peace with God, the union of above and below."[81]

NOTES

1. I deeply appreciate the interest, comments, and suggestions of my colleagues and students at the College of St. Benedict and St. John's University, particularly Martin Connell, whose advice was invaluable. I am also grateful to the contributors to this volume, several of whom provided suggestions that motivated revisions.

2. Joseph Ratzinger, "Form and Content in the Eucharistic Celebration," in *Feast of Faith: Approaches to a Theology of the Liturgy,* trans. Graham Harrison (San Francisco: Ignatius Press, 1986), 51.

3. Ibid., 50, 35. The second quote is a rhetorical question, but the context suggests that it represents Benedict XVI's opinion.

4. Ibid., 35–36.

5. Ibid., 34.

6. Ibid., 42.

7. Ibid., 41.

8. Ibid., 49. Eamon Duffy discusses Benedict XVI's understanding of liturgical development and authority in "Benedict XVI and the Liturgy," collected in *The Genius of the Roman Rite: Historical, Theological, and Pastoral*

Perspectives on Catholic Liturgy, ed. Uwe Michael Lang (Chicago: Liturgy Training Publications, 2010), 1–21.

9. Ratzinger, "Form and Content," 37.

10. Joseph Ratzinger, *Spirit of the Liturgy*, trans. John Saward (San Francisco: Ignatius Press, 2000), 77.

11. Ibid., 78.

12. Ibid.

13. Ibid., 200.

14. Joseph Ratzinger, "Theology of the Liturgy," in *Looking Again at the Question of the Liturgy with Cardinal Ratzinger: Proceedings of the July 2001 Fontgombault Liturgical Conference*, ed. Alcuin Reid, O.S.B. (Farnborough, UK: St Michael's Abbey Press, 2001), 24. This concern about modern reticence regarding expiation is repeated in Benedict XVI, *Jesus of Nazareth: Part Two: Holy Week: From the Entrance into Jerusalem to the Ressurection*, trans. Vatican Secretariat of State (San Francisco: Ignatius Press, 2011), 119.

15. Ratzinger, "Theology of the Liturgy," 23.

16. Benedict XVI, "Homily of the Holy Father at the Solemn Inauguration of the XI Ordinary General Assembly of Bishops," October 2, 2005. Available at www.vatican.va/news_services/press/sinodo/documents/bollet tino_21_xi-ordinaria-2005/02_inglese/b03_02.html.

17. Pope Benedict XVI, *Sacramentum Caritatis*, December 25, 2005, par. 2. Available at www.vatican.va/holy_father/benedict_xvi/apost _exhortations/documents/hf_ben-xvi_exh_20070222_sacramentum -caritatis_en.html.

18. Ibid., pars. 9, 10.

19. Benedict XVI, *Jesus of Nazareth*, II, 105–15.

20. Benedict XVI, *Christ Our Hope: The Papal Addresses of the Apostolic Journey to the United States* (Mahwah, NJ: Paulist Press, 2008), 6; see also 27.

21. Synod of Bishops, "XI Ordinary General Assembly: The Eucharist: Source and Summit of the Life of the Church, *Instrumentum laboris*," October, 2005, par. 33. Available at www.vatican.va/roman_curia/synod/documents/rc_synod_doc_20050707_instrlabor-xi-assembly_en.html.

22. Ratzinger, *Spirit of the Liturgy*, 35.

23. Ibid., 28.

24. Ibid., 22, 35.

25. Ibid., 28.

26. Ibid.

27. Ibid., 33.

28. Ibid.

29. Ibid., 25.

30. Ibid., 28, 45. See also Joseph Ratzinger, "God's Yes and His Love Are Maintained Even in Death: The Origin of the Eucharist in the Paschal Mystery," in *God Is Near Us: The Eucharist, the Heart of Life* (San Francisco: Ignatius Press, 2003), 33–34.

31. Ratzinger, *Spirit of the Liturgy,* 28.

32. Ibid., 35.

33. Ibid., 18.

34. Cf., e.g., ibid., 19.

35. Ibid., 35.

36. Ibid., 28.

37. Of course, these flawed understandings of sacrifice were not the only ones available in the late Middle Ages, but they were the ones that concerned Luther, and they have continued to hinder Catholic-Lutheran dialogue since Trent. For a history of doctrines of eucharistic sacrifice, see Edward J. Kilmartin, *The Eucharist in the West: History and Theology,* ed. Robert J. Daly (Collegeville, MN: Liturgical Press, 1998).

38. Ratzinger, "The Wellspring of Life from the Side of the Lord, Opened in Loving Sacrifice," in Ratzinger, *God Is Near Us,* 50.

39. Ratzinger, *God Is Near Us,* 29.

40. Ibid., 43–44.

41. Ibid., 49.

42. Ratzinger, *Spirit of the Liturgy,* 33.

43. Ibid., 35–44.

44. Ibid., 45.

45. Ibid., 47.

46. Ibid., 34.

47. Benedict XVI, *God Is Love,* par. 13.

48. Ibid., par. 6.

49. Ibid., par. 7.

50. Ibid., par. 10.

51. Hans Urs von Balthasar, *Theo-Drama: Theological Dramatic Theory. V. The Last Act,* trans. Graham Harrison (San Francisco: Ignatius Press, 1998), 74.

52. Ibid., 74.

53. Ibid., 66.

54. Ibid., 74.

55. Ibid.

56. Ibid., 86.

57. Benedict XVI, *God Is Love,* par. 10.

58. Ibid., par. 12.

59. Ibid., par. 10.

60. Ibid., par. 13.

61. Ibid., par. 14.

62. Ratzinger, *God Is Near Us*, 48.

63. Benedict XVI, *God Is Love*, par. 22.

64. Ibid., par. 14.

65. Ratzinger, *God Is Near Us*, 49.

66. Ibid., 21.

67. Ibid., 39.

68. Ratzinger, *Spirit of the Liturgy*, 102.

69. Ibid., 101.

70. Benedict XVI, *Sacramentum Caritatis*, par. 2.

71. Balthasar, *Glory of the Lord*, vol. 1: *Seeing the Form* (San Francisco: Ignatius Press, 1989), 22.

72. Ratzinger, *Spirit of the Liturgy*, 126.

73. Ibid., 118.

74. Benedict XVI, *Sacramentum Caritatis*, par. 12.

75. Ratzinger, *Spirit of the Liturgy*, 133.

76. Ibid., 119–20.

77. Benedict XVI, *God Is Love*, par. 42; *Spirit of the Liturgy*, 83. This emphasis on the Eucharist as a school for the capacity to see the invisible is thoroughly patristic; see, e.g., Georgia Frank, "'Taste and See': The Eucharist and the Eyes of Faith in the Fourth Century," *Church History* 70 (2001): 619–43.

78. Benedict XVI, *Sacramentum Caritatis*, par. 66.

79. Ibid.

80. Ratzinger, *Spirit of the Liturgy*, 59.

81. Ibid., 35.

chapter eleven

MARY IN THE THEOLOGY OF JOSEPH RATZINGER/ POPE BENEDICT XVI

MATTHEW LEVERING

In 1961, in preparation for the Second Vatican Council, Fr. Joseph Ratzinger, then a young theologian at the University of Bonn, wrote a speech for Joseph Cardinal Frings, archbishop of Cologne. In this speech Ratzinger urged that Mariology be placed fully in the context of ecclesiology. He wrote that Mary "is the living sign of the fact that Christian piety does not stand in isolation before God. . . . She is the sign that Christ does not intend to remain alone, but rather that redeemed, believing humankind has become one body with him, one single Christ, 'the whole Christ, head and members,' as St. Augustine said with unsurpassable beauty."[1] Twenty-five years later, Ratzinger made a similar point in his essay "The Ecclesiology of the Second Vatican Council." The inclusion of Mariology in *Lumen Gentium*, he said, shows that "the Church is not some piece of machinery, is not just an institution, is not even one of the usual sociological entities. It is a person. It is a woman. It is a mother. It is living. The Marian understanding of the Church is the most decisive contrast to a purely organizational or bureaucratic concept of the Church."[2] That "Christ does not intend to remain alone" means that we have an intimate communion with him in the Church. In order to understand Christ's presence to us (and our presence to him), we must study the person of Mary.

Inspired by this insight, I explore Ratzinger's Mariology in four steps, without pretending to offer a comprehensive treatment of his approach. First, I offer an overview of his mature theology of Mary, as found in his book-length interview with Peter Seewald, *God and the World*, originally published in 2000. Second, I briefly examine his major contribution to the theology of Mary's Assumption in his *Eschatology* (1977), where he argues against the influential theory that all humans die into resurrection life—a theory that if true would make the dogma of Mary's Assumption simply a truth about what happens to all of us. Third, I treat his most sustained Mariological work, *Daughter Zion* (1977). Here I emphasize his use of typological reasoning in expositing the Marian doctrines. Fourth and last, I examine three homilies for the Feast of Mary's Assumption that he has delivered as Pope Benedict XVI, and I show that these homilies contain his most characteristic themes. Through these four steps I hope to provide a sense of the main lines of his contributions to Mariology.

MARY IN RATZINGER'S *GOD AND THE WORLD*

Although not a formal scholarly treatise, *God and the World* provides an accessible compendium of Ratzinger's thought a few years prior to his election as pope. In the section on Mariology, Ratzinger begins by exploring the title "Mother of God." This title was the subject of the Nestorian controversy that led to the Council of Ephesus in the year 431. What was at stake was whether Mary simply gave birth to the human nature of Jesus. The Council of Ephesus answered that Jesus' divine nature and human nature are supremely united in his divine Personhood. Mary, in giving birth to Jesus, gives birth to the Person: she is the mother of the Son, the mother of God, although it is the human nature of the Son that derives from her flesh. Ratzinger draws a parallel with Eve. In Genesis 3:20 we read, "The man called his wife's name Eve, because she was the mother of all the living." Mary is the new Eve because she is the Mother of the life-giving Savior.

On this basis, Ratzinger finds in Mary an "expression of the closeness of God," not only with respect to God entering into human history in a highly personal way through the incarnation, but also with respect to Jesus' action at his crucifixion, when he commanded the beloved disciple to take Mary as his mother.[3] Mary is our mother because a relationship with her awakens us to how close to us God is in Jesus Christ: "Jesus is building a new family."[4] Because her motherhood is both physical and spiritual, Mary uniquely enjoys the closeness to God that Jesus has come to bring. She is the one who, at the birth of Jesus, marvels at the mysteries that have taken place (Lk 2:19). She is found at the foot of the cross, where she cares for her suffering Son (Jn 19) who shares in our condition and is our Redeemer rather than our Dominator.[5] By addressing Mary as "woman" (Jn 2:4), Jesus (and the evangelist John) represents Mary as the new Eve, who assists in Jesus' inauguration of the new creation.

Mary's relationship to the new Adam uniquely marks her. God sets her apart for Christ, and indeed "her belonging in a special way to Christ brings with it a complete state of grace."[6] She does not have this relationship to Christ only after the Annunciation. Rather, in God's plan, she is prepared from the beginning of her existence to be the mother of Christ, a mission that requires her free and complete spiritual assent, as we see in Luke 1:38, "Behold, I am the handmaid of the Lord; let it be to me according to your word." Ratzinger observes, "Since a new beginning takes shape in her, Mary cannot possibly belong to this sinful state of things: her relation to God is not disordered; she stands from the outset, in a special way, in the sight of God."[7]

This point brings Ratzinger to the doctrine of Mary's bodily Assumption into heaven. He first remarks that we cannot imagine "heaven"; nor can we imagine a glorified body. Yet the goal of baptism is to attain what the dogma of Mary's Assumption teaches us she has attained. Ratzinger points to Ephesians 2:6, where Paul proclaims that God "raised us up with him [Christ], and made us sit with him in the heavenly places in Christ Jesus." We do not yet sit with God as we will when God raises us from the dead and gives us eternal life. By contrast, the fullness of the baptismal gift that Paul describes has been given to Mary, and so Mary shows us the destiny of the whole Church in faithful response to Christ. Although we cannot now know what a glorified body entails, we know that her body has been glorified and that "she has entered into full community with Christ."[8] She is now "completely a 'Christian.'"[9]

Why has God done this for Mary, and how is the Church able to know that God has done it? In Ratzinger's view, Scripture when read as a whole presents Mary (and the Church) as "the New Eve."[10] In Christ the new Adam, the human race has a new beginning: the old family of the first Adam, marked by sin and death, has given way to the new family of the second Adam, the fulfillment that God's plan always had in view. According to Ratzinger, Mary's unique motherhood and sharing in Christ's mission led to her identification in Scripture as the second Eve, something that is apparent when the biblical texts are read as a whole. For the sake of the entire Church, God gave Mary, after her death, "full community with Christ," including bodily glorification.

DEATH AND ETERNAL LIFE: RATZINGER'S *ESCHATOLOGY*

Does death usher not only Mary but also all the blessed into resurrection life? In his *Eschatology*, Ratzinger argues that the blessed undergo a period of waiting prior to the general resurrection. He is aware that this position has encountered significant opposition, not only among those who deny that humans possess an immortal soul, but also among those who hold "the notion that death itself leads out of time into the timeless."[11] The theory of death into resurrection life, if it were true, would remove the main difficulties of the doctrine of Mary's Assumption by offering a portrait of life after death (and of the "end of time") that requires neither an immortal soul nor an intermediate period nor an actual end of temporal history. According to those who hold this theory, "The person who dies steps into the presence of the Last Day and of judgment, the Lord's resurrection and parousia," with the result that "what the dogma of the assumption tells us about Mary is true of every human being."[12]

Ratzinger identifies at least three serious problems with this theory. First, the result of this view is that people whose bodies are now lying in their graves are said to be alive in the flesh. If their bodies are risen, then how are their bodies in the grave? How can their bodies be both completely dead and alive? Ratzinger argues that this position does not really take bodies seriously. To claim that the dead body is dead in historical time but that the person now has his or her body in eternal life is to undermine the significance of historical bodiliness, one component of which is that when a person's body is dead, that person's body is certainly not alive. As Ratzinger remarks, "What we have here is a covert assumption of the continuing authentic reality of the person in separation from his or her body."[13] In attempting to solve this problem without the spiritual soul, theologians make the problem worse by positing a glorified body that has no real relation to the decomposing body in the tomb.

Second, Ratzinger asks, "Are we really confronted with a choice between the stark, exclusive alternatives of physical time on the one hand, and, on the other, a timelessness to be identified with eternity itself?"[14] Eternal life has a beginning for us, rather than being eternal in the strict sense. Although it is not an extension of historical time, eternal life therefore does not utterly do away with before and after. For this reason, a waiting period prior to the general resurrection is not ruled out by the concept of eternal life. To suppose otherwise would be to suppose that death is not the beginning of our eternal life but instead that we have always (or eternally) experienced eternal life on the eternal level, even while on the historical level we experience a temporal life. In fact, such a view would simply take to its furthest consequences the split between the historical level and the eternal level that results from the theory that death ushers all of us immediately into resurrection life.

Third, while making it easier to account for Mary's bodily Assumption, this theory calls into question what it means to say that Jesus died, was buried, and rose from the dead on the third day. It would seem that Jesus' death would accomplish his resurrection immediately on the eternal level. If so, then his Resurrection on the third day would be a mere manifestation of the reality that had already occurred at the very moment that his followers were grieving over his death. His burial and "descent into hell" would have no real meaning. By contrast, according to the New Testament, Jesus does indeed undergo an intermediate period between his death and his Resurrection.[15] Furthermore, if we die into resurrection life, then Jesus' Resurrection would be nothing more than a manifestation of what actually happens to every single person rather than the radical in-breaking of God's salvation that the first followers of Jesus proclaimed.[16]

THE CONTRIBUTION OF DAUGHTER ZION

Ratzinger's most sustained reflection on Mary is his short book *Daughter Zion: Meditations on the Church's Marian Belief,* which was written (and delivered as three lectures) in 1975 and published in 1977, just as Ratzinger moved from the University of Regensburg to become archbishop of Munich and Freising.[17] In this work he first notes that Marian doctrine can appear to be a "scaled-down duplicate of Christology" or simply a Christian version of pagan goddess worship, arising from a need for a feminine dimension in worship.[18] Ratzinger observes that if this is what Marian doctrine is, then it would have to be rejected entirely; but in fact it has a rich biblical grounding. He remarks that "the image of Mary in the New Testament is woven entirely of Old Testament threads" and identifies three Old Testament figures in particular: Eve, Hannah, and Israel as daughter Zion.[19] In a typological manner, the New Testament draws on each of these figures in portraying Mary.

Ratzinger first takes up the figure of Eve. God makes Eve from Adam's rib, because it is "not good" for Adam to be alone (Gn 2:18).

Humans are "fulfilled in the oneness of man and woman," just as it is as "male and female" that humans image God (Gn 1:27).[20] Eve is so named "because she was the mother of all living" (Gn 3:20), preserving her life-giving power even after the Fall. Both Eve's relation with Adam and Eve's association with life, Ratzinger says, will be typologically "taken up again in the dogma of the Assumption."[21]

The second figure Ratzinger discusses is Hannah. Hannah belongs in the Old Testament's line, beginning with Sarah, of infertile women who play a decisive role in transmitting the covenantal blessing of Israel. The blessing of the infertile woman shows that it is God's promise, not physical fertility, that ultimately gives life. To be blessed by God, we must rely on God's promise rather than on the resources of physical life. Hannah's song affirms that God not only makes the infertile woman to be a mother of many children but also "lifts the needy from the ash heap, to make them sit with princes and inherit a seat of honor" (1 Sm 2:8). All pride and arrogance are put to shame: the first will be last. This figure is taken up in Mary's immaculate conception (election and grace) and virgin motherhood.

The third figure or type, Israel as daughter Zion, Ratzinger finds in such women as Esther and Judith. Although Israel is enduring oppression, these women are spiritually strong and capable of overcoming Israel's enemies. Their strength comes solely from the Lord, and in this way they embody the true Israel, daughter Zion. In this light, Ratzinger notes that Israel is almost always personified as feminine in relation to God. He cites Hosea in particular, in which God depicts his indestructible love for his unfaithful wife, Israel. The covenant between God and Israel (Zion) is presented in terms of a marital covenant. As Ratzinger comments, "In the women of Israel, the mothers and the saviors, in their fruitful infertility is expressed most purely and most profoundly what creation is and what election is, what 'Israel' is as God's people."[22] The acceptance of the Song of Songs into the canon also exhibits this theology of Israel as God's bride. In the New Testament, the figure of daughter Zion finds its fulfillment in Mary, virgin and mother; Mary stands for Israel in assenting to the Incarnation. Ratzinger adds that the feminine personification of Wisdom, as the first creature or as the "answer" to God from the side of creatures, fits into the figure of daughter Zion as well. He states, "From the viewpoint of the New Testament, wisdom refers, on one side, to the Son as the Word, in whom God creates, but on the other side to the creature, to the true Israel, who is personified in the humble maid whose whole existence is marked by the attitude of *Fiat mihi secundum verbum tuum*."[23]

In sketching these three figures, Ratzinger's interpretation of the Old Testament is both literal and thoroughly typological. He argues that absent reflection on Mary, the full meaning of these Old Testament figures cannot be grasped. Rather than a pagan imposition on biblical faith, Marian doctrine is necessary for the understanding of the whole of Scripture from a Christian perspective. It follows that study of New Testament texts alone cannot provide the foundation for the Marian doctrines; they require for their intelligibility the whole of Scripture. As Ratzinger observes, "They can become visible only to a mode of perception that accepts this unity, i.e., within a perspective which comprehends and makes its own the 'typological' interpretation, the corresponding echoes of God's single history in the diversity of various external histories."[24] Since historical-critical biblical scholarship easily divides Old and New Testament texts without seeing their (often typological) unity, the biblical foundations of the Church's Marian doctrines tend to be less evident to exegetes and theologians today.

Even if one grants that the New Testament's typology indicates that Mary is the new Eve, however, the New Testament does not draw the conclusion that Mary is sinless or that she was assumed into heaven. Such conclusions involve a further typological extension, now made not by the New Testament authors on the basis of Old Testament figures but by the Church on the basis of reflection on the New Testament exposition of the Old Testament figures. Does this extension of the Marian typology count as biblical exegesis, inspired by the Holy Spirit, or is it simply the Church's imagination?

In response to this question, Ratzinger takes up the three central Marian doctrines in the following order: Mary as virgin and mother, indeed "mother of God"; Mary's sinlessness; and Mary's unique participation in her Son's Resurrection. Regarding the first, the apostle

Paul emphasizes the priority of the promise and says that Jesus is "born of woman" (Gal 4:4). Mary's virgin motherhood is presented in the Gospels of Matthew and Luke. Ratzinger notes that in Luke the annunciation of John the Baptist's conception occurs in the Temple, whereas, given Jesus' status as the new Temple, the annunciation of Jesus' conception occurs in Nazareth.[25] The angel's greeting to Mary corresponds to Zephaniah 3, with Mary in the role of daughter Zion: "Sing aloud, O daughter of Zion; shout, O Israel! Rejoice and exult with all your heart, O daughter of Jerusalem! The Lord has taken away the judgments against you, he has cast out your enemies. The King of Israel, the Lord, is in your midst" (Zep 3:14–15). The Holy Spirit that will overshadow Mary alludes to the creation (Gn 1:2) and to the cloud of glory overshadowing the Temple (1 Kgs 8:10–11). Mary is the infertile daughter Zion who bears the Savior of the world. Further, Mary's motherhood is not only a physical event but also a spiritual one: "To bear the 'Son' includes the surrender of oneself into barrenness," because the course of one's life is dictated by this event.[26] Ratzinger also takes up historical/textual questions in defending the historical occurrence of the virgin birth against views that place limits on God's involvement in human history.

When he turns to Mary's Immaculate Conception, he raises the central objection at once: "Facts . . . cannot be deduced through speculation, but can be known only through some communication (revelation). But such a communication regarding Mary does not exist."[27] A second objection asks how, if Mary is immaculately conceived, she can be said to need redemption. Along these lines, Karl Barth (for example) insists that God accepts the sinner Mary as the conceiver of her Son. Ratzinger responds that the priority of God does not require that there be no holy receptivity on the part of Israel. God promises Israel a righteous "remnant" (Is 37 and elsewhere), and Paul argues that this holy remnant (Rom 11:7) has indeed received Christ. Mary embodies this holy remnant, and she unites the Old and New Covenants by offering a holy response to God's Word. Her response derives entirely from God, and yet it is a true creaturely response (since God does not encounter opposition in her).[28] This brings Ratzinger back to the first and most difficult issue: how can we justify affirming that Mary is the sinless "remnant"?

The only way, he thinks, is through typology. As he points out, original sin itself is a typological doctrine. When Paul teaches that "one man's trespass led to condemnation for all men" (Rom 5:18), he does so by means of a typological argument based on Adam. If original sin can be accepted on the basis of Paul's typological exegesis, then the question is whether the New Testament offers any typology that would support the doctrine of Mary's Immaculate Conception. Ratzinger's answer is Ephesians 5. Here Paul states that Christ sanctifies the Church so that she may be "without spot or wrinkle or any such thing" and "holy and without blemish" (Eph 5:27). On the basis of Luke's and John's "typological identification of Mary and Israel," these statements in Ephesians about the Church are transferable to Mary, so that Mary is seen to embody personally "the rebirth of the old Israel into the new Israel, of which the Epistle to the Ephesians spoke."[29]

The Mary-Church typology, argues Ratzinger, belongs as much to the New Testament as does the Adam-Christ typology that undergirds the doctrine of original sin. An example is the correspondence of Mary in Luke 1:28 with "daughter Zion" of Zephaniah 3:14. For Mary to be preserved from original sin means that "Mary reserves no area of being, life, and will for herself as a private possession: instead, precisely in the total dispossession of self, in giving herself to God, she comes to the true possession of self."[30] Her virginal dispossession, her barrenness, enables her to bear the Savior. Mary truly is the holy Church, in person, who responds fully and freely to the Lord thanks to his grace. The link between the Mary-Church typology and Paul's typological presentation of Christ and the Church in terms of marriage (Eph 5) is a link that Paul himself, of course, does not make. Instead, the Church perceives this link by tracing and connecting the biblical typologies.

Turning to Mary's Assumption, Ratzinger observes that the dogma does not attest to a "historical tradition of an historical fact," since there was no such tradition and since the event was not "historical" in the public sense that Jesus' Resurrection was.[31] In light of the crucial distinction between Jesus' publicly witnessed Resurrection and Mary's hidden Assumption, Mary's Assumption is not termed "Resurrection" by Pius XII. The dogmatic definition does not present itself as the defense of Mary's Assumption on historical grounds but rather confirms the truth of centuries of liturgical veneration of Mary. Both the dogma of Mary's Immaculate Conception and the dogma of her Assumption are first and foremost acts of praise and veneration. Mary is recognized as most fully a "saint."

With this in mind, Ratzinger finds the biblical roots of the dogma first in the mandate that the Church venerate Mary, as in Luke 1:42, 45, and 48. In the Old Testament, extolling Abraham, Isaac, and Jacob means extolling the divine name; and the same is true in the New Testament for Mary. In Mark 12:26–27, Jesus makes clear that those who are venerated in this way will be resurrected. Death cannot keep them, because their God is the God of life. Given the connection between birth and death (Gn 3:16), Ratzinger considers it significant that Mary "bears him who is the death of death and is life in the full sense of the word."[32] As Mother of God, she bears the one who breaks the cycle of death; and her motherhood, then, belongs within this victory. This argument is essentially typological, rooted in and extending Jesus' insistence that God "is not God of the dead, but of the living" (Mk 12:27). Her motherhood breaks the cycle of birth and death, and her fullness of grace enables her assent to this motherhood. Mary's fullness of grace, her total self-dispossession, means that "death is absent, even if the somatic end is present. Instead, the whole human being enters salvation, because as a whole, undiminished, he stands eternally in God's life-giving memory that preserves him as himself in his *own* life."[33] In this way, Mary's Immaculate Conception implies her Assumption.

Ratzinger holds that it is to Mary alone, as the perfect Christian, that we can fully apply Colossians 3:3, "For you have died, and your life is hid with Christ in God," and Ephesians 2:6, "[God] raised us up with him, and made us sit with him in the heavenly places in Christ Jesus."[34] Because of her spiritual and physical motherhood, she possesses all the blessings of faith and baptism; she dies with Christ so as to be raised with him. She is most "blessed" (Lk 1:45) ultimately because, given her perfect self-dispossession, God has raised her up to sit with Christ in heaven. Along these typological lines of reasoning, it follows that "she who is wholly baptized, as the personal reality of the true Church, is at the same time not merely the Church's *promised* certitude of salvation but its *bodily* certitude also."[35] In her, we see that the new Israel will not fail or be cut off.

Ratzinger concludes with one final typological connection. King David, leading the Ark of the Covenant into Jerusalem, leaps and dances with joy before the Ark (2 Sam 6:14–16). The Hebrew term for leaping, when translated into Greek, is the same word as that found in Luke 1:44, where Elizabeth tells Mary that "when the voice of your greeting came to my ears, the babe in my womb leaped for joy." To understand Marian doctrine, we require this sense of joyous veneration, of leaping and dancing before the Ark of the Covenant which Mary truly is.[36]

For Ratzinger, then, the Marian doctrines flow from the Church's typological exegesis and liturgical praise of Mary. These doctrines would fall to the ground without the acceptance of typology as a real way in which God communicates truth about the mysteries of salvation. That God has used typology in this way is shown to us by Scripture, and indeed by Jesus himself. Guided by the same Holy Spirit, the Church over the centuries has liturgically and theologically interpreted Scripture's typological portraits of Mary by making typological connections that illumine the full reality of Mary's motherhood and her sharing in Christ's mission.

MARY IN THE TEACHING OF POPE BENEDICT XVI: THREE HOMILIES ON THE ASSUMPTION

This final section offers some selections from Pope Benedict XVI's first three homilies for the Feast of Mary's Assumption. Are his characteristic emphases present? In his 2005 homily, he focuses on the fact that "Mary was taken up body and soul into Heaven: there is even room in God for the body. Heaven is no longer a very remote sphere unknown to us."[37] Why, however, would Mary's Assumption be needed to show that "there is room in God for the body" or to make heaven less remote? Should not Jesus' bodily presence at the right hand of the Father already serve this purpose well enough?

Although Benedict XVI does not answer this question directly in his homily, he does suggest some ways to answer it. First, he points out that Jesus himself makes Mary our mother, namely, when Jesus tells his beloved disciple from the cross: "Behold, your mother!" (Jn 19:27). To have our mother in heaven with Jesus makes heaven less "remote" not because Jesus is insufficient but because Jesus raises her to himself so that she might share her "motherly kindness" with us, his brothers and sisters.[38] Because she "is with God and in God," says Benedict XVI, "she is always close to us and, being Mother of the Son, participates in the power of the Son and in his goodness."[39] In his supreme goodness, Jesus does not wish to be alone. We draw near to him not by avoiding his friends (above all his mother) but with and through his friends, those with whom he shares his goodness.

Second, Mary's greatness comes from placing her entire self, soul and body, entirely at the disposal of God: "Behold, I am the handmaid of the Lord; let it be to me according to your word" (Lk 1:38). Her words might seem to be self-abnegating and self-diminishing. But they are in fact the opposite. In assenting to conceive and bear her Son, Mary shows us not to fear "that God might be a 'rival' in our life, that with his greatness he might encroach on our freedom, our vital space. She knew that if God is great, we too are great."[40] Further, in assuming Mary bodily into heaven, God glorifies the body of a mere creature. There is "room in God," therefore, even for our bodies (and not simply for the body of his incarnate Son).

In his 2006 homily, Pope Benedict XVI observes that Mary, rejoicing in the Annunciation, "magnifies the Lord" by proclaiming his greatness, while at the same time she proclaims her own greatness: "For behold, henceforth all generations will call me blessed" (Lk 1:46, 48). Certainly, as she makes clear, her greatness comes from what God has done for her. Benedict XVI states that in this phrase, Mary "prophesies the Marian praise of the Church for all the future."[41] He adds that not only Mary but also her cousin Elizabeth sanctions the Church's praise of Mary. Elizabeth proclaims, "Blessed are you among women, and blessed is the fruit of your womb! . . . And blessed is she who believed that there would be a fulfillment of what was spoken to her from the Lord" (Lk 1:42, 45). Mary simply confirms and extends what Elizabeth has said. Benedict XVI comments, "It is a real prophecy, inspired by the Holy Spirit, and in venerating Mary, the Church responds to a command of the Holy Spirit; she does what she has to do."[42]

Why does God will for the Church to praise Mary? Benedict XVI answers that God, in guiding us to praise the mother of his Son, does not thereby guide us away from himself. Rather, praising God's gifts is a central way of praising God. The danger of praising God's gifts is that we might turn from God to his gifts. But if we do not praise God for his gifts, how can we praise him? One response might be that we can praise Jesus and leave it at that. Yet Mary prophesies that "henceforth all generations will call me blessed." The Incarnation means that Mary, both spiritually and physically, became God's "dwelling place on earth."[43] We cannot praise God as though his gifting were confined to Jesus alone. Benedict XVI comments, "We do not praise God sufficiently by keeping silent about his saints, especially Mary."[44] What do we praise when we praise Mary? We praise God for redeeming and elevating his creatures. We praise Mary, who has been assumed bodily into heaven, because by God's mercy and power, "she is united to God; she lives with God and in God."[45] Her Son does not discard the one who, in her soul and body, was his "dwelling place on earth." On the contrary, the wisdom and goodness of Christ is such that in heaven he now dwells with her, in her body-soul totality.

At the Annunciation, the angel tells Mary that, though she is a virgin, she will conceive "the Son of the Most High" when "the Holy Spirit will come upon you, and the power of the Most High will overshadow you" (Lk 1:32, 35). Benedict XVI notes that these words both promise that Mary will be the Mother of the Messiah and link Mary with the Ark of the Covenant and the Temple, in which God's glory dwelled. Because Mary "had made room for the Lord in her soul," she "really became the true Temple where God made himself incarnate."[46] Her body does not lose this dignity. As Benedict XVI states, "Mary is 'blessed' because—totally, in body and soul and for ever—she became the Lord's dwelling place."[47] Through faith, hope, and love, we too come to be God's dwelling place. Her bodily Assumption, then, precedes our resurrection in order to show us what it means to have God indwell us. Furthermore, as we learn in Revelation 12, the self-giving love of the seemingly powerless "woman"—who is both Mary and the Church—will be victorious thanks to God's power. Benedict XVI comments that the "woman clothed with the sun, with the moon under her feet, and on her head a crown of twelve stars" (Rv 12:1) is Mary. Her glorification underscores that not this world but "Paradise is the true goal of our earthly pilgrimage."[48]

Although Christ alone is the Redeemer, Mary certainly is united to his redemptive sufferings. Otherwise Simeon could not have said to Mary, on seeing her infant, that "a sword will pierce through your own soul also" (Lk 2:35).[49] Mary stands at the foot of the cross. As Benedict XVI observes in his 2007 homily, therefore, "Mother and Son appear closely bound in the fight against the infernal enemy until they completely defeat him."[50] Benedict XVI has in view Mary's status as the second Eve, who helps in the mission of the second Adam. He concludes that "just as Christ's glorious Resurrection was the definitive sign of this victory, so Mary's glorification in her virginal body is the ultimate confirmation of her total solidarity with the Son, both in the conflict and in victory."[51] Mary shares uniquely in Christ's Passion as his mother standing at the foot of the cross, and she receives a unique share, too, in his Resurrection. The second Adam draws the second Eve into the new creation, the true "Paradise." We can call upon our mother and sister Mary to help us as, with her, we follow her Son with the goal of attaining "the immortal destination of Paradise."[52]

CONCLUSION

Above I have briefly sketched the contours of Ratzinger's Mariology, whose characteristic emphases are present in his homilies as Pope Benedict XVI. At the level of speculative theology, Ratzinger's main contributions to contemporary Marian theology consist in his appreciation for typological reasoning and in his insistence that Mary's Assumption does not reveal what happens to all of us at the moment of death. His most important concrete insight about Mary is his awareness that "Jesus is building a new family" and that Mary has the role of the second Eve in this family.[53] With Genesis 2:18, Ratzinger underscores that humans are not intended to be alone. Christ Jesus, ascended to the right hand of the Father, does not remain alone. Rather, he brings the second Eve to be with him at her death. Because of her unique participation in Christ's mission, from the Incarnation through the cross, Mary fittingly receives bodily and spiritual glorification after her death.

In Mary, Christ has already accomplished the fullness of redemption in a merely human person, as he will do for the whole Church at the end of time. Heavenly glory already includes the unity of man and woman, Christ and his Bride the Church. As Ratzinger/Pope Benedict never tires of proclaiming, therefore, the fruits of Christ's Resurrection have truly begun in the new family of God.

NOTES

1. Joseph Ratzinger, "On the Position of Mariology and Marian Spirituality within the Totality of Faith and Theology," in *The Church and Women: A Compendium*, trans. Maria Shrady and Lothar Krauth (San Francisco: Ignatius Press, 1988), 67–81, at 72. See Emery de Gaál, *The Theology of Pope Benedict XVI: The Christocentric Shift* (New York: Palgrave Macmillan, 2010), 294–96.

2. Joseph Ratzinger, *Church, Ecumenism, and Politics: New Essays in Ecclesiology*, trans. Robert Nowell (New York: Crossroad, 1988), 20. De Gaál comments regarding Ratzinger's involvement in the debate at the Second Vatican Council over whether to produce a separate document on Mary or to include Mary in the document on the Church. As de Gaál says, Ratzinger "welcomed Cardinal König's intervention to incorporate Mariology into *Lumen Gentium*. . . . Later, Ratzinger would lament that this led to yet another misunderstanding. Rather than appreciating Mary as *Theotokos*, Mother of God, as the paradigm for the Church, Mariology was subsequently neglected. Yet only via Mary does one understand the truth about both Jesus Christ and the Church. A balanced appreciation of Mary's role in

salvation history prevents one from reducing the Savior to a mere human and from perceiving the Church as a mere congregation. For this reason, Ratzinger is now more favorably disposed to Marian titles than he perhaps was during the council." See de Gaál, *The Theology of Pope Benedict XVI*, 101.

3. Joseph Ratzinger, *God and the World: Believing and Living in Our Time: A Conversation with Peter Seewald,* trans. Henry Taylor (San Francisco: Ignatius Press, 2002), 296. This book-length interview reflects Ratzinger's work, over more than two decades, as the prefect of the Congregation for the Doctrine of the Faith.

4. Ibid.

5. See ibid., 301.

6. Ibid., 304.

7. Ibid.

8. Ibid., 305.

9. Ibid.

10. Ibid., 298.

11. Joseph Ratzinger, *Eschatology, Death, and Eternal Life*, trans. Michael Waldstein, 2nd ed. (Washington, DC: Catholic University of America Press, 2007), 107. In his essay "Between Death and Resurrection: Some Supplementary Reflections," included as Appendix I in *Eschatology*, 241–60, Ratzinger notes that Ernst Troeltsch and Karl Barth sought to overcome the apparent difficulty regarding Jesus' imminent eschatology by holding to "the complete incommensurability of time and eternity. The person who dies steps outside time. He enters upon the 'end of the world,' which is not the final day of the cosmic calendar but is, rather, something alien to the diurnal round of this world's time. . . . The end of time, as time's boundary, is not only very close but reaches into time's very midst" (251–52). Both Karl Rahner, S.J., and Hans Urs von Balthasar affirm the theory of death into resurrection life: see Karl Rahner, S.J., "The Intermediate State," in *Theological Investigations,* vol. 17: *Jesus, Man, and the Church,* trans. Margaret Kohl (New York: Crossroad, 1981), 114–24; Hans Urs von Balthasar, *Theo-Drama: Theological Dramatic Theory,* vol. 5: *The Last Act,* trans. Graham Harrison (San Francisco: Ignatius Press, 1998), 346–77. For this view, see also Gisbert Greshake, *Auferstehung der Toten: Ein Beitrag zur gegenwärtigen theologischen Diskussion über die Zukunft der Geschichte* (Essen: Ludgerus, 1969), 360–414; Gisbert Greshake and Jacob Kremer, *Resurrectio Mortuorum: Zum theologischen Verständnis der leiblichen Auferstehung* (Darmstadt: Wissenschaftliche Buchgesellschaft, 1986). For discussion and criticism of the theory of death into resurrection life, see Paul O'Callaghan, *Christ Our Hope: An Introduction to Eschatology* (Washington, DC: Catholic University of America Press, 2011),

318–26; Bryan Kromholtz, O.P., *On the Last Day: The Time of the Resurrection of the Dead according to Thomas Aquinas* (Fribourg: Fribourg University Press, 2010); Wolfhart Pannenberg, *Systematic Theology*, vol. 3, trans. Geoffrey W. Bromiley (Grand Rapids, MI: Eerdmans, 1998), 577–80; Andrew Hofer, O.P., "Balthasar's Eschatology on the Intermediate State: The Question of Knowability," *Logos* 12 (2009): 148–72; Avery Dulles, S.J., "The Dogma of the Assumption," in *The One Mediator, the Saints, and Mary: Lutherans and Catholics in Dialogue VIII*, ed. H. George Anderson, J. Francis Stafford, and Joseph A. Burgess (Minneapolis, MN: Augsburg Fortress, 1992), 279–94, at 292–93. See also the critique provided by the Congregation for the Doctrine of the Faith's "Letter on Certain Questions in Eschatology," published in *Acta Apostolicae Sedis* 71 (1979): 939–43; and by the International Theological Commission's "Some Current Questions in Eschatology," published in *Irish Theological Quarterly* 58 (1992): 209–43.

    12. Ratzinger, *Eschatology*, 108.

    13. Ibid., 109.

    14. Ibid.

    15. For exegetical support of this position, see N. T. Wright, *Surprised by Hope: Rethinking Heaven, the Resurrection, and the Mission of the Church* (New York: HarperCollins, 2008); James D. G. Dunn, *The Theology of Paul the Apostle* (Grand Rapids, MI: Eerdmans, 1998), 489; Andrew T. Lincoln, *Paradise Now and Not Yet: Studies in the Role of the Heavenly Dimension in Paul's Thought with Special Reference to His Eschatology* (Cambridge: Cambridge University Press, 1981), 69.

    16. After publishing his book, Ratzinger found that the Congregation for the Doctrine of the Faith was preparing the "Letter on Certain Questions in Eschatology" to address the issue of the soul and the intermediate state. This document, when published in 1979 (two years before Ratzinger himself became prefect of the Congregation), supported Ratzinger's rejection of the theory that we die into resurrection life. Ratzinger commented on the Congregation's Letter in an essay titled "Between Death and Resurrection: Some Supplementary Reflections," included as Appendix I in the English edition of his *Eschatology*. In the intermediate state, according to both the Congregation's Letter and Ratzinger, the dead live with Christ (cf. Phil 1:23, 2 Cor 5:8, Rv 6:9–11) and await the bodily resurrection and the final judgment that will come at the end of history. As he says, "a 'resurrection' which concerns neither matter nor the concrete historical world is no resurrection at all" (Ratzinger, "Between Death and Resurrection," 253). See also, for the same point, Ratzinger's "Afterword to the English Edition," written in 1987 and included as Appendix II in *Eschatology*, 261–74.

17. Joseph Ratzinger, *Daughter Zion: Meditations on the Church's Marian Belief,* trans. John M. McDermott, S.J. (San Francisco: Ignatius Press, 1983). The theme of daughter Zion is also central to the work of Ignace de la Potterie, S.J., *Mary in the Mystery of the Covenant,* trans. Bertrand Buby, S.M. (Staten Island, NY: Alba House, 1992); and Lucien Deiss, C.S.Sp., *Mary, Daughter of Sion,* trans. Barbara T. Blair (Collegeville, MN: Liturgical Press, 1972).

18. Ratzinger, *Daughter Zion,* 9.

19. Ibid., 12. See Tracey Rowland, *Ratzinger's Faith: The Theology of Pope Benedict XVI* (Oxford: Oxford University Press, 2008), 87; Aidan Nichols, O.P., *The Thought of Pope Benedict XVI: An Introduction to the Theology of Joseph Ratzinger,* 2nd ed. (London: Continuum, 2007), 143–44.

20. Ratzinger, *Daughter Zion,* 16.

21. Ibid., 18. See also Saint Gregory Palamas, *Mary the Mother of God: Sermons by Saint Gregory Palamas,* ed. Christopher Veniamin (South Canaan, PA: Mount Thabor Publishing, 2005), 73. For a particularly weighty example of Protestant exegetical scholarship that rejects the Marian typologies that Catholic and Orthodox interpreters have perceived, see John McHugh, *The Mother of Jesus in the New Testament* (Garden City, NY: Doubleday, 1975). For the Catholic and Orthodox perspective on Marian typology, see especially René Laurentin, *A Short Treatise on the Virgin Mary,* trans. Charles Neumann, S.M. (Washington, DC: AMI Press, 1991), 15–49, 269–83; Gary A. Anderson, *The Genesis of Perfection: Adam and Eve in Jewish and Christian Imagination* (Louisville, KY: Westminster John Knox Press, 2001), chap. 4: "Mary as Second Eve." See also, from a Protestant perspective sympathetic to typology, Max Thurian, *Mary, Mother of the Lord, Figure of the Church,* trans. Neville B. Cryer (London: Mowbray, 1985), 49–55, 176–83. For discussion regarding the relationship of typology and allegory (and whether one or the other should be preferred), see the contrasting views of Jean Daniélou, S.J., "Symbolism and History," in Jean Daniélou, *The Lord of History: Reflections on the Inner Meaning of History,* trans. Nigel Abercrombie (Chicago: Henry Regnery, 1958), 130–46; and Henri de Lubac, S.J., "'Typologie' et 'allégorisme,'" *Recherches de science religieuse* 34 (1947): 180–226. More recently, see especially Peter W. Martens, "Revisiting the Allegory/Typology Distinction: The Case of Origen," *Journal of Early Christian Studies* 16 (2008): 283–317; Hans Boersma, *Nouvelle théologie and Sacramental Ontology: A Return to Mystery* (Oxford: Oxford University Press, 2009), chap. 5; Frances M. Young, *Biblical Exegesis and the Formation of Christian Culture* (Cambridge: Cambridge University Press, 1997), 152–57.

22. Ratzinger, *Daughter Zion*, 23–24.

23. Ibid., 27.

24. Ibid., 32.

25. For further comparison of John the Baptist and Mary, see Yves Congar, O.P., *Christ, Our Lady and the Church: A Study in Eirenic Theology*, trans. Henry St. John, O.P. (London: Longmans, Green, 1957), 14.

26. Ratzinger, *Daughter Zion*, 52. See Joseph Ratzinger, "'Hail, Full of Grace': Elements of Marian Piety According to the Bible," in Joseph Ratzinger and Hans Urs von Balthasar, *Mary: The Church at the Source*, trans. Adrian Walker (San Francisco: Ignatius Press, 2005), 61–79, at 69: "When man's relation to God, the soul's open availability for him, is characterized as 'faith', this word expresses the fact that the infinite distance between Creator and creature is not blurred in the relation of the human I to the divine Thou. It means that the model of 'partnership', which has become so dear to us, breaks down when it comes to God, because it cannot sufficiently express the majesty of God and the hiddenness of his working. It is precisely the man who has been opened up entirely into God who comes to accept God's otherness and the hiddenness of his will, which can pierce our will like a sword. The parallel between Mary and Abraham begins in the joy of the promised son but continues apace until the dark hour when she must ascend Mount Moriah, that is, until the Crucifixion of Christ. Yet it does not end there; it also extends to the miracle of Isaac's rescue—the Resurrection of Jesus Christ."

27. Ratzinger, *Daughter Zion*, 62.

28. See also Joseph Ratzinger, "'Et Incarnatus Est de Spiritu Sancto ex Maria Virgine,'" in Ratzinger and Balthasar, *Mary*, 81–95, at 89–90.

29. Ratzinger, *Daughter Zion*, 68.

30. Ibid., 70.

31. Ibid., 72. On this point, see especially Laurentin, *A Short Treatise on the Virgin Mary*, 248.

32. Ratzinger, *Daughter Zion*, 78.

33. Ibid., 79.

34. Cf. the Pauline framework of the Anglican–Roman Catholic International Commission's statement, *Mary: Grace and Hope in Christ*. For this statement, see *Mary: Grace and Hope in Christ. The Seattle Statement of the Anglican-Roman Catholic International Commission: The Text with Commentaries and Study Guide*, ed. Donald Bolen and Gregory Cameron (New York: Continuum, 2005).

35. Ratzinger, *Daughter Zion*, 81. Original emphasis.

36. See also Pope Benedict XVI, *Saved in Hope—Spe Salvi* (San Francisco: Ignatius Press, 2008), §49: "With her 'yes' she opened the door of our world to God himself; she became the living Ark of the Covenant, in whom God took flesh, became one of us, and pitched his tent among us (cf. Jn 1:14)." For further reflection, see Ratzinger, "'Hail, Full of Grace,'" 65–66; Ratzinger, "'Et Incarnatus Est de Spiritu Sancto ex Maria Virgine,'" 87–88, 93–94. On Mary as the new Ark of the Covenant, see also John Saward, *Redeemer in the Womb: Jesus Living in Mary* (San Francisco: Ignatius Press, 1993), 27–31, 125–27.

37. Pope Benedict XVI, Homily on the Assumption of Mary, August 15, 2005, reprinted in *Maria: Pope Benedict XVI on the Mother of God* (San Francisco: Ignatius Press, 2009), 23.

38. Ibid.

39. Ibid.

40. Ibid., 25.

41. Ibid., 75.

42. Ibid. See also Ratzinger, "'Hail, Full of Grace,'" 62–63: "The Church neglects one of the duties enjoined upon her when she does not praise Mary. She deviates from the word of the Bible when her Marian devotion falls silent. When this happens, in fact, the Church no longer even glorifies God as she ought. For though we do know God by means of his creation—'Ever since the creation of the world [God's] invisible nature, namely, his eternal power and deity, has been clearly perceived in the things that have been made' (Rom 1:20)—we also know him, and know him more intimately, through the history he has shared with man."

43. Benedict XVI, Homily on the Assumption of Mary, August 15, 2006, 75.

44. Ibid.

45. Ibid.

46. Ibid., 79.

47. Ibid.

48. Ibid., 81. See also George T. Montague, S.M., "Eschatology and Our Lady," *Marian Studies* 17 (1966): 65–83.

49. For further reflection on the "sword," drawing a connection with 2 Samuel 12:9–10, see Ratzinger, "'Hail, Full of Grace,'" 76–79.

50. Pope Benedict XVI, Angelus on Mary's Assumption, August 15, 2007, in *Maria*, 119.

51. Ibid.

52. Ibid., 120. As he says elsewhere, "Marian piety is thus necessarily a Passion-centered piety. In the prophecy of the aged Simeon, who foretold

that a sword would pierce Mary's heart (Lk 2:35), Luke interweaves from the very outset the Incarnation and the Passion, the joyful and the sorrowful mysteries. In the Church's piety, Mary appears, so to speak, as the living Veronica's veil, as an icon of Christ that brings him into the present of man's heart, translates Christ's image into the heart's vision, and thus makes it intelligible. Looking toward the *Mater assumpta*, the Virgin Mother assumed into heaven, Advent broadens into eschatology." Joseph Ratzinger, "Thoughts on the Place of Marian Doctrine and Piety in Faith and Theology as a Whole," in Ratzinger and Balthasar, *Mary,* 19–36, at 35.

    53. Ratzinger, *God and the World,* 296.

CONTRIBUTORS

GARY A. ANDERSON is Hesburgh Professor of Catholic Theology at the University of Notre Dame. His field of inquiry is the Old Testament, with a special interest in its early history of interpretation.

KIMBERLY HOPE BELCHER is Assistant Professor of Theology, College of St. Benedict and St. John's University. Her first book, *Efficacious Engagement: Sacramental Participation in the Trinitarian Mystery*, was published in 2011.

SIMONA BERETTA is Professor of International Economics, Università Cattolica del Sacro Cuore (UCSC), Milan. Her research interests are institutions and development, international finance, the ethical dimension of economic actions, and policy decisions. She is a member of the UCSC Center for Catholic Social Doctrine, consultant for the Pontifical Council for Justice and Peace, and member of the Scientific Committee of the Italian Catholic Social Weeks.

PETER CASARELLA is Professor of Catholic Studies and Director of the Center for World Catholicism and Intercultural Theology at De-Paul University in Chicago. In addition to promoting collaborations with the Catholic Church in the global South, he has published on global civil society, Hispanic/Latino theology, Hans Urs von Balthasar, Nicholas of Cusa, and Saint Bonaventure.

JOHN C. CAVADINI is Professor of Patristic Theology in the Department of Theology and McGrath-Cavadini Director of the Institute for Church Life at the University of Notre Dame. He served as chair of the Department of Theology from 1997 to 2010.

LAWRENCE S. CUNNINGHAM is John A. O'Brien Professor of Theology Emeritus at the University of Notre Dame.

ROBERT M. GIMELLO is Research Professor of Theology and of East Asian Languages and Cultures at the University of Notre Dame. He is a specialist in the history of Buddhist thought and practice in East Asia, especially the Chan (Zen), Huayan, and esoteric traditions of medieval and early modern China. In addition, Gimello works on issues in the comparative philosophy of religion, comparative mysticism, and Catholic theology of religions.

MATTHEW LEVERING is Professor of Theology and Director of the Center for Scriptural Exegesis, Philosophy, and Doctrine at the University of Dayton and coeditor of *Nova et Vetera*. He is currently working on a theology of Mary's Assumption.

FRANCESCA ARAN MURPHY is Professor of Systematic Theology at the University of Notre Dame. She has written and edited a dozen books, including most recently a commentary on I Samuel.

EDWARD T. OAKES, S.J., is Professor of Systematic Theology at the University of St. Mary of the Lake/Mundelein Seminary. His most recent book, *Infinity Dwindled to Infancy: A Catholic and Evangelical*

Christology (Eerdmans) won the 2012 Book Prize from the Center for Catholic and Evangelical Dialogue. He is also the author of *Pattern of Redemption: The Theology of Hans Urs von Balthasar* (Continuum) and coeditor of *The Cambridge Companion to Hans Urs von Balthasar* (Cambridge).

CYRIL O'REGAN is Huisking Professor of Theology at the University of Notre Dame. He is a systematic theologian who works at the intersection of philosophy and theology. He has published monographs on Hegel, Gnosticism in modernity, and apocalyptic theology. O'Regan's two-volume study on Hans Urs von Balthasar and his critical engagements with Hegel and Heidegger respectively is forthcoming from Crossroad.

DANIEL PHILPOTT is Associate Professor of Political Science and Peace Studies, University of Notre Dame. He is the author of *Just and Unjust Peace: An Ethic of Political Reconciliation* (Oxford, 2012) and coauthor with Monica Duffy Toft and Timothy Samuel Shah of *God's Century: Resurgent Religion and Global Politics* (Norton, 2011).

INDEX

community, 47, 74, 145, 202–3, 205,
269
charity and, 198
morality and, 73, 74
*Compendium of the Social Doctrine of
the Church*, 73, 178, 191
Comte, Auguste, 57n52
confession, 145, 179, 237, 239–40,
243, 246
Confucianism, 121, 137–38
Congregation of the Doctrine of the
Faith (CDF), 30, 79–80, 87,
118, 293n16
conscience
acts of, 79, 81–82
Benedict XVI, prioritization of,
64, 68, 70, 71–73, 76, 80
Bonaventure, doctrine of, 75, 76
Christian, 76, 81
culture and, 64, 68, 81–82
erroneous, 72
formation of, 5, 73
freedom of, 79
God and, 72, 74, 76
human nature and, 81
natural beauty of, 78
Newman, theology of, 68–69
as safeguard against relativism,
72
truth and, 68, 69, 71, 77, 80
conscientia, 71, 84n29
consciousness, 68, 72
social, 73, 74
Conversation of Faith and Reason
(Nichols), 149
1 Corinthians, 103–4, 232
correlation, principle of, 94
Council of Ephesus, 277
Council of Trent, 170, 231, 254
creation, 52n14, 127–28, 149, 202

creative anti-realism, 160
Credo (Barth), 216
cross, 79, 230, 231, 266, 269
power of, 77, 150
sacrifice of, 17, 264–65, 268–69
and salvation history, 54n23
crucifixion, 150, 246–47, 264, 270,
278
Crusades, 108
culture
advent and, 64, 65–66, 67
Christianity and, 44–46, 50, 65
conscience and, 64, 68, 81–82
faith and, 23, 28, 44–46
Ratzinger/Benedict XVI on, 64, 65
religion and, 65, 66–67, 101, 123
Cyran, Saint, 38

Dalai Lama, 135
Daniel, Book of, 35
Daniélou, Jean, 60n95
Dante Alighieri, 29
Daoism, 121
Darwin, Charles, 92
Day, Dorothy, 1–2
death, 65, 191, 286
love and, 219, 263
and resurrection, 242, 243, 247,
263, 269–70, 279–81, 292n11
The Death of Socrates (Guardini), 69
De Doctrina Christiana (Augustine),
4, 9, 25, 40, 44–45
de Gaál, Emery, 83n14, 111n21,
291n2
de Gasperi, Alcide, 166
de Gaulle, Charles, 79, 166
de Gruchy, John, 165
deism, 74
Dei Verbum, 43, 44, 217
Delp, Alfred, 207